SEMIOTICS OF PROGRAMMING

This book provides a semiotic analysis of computer programs along three axes: models of signs, kinds of signs, and systems of signs. Since computer programs are well defined and rigid, applying semiotic theories to them will help to reorganize the semiotic theories themselves. Moreover, semiotic discussion of programming theory can provide possible explanations for why programming has developed as it has and how computation is fundamentally related to human semiosis.

The goal of this book is to consider the question of what computers can and cannot do by analyzing how computer sign systems compare to those of humans. A key concept throughout is reflexivity, that is, the capability of a system or function to reinterpret what it has produced by itself. Sign systems are reflexive by nature, and humans know how to make the most of this characteristic but have not yet fully implemented it into computer systems. Therefore the limitations of current computers can be ascribed to insufficient reflexivity.

Kumiko Tanaka-Ishii is currently an associate professor in the Department of Creative Informatics at the Graduate School of Information Science and Technology at the University of Tokyo, Japan. Her major areas of interest are computational linguistics, natural language processing, and computational semiotics. Her previous books include *Text Entry Systems: Mobility, Accessibility, Universality* (co-edited with I. Scott MacKenzie) and a joint translation (with Kyo Kageura) of *Troisième cours de linguistique générale (1910–1911): d'après les cahiers d'Emile Constantin* by Ferdinand de Saussure.

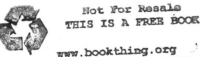

Semiotics of Programming

KUMIKO TANAKA-ISHII

University of Tokyo

CAMBRIDGE
UNIVERSITY PRESS

CAMBRIDGE UNIVERSITY PRESS
Cambridge, New York, Melbourne, Madrid, Cape Town, Singapore,
São Paulo, Delhi, Dubai, Tokyo

Cambridge University Press
32 Avenue of the Americas, New York, NY 10013-2473, USA

www.cambridge.org
Information on this title: www.cambridge.org/9780521736275

First published 2010

Printed in the United States of America

A catalog record for this publication is available from the British Library.

Library of Congress Cataloging in Publication data

Tanaka-Ishii, Kumiko.
Semiotics of programming / Kumiko Tanaka-Ishii.
p.   cm.
Includes bibliographical references and index.
ISBN 978-0-521-51655-6 (hardback) – ISBN 978-0-521-73627-5 (pbk.)   1. Programming
languages (Electronic computers)   2. Semiotics.   3. Human-computer interaction.   I. Title.
QA76.7.T35   2009
004.01′9–dc22   2009038892

ISBN   978-0-521-51655-6 Hardback
ISBN   978-0-521-73627-5 Paperback

Contents

2 KINDS OF SIGNS AND CONTENT

Acknowledgments

This book owes a great deal to the support of the following people.

This book was motivated by a conversation in 2001 in which Professor Toru Nishigaki of the University of Tokyo suggested that I clarify the relationship between object-oriented programming languages and the semiotic theories of Charles Sanders Peirce. Although the final coverage of this book has extended to a broader perspective concerning the fundamentals of semiotics and various programming language paradigms, I would never have started the book without this thoughtful and timely suggestion.

Since that time, I have been working on the drafts forming the core of this book. At the beginning, I was unable to find a forum in which to properly discuss the content because the two domains of semiotics and programming have not often intersected: the former is mainly humanistic, whereas the latter is quite the opposite, belonging to computer science. I was very fortunate to encounter four outstanding people who have given me positive comments and support for this endeavor.

First, and above all, is Professor Kyo Kageura of the University of Tokyo. He encouraged me to continue and write down my ideas with respect to this book, and he kindly went through many discussions of its content. Kyo's comments were always essential in nature, positive, and supportive, and his enthusiasm for semiotics was the main driving force for me to complete this book: without Kyo's competence and good will this book would never have been completed.

Second is Professor Marcel Danesi of the University of Toronto. As the editor of Walter de Gruyter's journal, *Semiotica*, he went through my articles every time I submitted to the journal. He was the first person to publicly acknowledge these articles, and he encouraged me to continue my work. Also, it was Professor Danesi's suggestion to collect several of my early articles appearing in *Semiotica* into the form of a book.

Third is Professor John H. Connolly of Loughborough University. During the publication process, he kindly served as the book's reviewer at Cambridge

University Press. Through communication via Cambridge, he gave me excellent questions and comments, which helped me greatly improve and finish the book. In particular, his comments regarding the contrast between semantics and pragmatics with reference to Harder's statement helped ground the rationale of the argument in Part 1. The other parts were also improved by addressing his essential comments and questions.

Fourth is Assistant Professor Peter Marteinson of the University of Toronto. He is the coeditor of the *Journal of Applied Semiotics* and gave me professional comments from the semiotic and philosophical viewpoints on one of the articles that I sent to the journal. In addition, he kindly went through the draft of this book and gave me essential comments, including suggestions to improve the text.

In 2008, I was introduced to Mr. Eric Schwartz, Ms. Simina Calin, and Ms. Jeanie Lee, editors at Cambridge University Press, via Ms. Keiko Hirano of Cambridge Japan and Mr. Kensuke Goto of The University of Tokyo Press. These editors are wonderful people with professional knowledge of state-of-the-art publication, and they offered me this precious opportunity to publish my book. I am especially happy to have worked with Ms. Calin and Ms. Lee, the chief editors of the book: they were always very supportive during the process of publication. Moreover, Mr. James See helped improve the text once the book was finished. Ms. Tomoko Nishigaki was supportive during this process of final improvement. During the production process, Mr. Mark Fox of CUP and Mr. Frank Scott and his team of Aptara Corporation professionally put this book into this final form. I also thank my assistant, Ms. Mikako Yanagicuhi, who always supported me while contacting various organizations and doing paperwork, among many other tasks.

Before final publication, Emeritus Professor Eiiti Wada, of the University of Tokyo, kindly read the text and gave me detailed comments from the viewpoint of a professional programmer. His great enthusiasm for programming has influenced me, since I was an undergraduate, to learn the computer programming theories appearing in this book.

Last, this book could not have taken its final form without the support of Yuichiro Ishii, my husband. Although he is currently working professionally in the legal domain, he is one of the most talented programmers I know. I am exceedingly fortunate to have his talent on hand for discussion at home. Many of the core concepts of chapters of this book were articulated through our private weekend discussions. Also, he went through every chapter and helped me improve the text.

I do not know how to fully convey my appreciation to all these wonderful people. I am blessed to have met them and had their support throughout. This book is dedicated to all the people mentioned here.

1

Introduction

1.1 The Aim of This Book

The theme of this book is to reconsider reflexivity as the essential property of sign systems. In this book, a *sign* is considered a *means of signification*, which at this point can be briefly understood as something that stands for something else. For example, a sequence of letters, 'computer', stands for an electronic machine. Such sign-based proxy relationships are powerful tools for communication. Signs function in the form of a *system* consisting of a relation among signs and their interpretations.

As will be seen further along in the book, a sign is essentially reflexive, with its signification articulated by the use of itself. Reflexivity is taken for granted, as the premise for a sign system such as natural languages. On the other hand, the inherent risk of unintelligibility of reflexivity, has been noted throughout human history in countless paradoxes. For example, in a Greek myth, Narcissus became immobile as a result of staring at his own reflection in the water. As shown by such examples, reflexivity has been an issue since ancient times in philosophy, logic, and language. Still, unless reflexivity causes contradiction or nonsensicality, reflexivity will stay as the manifest mechanism hiding the way in which sign systems work. Reflexivity becomes the theme mainly at the border between significance and insignificance. With artificial languages, however, it is necessary to design the border of significance and insignificance and thus their consideration will serve for highlighting the premise underlying signs and sign systems.

The artificial languages considered in this book are programming languages. They are artificial languages designed to control machines. The problems underlying programming languages are fundamentally related to reflexivity, and it is not too far-fetched to say that the history of programming language development is the quest for a proper handling of reflexivity. This book does not merely survey the consequences, but attempts to consider programming languages from a broader viewpoint of signs and sign systems in general. The domain serving this purpose is *semiotics*, the theoretical framework in which the general properties of signs and sign systems are described. In particular, the aim of the book is to consider the nature of signs and sign systems through discussion of programming languages by semiotics.

Such an endeavor highlights the difference between computer signs and human signs. The comparison of machines and humans is a recurring theme in conversations in daily life, in science fiction, and in philosophical discussions in academic domains, despite the fact that humans and machines are utterly different, with one being biological and the other mechanical. Countless metaphors compare computers to humans, and vice versa. This very fact suggests machine-based and human systems can be considered similar, to some extent.

A common test bed applied in this book regarding this similarity is the sign systems. Readers might doubt the plausibility of this comparison of human and computer sign systems. The world of computer software indeed consists only of signs, because all information processed on computers is ultimately made up of zeros and ones. Still, computer languages often appear very limited as compared to human language, especially to those who are not programmers. This delineation of human and computer language, however, is not as trivial as a division based on human language being complex and computer language being simple; rather, the delineation is a difficult issue, as seen in controversies over formal theories of language. At the same time, some readers might also wonder to what extent humanity can be considered merely in terms of signs and sign systems. Such an approach, however, is indeed extant in the humanities, particularly in semiotics, linguistics, and philosophy. It is therefore not an oversimplification to compare human language and computer language on the common test bed of sign systems.

Considering both as sign systems, their comparison seems to lead to highlight the premise upon which our sign system is founded. Namely, the application of semiotic theories to programming enables the consideration, in a coherent manner, of the universal and specific nature of signs in machine and human systems (see Figure 1.1). Such a comparison invokes the nature of descriptions made by humans in general, of the kinds of features a description possesses, and of the limitations to which a description is subject. These limitations, this book suggests, are governed by reflexivity. Moreover, the difference between computer signs and human signs lies in their differing capability to handle reflexivity, which informs both the potential and

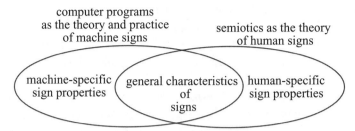

FIGURE 1.1. Human signs and machine signs.

the limitations of the two sign systems. While people do get puzzled, they seldom become uncontrollable because of one self-reference. In contrast, for computers, reflexivity is one of the most frequent sources of malfunction.

Given this key concept of reflexivity, this book straddles the domains of semiotics and computation, as well as those of the humanities and engineering, and the study of machines and humans. Such an interdisciplinary approach can be expected to bring forth contributions to each participating realm.

1.2 Computational Contributions to Semiotics

The purpose of semiotics, in general, is to explain signs and sign systems, to describe their general characteristics and structure, and thus to establish a methodology for their explanation. Behind these considerations is the question of the meaning of meaning, or how signs convey meaning. The domain of modern semiotics was established by Saussure and Peirce, with roots dating back to the ancient Greeks and the scholastics. Before the nineteenth century, the distinction between the arts and sciences was not recognized, but scholars have since subdivided academia in this way. As a consequence, the semiotic discipline was initially developed mainly by scholars in the arts, and the preponderance of the existing literature on semiotics is humanities oriented.

The object of semiotic analysis has traditionally been sign systems for human interpretation: natural language, texts, communication, codes, symbolic systems, sign language, and various art forms. There are some exceptions, such as biosemiotics, but the majority of studies examine human communication. Unfortunately, this means that semiotic studies have normally been conducted without a clearly delineated separation between the sign system to be analyzed and that used for its study. As a consequence, a solid theoretical foundation for semiotics has yet to be established. For example, even considering models of signs alone, various philosophers have each presented their own ideas, and how these ideas correspond has remained unclear.

The use of computer languages as a semiotic subject does not suffer from this failing, however, because human beings do not think in machine language. Computer languages have their own type of interpretive system, external to the interpretive systems of natural languages. All computer language expressions are meant for interpretation on machines. Here we may remark how computer programs have marked characteristics in terms of possessing explicit, external interpretation schemes. They are open and explicit only for artificial notations, and this holds for other artificial notational systems, such as those in mathematics, logic, and even music and dance. Still, these notations are meant for human beings to interpret. For example, mathematics is another well-formed, rigorous sign system, but it is ultimately interpreted by human beings, and therefore certain repetitive elements are frequently omitted.

In contrast, every computational procedure must be exhaustively described in a programming language, inclusive of all repetitions, so that the processing comes to a halt and is valid for the intended purpose. With respect to interpretation, in a sense, there is in theory no system better than that of computer languages because they are truly formal, external, and complete in scope. Since this interpretation is performed mechanically, it is explicit, well formed, and rigorous. Computer languages are the only existing large-scale sign system with an explicit, fully characterized interpreter external to the human interpretive system. Therefore, the application of semiotics to computer languages can contribute, albeit in a limited manner, to the fundamental theory of semiotics.

Regarding this point, the reader might object that computation is quite different from human interpretation, which is true. Indeed, as we shall see in more detail in Chapter 4, computation is equivalent to chains of mere substitutions. Substitution, however, is a simple scheme that could also be considered a fundamental procedure underlying human interpretation. Moreover, even though the interpretation of artificial languages differs from that of natural languages, its study can bring forth a better understanding of interpretation in general, as compared with neglecting such an approach.

Consequently, applying semiotics to the external, rigorous system of computer programs helps formalize certain aspects of the fundamental framework of semiotics. Understanding the semiotic problems in programming languages leads us to formally reconsider the essential problems of signs. Such reconsideration of the fundamentals of semiotics could ultimately lead to an improved and renewed understanding of human signs as well.

1.3 Semiotic Contributions to Computing

Computers are now indispensable in our daily lives. Behind every computational system is a program. Programming languages are among the most widely applied artificial languages. People have attempted to describe various conceivable phenomena in terms of computer programs, and the only form of language exceeding this coverage is natural language. Computer programming is thus the most successful application of artificial language, and the scale of its practice is vast.

Most programs are generated by human beings. As expressions written in programming languages are interpreted by both humans and machines, these languages reflect the linguistic behaviors of both. The history of the development of computer languages can be characterized as the history of an effort to transform a mere mechanical command chain into more human-friendly expressions. Thus, an analysis of recent, well-developed programming languages may reveal significant aspects of human linguistic behavior.

Many of the concepts, principles, and notions of computer programming, however, have derived from technological needs, without being situated within the broader context of human thought. An example is that the paradigm of object-oriented programming is considered to have been invented in the 1960s. This was, however, no more than the rediscovery of another way to look at signs. The technological development of programming languages has thus been a rediscovery of ways to exploit the nature of signs that had already been present in human thought.

The application of semiotics to programming languages therefore helps situate certain technological phenomena within a humanities framework. To the extent that computer programs are formed of signs, they are subject to the properties of signs in general, which is the theme of this book. That is, the problems existing in sign systems generally also appear in programming languages. This semiotic discussion of programming theory has sought to provide a possible explanation of why programming and current computer systems have necessarily converged to their current status and how computation is fundamentally related to human semiosis.

1.4 Related Work

Generally, the relation between signs and reflexivity, without noting specific examples at this juncture, has been a recurring theme appearing in many investigations, in which at least two broad genres are apparent. First is the reflexivity existing in natural languages and in human knowledge based upon natural language. Second is the reflexivity existing in a specific and formal language, such as in mathematics or logic. As seen in these domains, the former was developed mainly in the humanities, whereas the latter belongs more to science and engineering. In these two major scholarly domains, there have been similar considerations. This book addresses the theme of the reflexivity of signs but attempts to bridge the two genres of natural and formal language to situate reflexivity as the general property of signs and sign systems.

From the more specific viewpoint of semiotics in computing, in recent decades, there has been evidence of a growing interest in semiotics on the part of those concerned with computer science and on the part of those applying information technology to the domain of the humanities. The earliest mention of this topic was a brief four-page article in *Communications of the ACM* (Zemanek, 1966), which emphasized the importance of the semiotic analysis of programming languages. Publication of an actual study analyzing the computing domain, however, had to wait until publication of studies by Andersen (1997) and Andersen, Holmqvist, and Jensen (1993, 2007). Their work modeled computer signs within information technology in general. Such work was important because it opened the domain of the semiotic analysis of computing, and it has been continued further by authors such as Liu (2000). Ever since then, this domain has progressed through papers in Walter de Gruyter's *Semiotica* and the *Journal of Applied Semiotics*, through conference/workshop papers on *Organizational Semiotics*, and also through Springer's *Journal of Minds and Machines*, which takes a more philosophical approach. Other related publications are those of Floridi (1999, 2004), which provide wide-ranging discussion of philosophy as applied to the computing domain. In terms of application, the most advanced domain in this area of semiotics is human–computer interaction, the advances in which have been elucidated in a book by de Souza (2006).

The appearance of all these titles and papers would seem to suggest a growing interest in books relating to the technological application of the humanities. Nevertheless, in this domain much more remains to be done in exploring the relationship between computing and semiotics. This book is specifically concerned with semiotics in relation to programming languages, which represents an area of computing not yet covered in great detail by any existing book on computational semiotics.

1.5   The Structure of This Book

The fundamentals of semiotics can be examined from three viewpoints: first, through *models* of signs as an answer to the question of what signs are; second, through *kinds* of signs and the content that signs represent; and third, through *systems* of signs constructed by those signs. Accordingly, the main part of this book is organized into three corresponding parts. Part I starts by formalizing models of signs through consideration of the correspondences between two large trends in sign models. Since each trend incorporates the notion of kinds of signs and entities, Part II considers these trends' correspondences, based on Part I, and how they appear in computer programs. Finally, Part III compares and contrasts human and machine systems in terms of the foundations established in Parts I and II.

This structure differs from studies on language in general, which are usually organized according to the domains of syntax, semantics, and pragmatics. I chose the organization described above because the approach of this book arises from semiotics, which is situated at the most fundamental level of language, even before considering elements of linguistic structure such as syntax. The levels of syntax, semantics, and pragmatics do appear in the book but are distributed throughout the various chapters at appropriate points, when necessary. In this sense, the term *language* in this book does not signify a language in the context of linguistics, that is, a system with morphology, syntax, semantics, and pragmatics. The signification of language in this book is in its most abstract form, referring to a kind of sign system in which the signs are linguistic elements. In other words, I treat a language as a relation among linguistic elements and their interpretations.

Additional guidance on the structure of this book is provided in Figure 3.8 in Section 3.5, which shows a map of the chapters, indicating which part of the sign system is the focus of each chapter. This map appears after the definitions of basic concepts and terms in Chapters 2 and 3.

As mentioned previously, this book follows an interdisciplinary approach covering both semiotics and computer programming. Both domains require a degree of expertise, and for this reason an introduction to each is needed. An interdisciplinary book such as this one usually has several chapters of introductory material followed by the main content. This book, however, does not include such introductory chapters in either semiotics or computer programming. Rather, introductory material is provided throughout as needed.

For semiotics, the reason for not providing introductory material at the start is that I have not simply taken a theory established by just one semiotician and applied it to computer programs. When I began writing this book, semiotic theory was not sufficiently established to be straightforwardly applied in a complete form that could be introduced at the beginning of the book. Application of semiotic theory to a well-formed corpus required dismantling, reconsidering, and reconstituting the constituent theories. Most of the chapters in this book treat a semiotic problem that I find fundamental, and the problem is analyzed and hypothetically solved by some adaptation of semiotic theory through its application to computer programs. These hypothetical conclusions currently apply, in the most rigorous sense, only to computer programs. To show the potential of these conclusions, however, they are also applied to the artwork at the beginning of each chapter, thus offering an intuitive or metaphorical introduction to the hypothetical problem explored in the chapter. Although I am no more than an amateur with regard to the fine arts, these parts are included in the hopes of helping the reader intuitively grasp the significance of each chapter and to make the book more interesting.

In contrast, for programming languages, I refer only to theories and concepts already extant within the computer programming domain and merely utilize them for semiotic analysis: since a programming language is well-formed and rigorous, the relevant theory is fundamentally clear. Where necessary, introductions to a programming language and its related theoretical material are made at certain points in the book to clarify the point of an argument. For example, the next chapter introduces two programs and explains the purposes of the programs to an extent sufficient to fulfill the purpose of the chapter, which is to define what I mean by computer signs. A more substantial explanation of the underlying concepts of the two programming languages introduced in the next chapter is given in Chapter 3, along with a semiotic interpretation of these languages' differences. This is by design because this book considers various programming languages: each chapter is based on specific programming languages that best highlight the point of the argument. A thorough introduction to each language would itself require an entirely separate book. Among numerous programming languages, the two representative ones introduced here are Haskell (Chapters 3, 7, and 10) and Java (Chapters 3, 5, and 6). Moreover, Chapter 4 is based on the lambda calculus and other languages appear here and there throughout the book. Since there are many good books about each of the languages appearing here, readers interested in a more thorough understanding of these languages are invited to refer to these additional sources.

Both semiotics and computer programming have their own technical terms; these terms sometimes overlap, making the situation more complex. For example, the term *argument* can mean the persuasive thrust of a discussion in general, but in semiotics it often signifies a Peircian argument, whereas in computer science it refers to a parameter given to a function. To clarify such terminology, a glossary providing basic definitions, concepts, and the reasoning behind certain of my lexical choices is included at the end of the book, with separate term lists for both semiotics and programming. The usage throughout the book follows the definitions given in the Glossary.

The notations used in this book are as follows. Executable program code is shown in `typewriter face`, whereas mathematical notations, titles, emphases and important terms are in *italics*. Sample terms and phrases appearing in the book are enclosed in single quotation marks, whereas inline quotes taken from other references are enclosed in double quotation marks. Strings appearing in programs are enclosed in double quotation marks, and parentheses within program code are sometimes added, even when unnecessary, to explicitly indicate a program's composition. Some references have detailed information, such as chapters, page numbers, and paragraphs, indicated within square brackets. The format of this information differs according to the reference: for example, the format for Peirce (1931) is the composite of two numbers, such as [2.345], where the first number indicates the volume and the latter number gives the section number in the *Collected Papers* published by the Harvard University Press. I do not explain how to read the reference format for every reference; interested readers can consult the referred documents.

The individual chapters are based on my papers published in Walter de Gruyter's *Semiotica*, in the *Journal of Applied Semiotics*, and in the *Journal of Minds and Machines*. Specifically, for Part I, the original basis of Chapter 3 appeared in Tanaka-Ishii (2006), that of Chapter 4 in Tanaka-Ishii and Ishii (2008b), and that of Chapter 5 in Tanaka-Ishii and Ishii (2008a); for Part II, Chapter 6 appeared in Tanaka-Ishii and Ishii (2007), Chapter 7 in Tanaka-Ishii and Ishii (2006), and Chapter 8 in Tanaka-Ishii (2009); and for Part III, Chapter 9 appeared in Tanaka-Ishii (2008) and Chapter 11 in Tanaka-Ishii (2010). The content of these journal papers was modified for the purpose of archiving and also elaborated to make the overall arguments consistent.

2

Computer Signs in Programs

2.1 Introduction

A programming (or computer) language is an artificial language designed to control computers and machines. A text written in a programming language is called a program, and machines are thus controlled using programs. Programming languages follow strict rules on syntax and semantics, and a programmer must follow these rules to generate a program with the expected behavior. Once written, the program text is syntactically analyzed, optimized, or compiled if necessary, depending on the language, and then it is executed, or run, on machines.

Since the major theme of this book concerns signs, this chapter introduces the nature of the computer signs employed in programs before embarking upon the primary focus of the book in the next chapter. Recent programming languages are highly developed and have many distinct features and functions. A proper formal introduction to these programming languages would therefore require a book for each language. Because this book considers different languages in parallel, a thorough introduction to these languages is beyond the scope of the book. This chapter therefore limits the introduction of programming languages to the extent that is necessary to proceed to the main part of the book.

The introduction is briefly made through two comparable executable example programs written in two different programming languages. From among the substantial number of different programming languages, Haskell (Bird, 1998) and Java (Arnold *et al.*, 2000) were chosen because these languages represent two paradigms – a functional language and an object-oriented language – that have interesting features from a semiotic viewpoint. These two examples represent the essences of the languages needed for semiotic discussion throughout this book, which can also be seen in any other programs written in the same languages. I have made the examples as simple as possible, and the expressions appearing in these examples were chosen giving consideration to providing further explanation and consistency.

The examples should be easy for a reader from the computer science domain to understand. After a glance at the two sample programs below, these readers can readily skip the lengthy explanation appearing in the following section. The explanation is given for the sake of ambitious readers from the humanities domain, who might use computers every day but have never written programs. Such readers are invited to go through the following section while frequently consulting the glossary. In this chapter, for the moment, as long as readers roughly understand what is done, and where it is done, in the example programs, they should not have great difficulty proceeding further into the book, even if the details of the programs remain elusive. Even though the programs are short, they include a large number of concepts in computer science, each of which requires at least several pages of explanation. Explanation of some important concepts appear in the main part of the book. Here, I explain only the broad purposes of the blocks and expressions in these programs so that I can continue with the subsequent sections of this introductory chapter. I repeatedly come back to these two examples with further explanation throughout the main part of the book to elucidate the underlying concepts. Additional, related examples are given later in the book.

2.2   Two Sample Programs

Each of the two sample programs calculates the areas of three simple shapes: the rectangle, the circle, and the ellipse. These shapes are *represented* in the programs by an exact or approximated *modeling* sufficient for the purpose of area calculation. The rectangle and the ellipse here are modeled by the width and the height, whereas the circle is modeled by the radius. The width, the height, and the radius are represented by decimals.

The example Haskell program is shown in Figure 2.1. The program has three blocks, with the first block consisting of lines 1 to 3, the second block consisting of lines 5 to 7, and the third block consisting of lines 9 to 15.

The first block defines the data structure for the three shape types, where the `Rectangle` and the `Ellipse` each have two decimals and the `Circle` has one decimal. A decimal in Haskell is represented by a type denoted as `Double`, which is a basic data type provided by the language system. All three shapes are represented by the type `Shape`.

```
1: data Shape = Rectangle Double Double
2:            | Ellipse   Double Double
3:            | Circle    Double
4:
5: area (Rectangle width height) = width*height
6: area (Ellipse width height) = pi*width*height/4.0
7: area (Circle radius) = area (Ellipse (radius*2.0) (radius*2.0))
8:
9: main = let
10:          r = Rectangle 5.0 8.0
11:          u = Ellipse 3.0 4.0
12:          v = Circle 3.0
13:          ss = [r, u, v]
14:       in
15:          for (\s -> putStr("area: "++show (area s)++"\n")) ss
```

FIGURE 2.1. A Haskell program for calculating the areas of simple shapes.

The second block defines three functions, each of which represents a calculation procedure to obtain the area of a shape type. In the case of a Rectangle, given a width and a height, the area is calculated by multiplying the two, with multiplication denoted by *. Similarly, the area for an Ellipse is calculated from its width and height. The circle is slightly different in that the calculation is defined by using the area function defined for the Ellipse. To achieve this, the radius is doubled and the shape type is converted to Ellipse before calling the area function for Ellipse. Such reuse of the area function for Ellipse might not seem efficient because of the multiplication of the radius twice by 2.0 in line 7 and division of the whole area by 4.0 in line 6. This program is designed in this way for correspondence with the next sample program, which is written in Java.

The third block demonstrates the use of the defined data and functions. The let expression has two blocks; the first block is between let and in (lines 10–13) and the second block is after in (line 15). This *let-expression* (namely, let...in...) means that the second block should be calculated under the conditions of the settings given in the first block. The first block specifies the actual shapes of a rectangle (with a width of 5.0 and a height of 8.0), an ellipse (width of 3.0 and height of 4.0), and a circle (radius of 3.0), which are represented by the signs r, u, and v, respectively. Because the calculations for these shapes consist of applying the area function defined in lines 5–7, the shapes are put into a *list*, a data structure designed to handle multiple data items, one after another, with the list represented by the sign ss.

In the second block of the let-expression, in line 15, each shape is extracted from list ss and provisionally represented by the sign s. For each shape, a string (i.e., a set of characters) is generated and printed out, where the string consists of "area: " concatenated (i.e., combined) with the value of the area,[1] obtained by applying the function area to s, followed by a newline (a control character moving the output to the next line, in the context of printing text on-screen). The syntax in line 15, using \s ->, looks complicated but is explained in Section 7.4 in Chapter 7 and relies on the lambda calculus, which is introduced in Chapter 4.

The program therefore consists of a *definition* part and a *use* part, which operate both globally and locally. Globally, the first two blocks represent definitions and the third block represents use. Locally, the first block in the let-expression defines the four signs of r, u, v, and ss, while the second block gives their use. A definition is a kind of *statement* – the basic unit of execution in a computer program – whereas the use is described through an *expression*. Every expression has a value, which is not necessarily required for a statement. For example, 3, 4, 3+4, 2*(3+4), and pi*width*height/4.0 (in line 7) are all expressions. Definitions and expressions are inter-related: a definition contains an expression (on the right-hand side of the =) and an expression may include definitions, as in the first block of the let-expression.

One way to execute this program is by starting a Haskell language interpreter and loading the program.[2] The program is run by typing main. The first block of the let-expression is executed initially, and actual shape instances are allocated according to the definitions given in the first three lines of the program. Then, the second block of the let-expression is executed by using the definitions of the area functions (lines 5–7). The program output is the following:

```
area:  40.0
area:  9.42477796076938
area:  28.2743338823081,
```

---

[1] The necessary type conversion from a decimal to a string is performed by the function show in line 15.

[2] The program in Figure 2.1 can be made executable by adding the following two lines, which define the function for. This function is introduced for correspondence with the Java program shown in Figure 2.2.

```
for f []    = do return ()
for f (s:ss) = do { (f s) ; for f ss }
```

```
 1: abstract class Shape {
 2:   double width, height;
 3:   Shape(double w, double h) { width=w; height=h; }
 4:   public double area() { return width*height; }
 5: }
 6:
 7: class Rectangle extends Shape {
 8:   Rectangle(double w, double h) { super(w,h); }
 9: }
10:
11: class Ellipse extends Shape {
12:   Ellipse(double w, double h) { super(w,h); }
13:   public double area() { return Math.PI*width*height/4.0; }
14: }
15:
16: class Circle extends Ellipse {
17:   Circle(double r) { super(r*2.0,r*2.0); }
18: }
19:
20: void run() {
21:   Rectangle r = new Rectangle(5.0,8.0);
22:   Ellipse   u = new Ellipse(3.0,4.0);
23:   Circle    v = new Circle(3.0);
24:
25:   Shape[] ss = new Shape[] {r, u, v};
26:   for (Shape s : ss) { putStr("area: " + s.area() + "\n"); }
27: }
```

FIGURE 2.2. A Java program for calculating the areas of simple shapes.

where the three lines represent the areas of a rectangle of width 5.0 and height 8.0, an ellipse of width 3.0 and height 4.0, and a circle of radius 3.0, respectively.

Let us move on now to the corresponding Java program shown in Figure 2.2. The code contains five blocks, with the first four starting with the term class. These blocks define the data structures for the shape types: Shape, Rectangle, Ellipse, and Circle.

The class Shape first declares the width and the height as decimals (declared as double in lowercase, following the style for Java's basic data types). This class has two other functions, Shape and area. The Shape function (line 3) is needed for initial construction of an *instance* of shape data. The function area is for calculating the area.

The class Shape is a data type representing the other three shapes. Also, Ellipse is more abstract than Circle, because any circle is an ellipse, but not all ellipses are circles. Considering these relations among shape types from the viewpoint of mathematical sets, the classes are related by the keyword extends. A class that extends another class *inherits* the properties of that class, and the inherited properties can be used without declaration. For example, because the class Rectangle extends the class Shape (line 7) and inherits the properties of Shape, namely, the width and height declared in line 2 and the function area in line 4,[3] the width and height and the function area become properties of the shape type Rectangle even though they are not declared in the class Rectangle (lines 7 to 9). A more proper explanation of inheritance is provided in Chapter 5.

The function area is defined to calculate the area as the width multiplied by the height (line 4), and this is the *default* way to calculate the area for all classes that extend Shape. Since this calculation applies to rectangles, the class Rectangle does not require redefinition of the function area. For the other shapes, Ellipse and Circle, this calculation is inaccurate and must be refined. In this case, the function area is redefined (overridden) in line 13 for the class Ellipse; this new definition is also inherited by the class Circle, which extends Ellipse.

After the first four blocks forming the definition part of the program, the last block gives the use part. As was the case in the Haskell example, three instances, one of each shape type (rectangle r, ellipse u, and circle v), are newly allocated in lines 21 to 23. An array (a set of ordered data corresponding to the list in Figure 2.1) of type Shape is allocated in line 25 and represented by ss, and the shape instances are added to this array in the same line. Their areas are printed in line 26.

This program also consists of both global and local parts in terms of definition and use. Globally, the first four blocks represent definitions and the last block represents use. Locally, lines 21 to 25 define r, u, v, and ss, and line 26 gives their use. Similar to the Haskell case, in Java too, a definition is a statement and the defined signs are used in expressions. In addition, a sign is declared in terms of how it will be used in the program, before it is defined. A *declaration* is another type of statement declaring the use of a sign in a program. For example, in line 21 (Rectangle r = new Rectangle(5.0,8.0);), the first part, Rectangle r, declares that r will be used in the program and also that it represents data of the type Rectangle.

---

[3] The initialization function (i.e., the constructor) is treated differently from normal functions under inheritance in Java, whereas some object-oriented languages treat both the same.

The program is first compiled by a Java compiler and then executed[4] by a Java VM.[5] The program output is the following:

```
area:  40.0
area:  9.42477796076938
area:  28.2743338823081,
```

which is exactly the same as the output for the program shown in Figure 2.1.

2.3 Identifiers

The actual semiotic comparison and analysis of these programs starts in the next section. Leveraging these two examples, the rest of this chapter is dedicated to explaining which signs are of concern in this book and their semantic levels.

In short, four kinds of signs appear in computer programs:

Literals. Literals consist of constant values, such as numbers or a string of text.

Operators. Operators consist of special signs such as + (addition), * (multiplication), parentheses, quotation marks, and so on.

Reserved words. Reserved words are signs defined in the language system design.

Identifiers. Identifiers are signs defined and utilized within programs by programmers. An identifier represents a data structure and/or a function.[6] The choice of names is left to the programmer.

---

[4] The program can be made executable by placing the code in Figure 2.2 within the following code:

```
class SampleProgram{
//place the program here

void putStr(String s){
 System.out.print(s);
}

public static void main(String argv[]){
  (new SampleProgram()).run();
 }
}.
```

[5] Java VM stands for Java Virtual Machine, an interpreter for compiled Java code.

[6] Precisely speaking, identifiers include many other user-defined names, such as module names. In this book, such variants are generally considered to be classified as either data structures and/or functions.

All signs that begin with alphabetic characters are either reserved words or identifiers. Among the identifiers are those defined in the language *library*, which is the set of basic data structures and functions defined by the system designer and associated professional programmers.

In the case of the Haskell example in Figure 2.1, the literals are 2.0, 3.0, 4.0, 5.0, 8.0, and "\n"; the operators are *, /, [,], ++, (, and); the reserved words are |, =, data, let, in, \, and ->; and all other signs are identifiers. Among the identifiers, putStr and show are functions defined in the Haskell library, whereas the other signs are defined within the program.

Signs must be defined before being used, but the definition can be made by the user or within the system design. The first three kinds of signs are defined within the language system, and programmers merely utilize them. The definition and processing of these are specified in another programming language used to create the language system (further explanation and discussion of this concept are given in Chapter 11). In contrast, identifiers are defined by the programmer, and a program consists of hierarchical blocks of identifier definitions and uses.

An identifier usually corresponds to an address inside the computer's memory where the actual value is stored in the form of bits. The memory includes registers, main memory, and secondary memory. Values are represented by the corresponding identifiers and defined within the program. Among these values are data and functions, and both of these are stored at addresses represented by their corresponding identifiers: in the case of data, the data representation in bits is stored at the memory address associated with the identifier; in the case of a function, its code in bits is stored at the associated memory address. Some identifiers represent complex structures consisting of data and functions. For example, Rectangle indicates an ensemble of the data width and height, the constructor Rectangle(), and the function area(). Such an identifier also corresponds to a memory address indicating where the ensemble structure is located, and it is further subdivided in terms of the identifiers of data and functions.

Some identifiers can be removed during the optimization process (as will be seen in Chapters 7 and 10); however, programs can be executed without such optimization. Therefore, each identifier can be regarded as corresponding to a memory address. Historically speaking, identifiers *were literally* memory addresses in early programming languages. In many early assembly languages, programmers had to calculate free locations in memory and indicate the specific addresses for temporary data/code storage. This put a considerable burden on programmers with regard to the management of free memory, as well as significantly reducing program reusability, because addresses had no particular meaning for other programmers. Fortunately, the whole process of memory management is now automated. Today's identifiers are abstract representations of memory addresses in the form of signs.

The analysis in this book focuses mainly on these identifiers. Most other language-specific signs are defined as identifiers in the metalevel language that describes the language, as will be seen in Chapter 11. Moreover, many computer signs, such as visual icons for mouse clicking or operating system sounds, are implemented once through representation by some identifier within a program. That is, most signs used in computing are introduced as identifiers and defined at some programming level before being put to actual use. Therefore, the focus here on identifiers, in fact, covers most signs on computers. We use the term *computer sign* to denote these identifiers appearing in programs and we focus on them as our analysis target.

2.4   Semantic Levels of Identifiers

In the generation and execution of programs, different levels of semantics are used for the interpretation of identifiers.

2.4.1 Computer Hardware Level

The memory address assigned to an identifier is, in fact, what the identifier actually is, giving it meaning. An identifier represents the memory address as direct content. The address indicates the location of the actual value, in bits, represented by the identifier. The actual value in bits is obtained as a result of calculation. Such calculation is described in the program through the definitions and uses of the identifiers.

An identifier therefore represents both an address and a value in bits at the hardware level. With many programming languages, a programmer does not need to think about which address to assign to an identifier because the allocation of a memory address for each identifier is automated, as mentioned at the end of the previous section. Moreover, optimization of this automatic process has been much studied in compiler theory. This semantics at the computer hardware level is now becoming more the domain of professionals who build compilers and optimizers, whereas programmers tend to handle programs only at the higher levels of programming languages and natural language.

In this book, Chapter 10 concerns this level of the computer hardware.

2.4.2 Programming Language Level

All identifiers are defined and used in a program. This definition and use form another semantic level. For example, r, u, v, and ss are defined as identifiers and used in the last block of each of the two example programs.

The identifiers Shape, Rectangle, Ellipse, and Circle are defined in the first several blocks and used in the last block of both programs to define the content of r, u, and v. Such definition and use stipulate what these signs are. In all remaining chapters except for Chapters 6 and 10, the focus in terms of the semantic level is this programming language level as determined through the definition and use of identifiers.

In addition to definition and use, there are two other layers of interpretation within a programming language.

Layer of type. Many contemporary programming languages feature types, where a *type* indicates an abstraction of a kind of data, a function, or a combination of the two. A *typed* language means a language in which the type is declared explicitly in programs. The type of an identifier limits the kind of data that it represents and the kinds of expressions in which it can be used. Both Haskell and Java are typed. In typed languages, basic types are provided by the language system; typical basic types include integers, Boolean values (i.e., true/false), decimals, and characters. A complex type, namely, a large data structure formed as a combination of multiple basic types, is generated by a programmer by combining these basic types. For example, Double in Figure 2.1 and double in Figure 2.2 are basic types, whereas types such as Shape, Rectangle, Circle, and Ellipse are user-defined complex types. The rectangles represented by r in Figures 2.1 and 2.2 are both of type Rectangle and of type Shape as well. An identifier thus has interpretations at this level of the type. The corresponding semiotic question is considered in Chapter 6.

Layer of address. As noted in the previous subsection, an identifier is finally transformed into an address in memory, which indicates what the identifier actually is. An address is specified automatically by the language system, and before compilation or execution it is used as an address in the abstracted sense of an address that is relocatable (Levine, 2001) depending on the conditions of execution. Within a program, an identifier usually represents a value, but it often happens that addresses must also be represented and processed via identifiers. This is implemented using a special syntax or pragmatics predefined within the programming language. This direct meaning as an address within the program gives a meaning to the identifier. A related semiotic question is discussed in Chapter 6.

2.4.3 Natural Language Level

Programs are interpreted by people as well as by machines. They are read not only by the programmers who initially write them but also by other programmers who will modify and reuse these programs. The activity is helped greatly by attaching comments to program lines in natural language intended for human consumption. Another, more important issue at this level is the interpretation of identifiers that are apparently formed of natural language terms. For all programmers, identifiers give clues as to the intent of a program. For example, an identifier named `Rectangle` suggests that the corresponding data is *supposed* to represent a rectangle.

As explained previously, any identifier is defined and introduced by a programmer, and in this sense identifiers are arbitrary. For example, a term like `HiThere` could be used instead of `Rectangle` in the sample programs without changing their actions at all. If a programmer wants his program to be readable, however, `Rectangle` is a better identifier because it transmits the supposed meaning of the data structure in natural language. Therefore, programmers are trained to choose and design meaningful identifiers from a natural language viewpoint.

Since the identifiers are thus borrowed from natural language, they are considered subject to normal semiotic analysis of terms in natural language.

2.5 Pansemiotic View

Setting the interpretation level at the programming language level means considering the interpretation of signs *within* the semiotic system. It does not require external entities such as the physical objects that a program represents.

Such a viewpoint is called the *pansemiotic* view and is attributed to Charles Sanders Peirce's notions of human thought. For example, Peirce presented his drastic idea that "the fact that every thought is a sign, taken in conjunction with the fact that life is a train of thought, proves that man is a sign" (Peirce, 1931, 5.314). The reader might consider the pansemiotic view too extreme, especially in regard to humans. Humans are biological systems, and many humanistic phenomena might not be representable by discrete, digital signs. This basic premise, however, has been mentioned by many other philosophers as well. For example, Ferdinand de Saussure, another major semiotician and linguist whose work informs this book, said that "there is nothing at all distinct in thought before the linguistic sign" (de Saussure, 1911, p. 138). Similar ideas also appear already in the writings of Saint Augustine of Hippo (Yamanouchi, 2008, p. 141). Note that not all of these ideas deny the existence of entities apart from signs: entities exterior to signs do exist, of course, but the pansemiotic viewpoint suggests that they can be grasped in the mind only through representation by signs.

I will not argue here whether the pansemiotic view applies to human thought (although I personally believe that every rational thought process is pansemiotic). Putting aside whether it applies to human thought, the pansemiotic view is taken in this book because it allows comparison of computers with humans at the same level of the sign system. Indeed, the world of computing is a world made only of signs because all information handled by computers ultimately consists only of zeros and ones, or bits, represented by electric signals passing through circuits. These bits are combined into various patterns and computers are controlled by processing the bit patterns defined in programs. The computing world is a rare case in which the basic premise of pansemiotic philosophy holds.

PART 1

MODELS OF SIGNS

3

The Babylonian Confusion

It is natural, now, to think of there being connected with a sign (name, combination of words, written mark), besides that which the sign designates, which may be called the *Bedeutung*[1] of the sign, also what I should like to call the *sense* of the sign, wherein the mode of presentation is contained.

From *The Frege Reader* by Gottlob Frege. Edited by M. Beaney.
Oxford: Wiley-Blackwell. (Frege, 1892, p. 152)

3.1 Two Models of Signs

Consider the two images shown in Figures 3.1 and 3.2. Both are still-life paintings, and each shows an assemblage of objects in a frame. The painting in Figure 3.1 was produced by Jean-Baptiste-Siméon Chardin, who often painted household objects having various shapes and textures. Most of Chardin's still-life paintings are realistic and accurately reproduce the texture and the structure of the original object placement.

In contrast, the painting in Figure 3.2 was produced by Lubin Baugin and is representative of *vanitas* paintings. Each object represents one of the five senses: the mandolin is auditory; the flowers are olfactory; the chessboard, cards, and pearls are tactile and visual; and the bread is gustatory. Thus the painting as a whole represents human life. This is opposed to the mirror on the wall reflecting only empty darkness, representing death. The painting is considered to connote the vanity of life and has another title: *Allegory of Five Senses* (Martin, 1977).[2]

---

[1] The term *Bedeutung* was left untranslated in the cited translation. The usual English translation for the term is *meaning* or *signification*.

[2] Some interpretation goes much further (Réunion des Musées Nationaux, 2002). The mandolin represents a woman (because it is sometimes regarded as a woman's musical instrument), and the card represents a man (because it is a jack). In between is a purse (representing fortune), suggesting the relation of a man and a prostitute. These are all oriented toward the lower right

FIGURE 3.1. Jean-Baptiste-Siméon Chardin (1699–1779), *The Copper Fountain*, The Louvre. Photo credit: Réunion des Musées Nationaux/Art Resource, NY.

Chardin's objects mostly exclude deeper meaning, and therefore his painting may be described as the more realistic of the two. The representation consists of the visual image on canvas and its content is seen as a set of objects, so the representation is essentially dyadic. On the other hand, every object in Baugin's painting carries a meaning and interpretation, and as a whole the painting conveys a message. The representation is especially suited to the triadic model: in addition to the image and its content as object, each item in the painting evokes a subtext as well. The two paintings represent objects within a frame, but they differ in whether each object is associated with a further interpretation.

Similar contraposition has been present in a more general form in the domain of semiotics. The most fundamental semiotic question that philosophers and linguists have considered from ancient times is that of the basic unit of signs. The hypotheses in response to this question can briefly be classified into two sign models: the dyadic model and the triadic model. A sign

corner, suggesting convergence, or the end of the relation. In contrast, the bread and wine at the back of the painting represent Christianity, and the carnation represents chastity. As a whole, the painting conveys a warning against indulging in short-term pleasure and in favor of living under God's love in pursuit of pure spirit.

FIGURE 3.2. Lubin Baugin (1610–1663), *Still Life with Chessboard*, The Louvre. Photo credit: Réunion des Musées Nationaux/Art Resource, NY.

consists of two components, or relata, in the former model versus three in the latter model. The inherent difference separating these two models has been recognized since the beginning of the philosophy of language. Figure 3.3 summarizes the dyadic model and the triadic model.

The root of the dyadic model is found in the philosophy of Augustine in the fourth century (Nöth, 1990, pp. 87–88). Among the scholastics following this tradition, signs were regarded as *aliquid stat pro aliquo*, that is, *something standing for something else*. A sign consisted of a label or name (aliquid) and a referent (aliquo). For example, considering the sign 'tree', first there is the real-world 'tree', to which is attached the label 'tree'. Philosophers and linguists such as John Locke also considered signs dyadic (Nöth, 1990, p. 88). At the beginning of the twentieth century, Saussure advocated that the function of a label is not mere labeling but rather that the label articulates the content of the sign.[3] With the example of 'tree', it is not that a tree invokes the label but rather that the term 'tree' invokes the concept of the tree. To escape from the notion of *labeling*, Saussure referred to the two sides of a sign as the *signifier* (corresponding to a label) and the *signified* (corresponding to the meaning or content), and he asserted that these are two inseparable sides of a sign. This thought was inherited and further elaborated by linguists and semioticians such as Louis Hjelmslev (1943).

The root of the triadic model appears in Greek philosophy, in Plato and Aristotle (Nöth, 1990, pp. 89–90). Here, a real-world object is considered to

[3] This Copernican change is discussed in much more detail in Chapter 4.

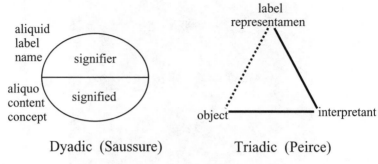

FIGURE 3.3. Dyadic and triadic sign models.

evoke its *idea* in the human mind and thus leads to its label. For example, a real-world tree reminds one of the idea of a tree, leading to the label 'tree'. Thus, in addition to a label and its referent, there is a third relatum – an *idea* or a *sense* – that is regarded as connecting the other two relata. An elaborate triadic sign model was developed by the Stoics (Deledalle, 1979, p. 194). After philosophers such as Gottfried Leibnitz, who favored triadic modeling, Peirce, in parallel with the development of the dyadic model in the nineteenth century, wrote that the order of the three elements appearing in the mind is not as Plato said: it is the *representamen* (label) that evokes the *interpretant* (idea or sense) defining the *object* (referent) (Peirce, 1931, 2.228).[4] In the example of the tree, the label 'tree' evokes the idea of the tree, which designates the referent tree. Since then triadic modeling has been accepted and promoted by linguists such as Ogden and Richards (1989) and Morris (1946).

Numerous philosophers have developed original sign models, and all have presented their own ideas about what should be considered as the relatum of the sign. Even among triadic models, as will be explained further on, the models of Plato and Peirce differ and cannot be considered as the same model. Still, if we consider only the number of relata within the sign model, the dyadic and triadic models and their variants have been the dominant sign models throughout human history. This naturally raises the question of how they are related. Understanding their correspondence promotes a better

[4] It has been controversial whether the main parts of Peirce's sign theory can be attributed to Peirce himself. Many have shown how parts of Peirce's major lines of thought originate in the philosophy of Aristotle and how Peircian philosophy on signs is deeply rooted in Stoic philosophy. For example, (Deledalle, 1979, p. 193) shows how triadic sign modeling, the distinctions among the representamen, interpretant, and object, and other important concepts in Peirce's sign theory already existed in the language philosophy of the Stoics. Clarification of the originality and newness of Peirce's theory is all the more complicated because of inconsistencies seen in his writings. The controversy over the originality of Peirce's academic contribution, however, is outside the scope of this book.

understanding of each model and also of the universal functions of each of the relata. Above all, readers from a relatively formal domain would doubt the impact of semiotics if such a fundamental concept as sign modeling was left undetermined.

Nöth (1990, p. 93) states, however, that the correspondence "before and after Frege is a Babylonian confusion." Above all, proper consideration of the relation between the two models has been infrequent, and even in the literature concerning this problem the conclusions have been controversial. The situation is made even worse by the fact that every time a new philosopher has contemplated sign models the relata of signs have acquired new names with original meanings.

The theme of this chapter is to establish a hypothesis for solving this Babylonian confusion through analysis of signs in computer programs. Above all, if the two models are both essential and important, then a concept in one model must be found in the other. Moreover, such contrast must appear in some form in computer signs too.

Because the names of relata proposed by philosophers have varied greatly, I select a representative naming convention for each sign model: from Saussure, representing the dyadic model, we have two relata, the signifier and the signified; and from Pierce, representing the triadic model, we have three relata, the representamen, the object, and the interpretant. The choice is based on the fact that these two men are considered the founders of semiotics.

3.2   Two Hypotheses

There is one point upon which everyone agrees: the relatum correspondence between Saussure's signifier and Peirce's representamen. Every dyadic model and every triadic model must include a dimension corresponding to the label (apart from its functionality), and the authors of the existing literature generally agree that this dimension corresponds to Peirce's representamen and Saussure's signifier.

Assuming correspondence of the remaining relata leaves only three possibilities:

* Saussure's signified corresponds to Peirce's object,
* Saussure's signified corresponds to Peirce's interpretant, or
* Saussure's signified corresponds to both.

Most importantly, in the first case, the location of Peirce's interpretant must be situated within the dyadic model; similarly in the second case, the location of Peirce's object must be identified.

Among those who have considered this correspondence, the two key representatives are Winfried Nöth and Umberto Eco. Nöth referred to the three relata of the sign model as the sign vehicle, reference, and sense. Nöth (1990, p. 83) states this issue as follows:

Triadic models distinguish between sign vehicle, sense, and reference as the three relata of the sign. Dyadic models ignore either the dimension of reference or that of sense.

Given the eminent scholars favoring the dyadic model, however, is it possible that they all ignored or overlooked something as fundamental as a sign relatum existing in triadic modeling? With this question in mind, let us first look at the existing hypothesis.

3.2.1 A Traditional Hypothesis

Many semioticians currently consider the signified to correspond to the interpretant. For example, Nöth characterizes Saussure's model as follows (Nöth, 1990, Section 3.1):

The distinctive feature of its bilaterality is the exclusion of the referential object.

Moreover, in one chapter of Nöth (1990, p. 94, Fig. M 3), he gives a table demonstrating the contrast between reference and sense, where sense corresponds to Saussure's signified and reference corresponds to Saussure's thing. Here, Saussure's thing is what Nöth considered the referential object in the above statement, which is excluded from the sign model in Saussure's theory. For Saussure, "language is located only in the brain" (de Saussure, 1911, p. 68), and therefore a thing cannot form a part of the sign model. Alternatively, in Nöth, sense corresponds to Peirce's interpretant and reference corresponds to Peirce's object. From these correspondences it can be inferred that Nöth regards Peirce's interpretant as corresponding to Saussure's signified and Peirce's object as corresponding to Saussure's thing.

Eco also discusses the correspondence between the dyadic and triadic models (Eco, 1979, 1988) and suggests correspondence between Saussure's *concept* and Peirce's *interpretant*. Saussure repeatedly uses the term *concept* to explain and define his signified (de Saussure, 1911), again indicating that Peirce's interpretant corresponds to Saussure's signified. Elsewhere (Eco, 1979, p. 60), Eco states that "objects are not considered within Saussure's linguistics."

Consequently, Nöth and Eco indicate that the two sign models of Saussure and Peirce can be related as follows:

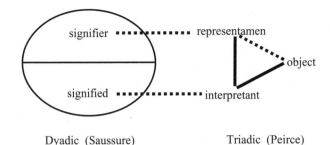

Dyadic (Saussure)   Triadic (Peirce)

FIGURE 3.4. Traditional hypothesis relating dyadic and triadic sign models.

- Saussure's signifier and Peirce's representamen correspond,
- Saussure's sign model does not include the referential object, and
- Saussure's signified and Peirce's interpretant correspond.

This traditional hypothesis is summarized in Figure 3.4.

3.2.2 A New Hypothesis
To consider the correspondence of Saussure's signified, the definitions of the relata in the sign models of Peirce and Saussure should be examined. First, Peirce (1931) explains his object as follows:

The Sign stands for something, its object. It stands for that object, not in all respects but in reference to a sort of idea. [2.228]

In the latter sentence, "not in all respects" is explained mainly by his distinction between two kinds of objects: the *immediate* and *dynamical* objects. The immediate object is "as the Sign itself represents it, and whose Being is thus dependent upon the Representation of it in the Sign" (Peirce, 1931, 4.536). This is expressed by Peirce as "a sort of idea", which is interpreted as "the mental representation of an object" in (Nöth, 1990, p. 43). In contrast, the dynamical object is the "Object outside of the sign"(Nöth, 1990, p. 43) or "the Reality which by some means contrives to determine the Sign to its Representation" (Peirce, 1931, 4.536). Therefore, Peirce's object in his sign model is the immediate object, which is actually the mental representation of a real-world entity. I must emphasize here the difference between Peirce's model and other triadic models from that of Plato to even recent ones such as that presented by Ogden and Richards (1989), the difference being that the dimension corresponding to Peirce's object is the material object. In contrast, Peirce considered the object as the concept of the object. This is demonstrated by Baugin's painting in Figure 3.1 in which the visual representation of the mandolin indicates the content of a mandolin as a concept in the mind, which differs from an actual mandolin external to the mind. The concept of the mandolin is Peirce's immediate object, whereas a real-world mandolin corresponds to the dynamical object. Peirce's model is particular in that the dimension of the object represents the concept of the real-world object. This is natural under Peirce's pansemiotic view, in which everything is a sign – inclusive of the concept of objects – as introduced in Section 2.5. Assuming a sign to be mental, their elements must be mental too.[5]

Considering that there are two types of triadic modeling, regarding the object as either mental or real, and that triadic modeling has historically re-garded the object as real, it is in some sense understandable that Nöth and Eco considered Peirce's interpretant to correspond to the signified, because both are mental. However, Peirce's distinction between the immediate and dy-namical objects raises the question of whether his object actually corresponds to Saussure's thing, because Saussure's thing is a material object external to his sign. More precisely, Peirce's dynamical object corresponds to Saussure's thing, with both referring to a real-world object. Peirce's immediate object, however, does not similarly correspond because it is mental in nature. It is more likely to correspond to Saussure's signified, which is explained in (de Saussure, 1911, p. 93) as follows:

The signifier[6] <(auditory)> and the signified <(conceptual)> elements are the two elements that make up the sign.

In other words, Saussure's signified is conceptual and therefore corresponds well with Peirce's immediate object. Such consideration is advantageous

---

[5] From this view of whether a sign is mental, in my opinion, it might be possible to consider the historical consequences of dyadism and triadism as follows. Originally, the ancient Greek philosophers tended to consider triadic modeling, in which the object was the real-world object. After Augustine proposed the dyadic model, the sign became abstracted and was considered to have mental existence. The dyadic model remained prominent until modern times, but today triadic modeling has regained its importance while incorporating the notion of a sign being mental. Foucault (1966, pp. 238–239) indicates that the following change occurred at the end of the eighteenth century:

Representation has lost the power to provide a foundation – with its own begin, its own deployment and its power of doubling over on itself – for the links that can join its various elements together.

The basis of perception via signs is founded on objects. When the objects were those of the real world, they functioned as the foundation of signs. Through the dyadic era, the notion of signs as mental drove them to become virtual, depriving them of a real-world foundation. When triadic modeling was revived, the notion of *use* appeared, doubling the signification while reinforcing the virtualization of signs.

[6] The original translation uses the term *signifying* extensively, but I've used the term *signifier* here because it is more common in modern semiotics.

because both dyadic and triadic models apply to many abstract signs without a real-world object, such as 'justice' or 'if'. The object or the signified within the sign must be a mental image. Consequently, there is the possibility that Saussure's signified corresponds to Peirce's immediate object.

Peirce (1931, 2.228) defines his other relatum, the interpretant, as follows:

A sign addresses somebody, that is, creates in the mind of that person an equivalent sign, or perhaps a more developed sign. That sign which it creates I call the interpretant of the first sign.

Peirce's objective in semiotic study concerns the formulation of human semiosis – the semiotic process – and the interpretant plays a crucial role in semiosis production. The interpretant of a sign calls other signs that evoke interpretants, which call other signs, and so on, leading to infinite semiosis. Peirce (1931) explains the interpretant with respect to the term *interpretation* [8.184]. Thus, the interpretant serves to evoke interpretation of signs in the form of semiosis, and this function is included in Peirce's sign model.[7] For example, the interpretation of the mandolin in Baugin's painting in Figure 3.2 is 'auditory among five senses', evoked from the concept of the mandolin. Peirce's sign model thus encapsulates not only the mental representation of an object but also its interpretations.

Now, clarification is needed as to where such interpretation is situated in Saussure's model. If Saussure encapsulates this in his sign model, then it should be contained inside the signified (because there is no other possible relatum), but how much Saussure's signified and concept constitute interpretation is not clarified in his students' notes (de Saussure, 1911, 1916, 1968).

Since Peirce's interpretant concerns semiosis, another way to find a solution is to look for the notion of semiosis within Saussure's philosophy. In Saussure's thought, the meanings of signs exist not only in the signified but also outside his model. Saussure (1911, p. 141) uses the notion of *difference*, which is explained as follows:

What I have said by focusing on the term *value* can be alternatively expressed by laying down the following principle: in the language (that is, a language state) there are only differences. Difference implies to our mind two positive terms between which the difference is established.

This thought can also be seen in his emphasis on the sign world as a holistic system, where the meanings of signs exist within the total language system

---

[7] Here, some readers might wonder about the relation between the interpretant and connotation. The term connotation in this book is considered solely according to Hjelmslev's notion, explained in Chapter 6.

(further explanation is given in Chapter 9). The differences among signs appear only in the presence of other signs within use. Then, it is likely that in Saussure's model the use of a sign is not incorporated in the sign model but exists as a holistic value within the system.

Overall, this raises another hypothesis, that Saussure's signified corresponds to Peirce's immediate object and Peirce's interpretant is located in Saussure's language system outside the sign model. The dimension of reference or sense is not *ignored* by Saussure; rather, the interpretant is simply situated outside the sign model, appearing as difference in use. This hypothesis is also consistent with the two different views of Peirce and Saussure as to how semiosis, a chain of signs as language use, is generated. Peirce thought that semiosis is generated successively by evoking the interpretant incorporated in each sign. The value of a sign generated by its use is embedded within the sign itself. In contrast, Saussure thought that a sign is used by some other sign, which is used by some other sign, and so on. The value of a sign generated by its use does not exist in the sign model itself, but in the language system.

Justification for which hypothesis is more accurate – whether the signified corresponds to Peirce's object or interpretant – cannot be done without concrete examples, and therefore it is now time to consider computer signs. If dyadic and triadic modelings are fundamental, then they should apply in the computer sign world too. Hence, this problem of correspondence must be understood by considering correspondence within the realm of computer signs.

3.3 Two Programming Paradigms and the Sign Models

Recall the two programs shown in Chapter 2. Note that the semantic level of an identifier is considered here in terms of its definition and use within a program. There is a large difference between the first program example and the second. In the Haskell program, shown in Figure 2.1, the functions for calculating the `area` of each shape are located *outside* the definition of the `Rectangle`, `Ellipse`, and `Circle` data, whereas in the Java program, shown in Figure 2.2, these functions are encapsulated *inside* each of the classes. The question addressed here is where to locate the calculation of the common function `area` with respect to the definition of the shape.

For the program in Figure 2.1, this question is addressed on the function side by changing the calculation method according to what shape it receives as an argument.[8] The `area` functions are defined in lines 5 to 7 for each different shape, separately from the data type definition in lines 1 to 3. In contrast, for

---

[8] See the glossary for an explanation of 'argument' as a programming term.

the program in Figure 2.2 the question is addressed by having the function area belong to each of the classes Shape and Ellipse (and through the effect of extends, the classes Rectangle and Circle also include the function area). The function area is regarded as functionality *belonging* to the data classes of each shape.

This difference also appears in the use of the function to calculate the areas of the shapes. In line 15 of Figure 2.1, the expression is (area s); namely, it is *the function that takes* each shape represented by s as the argument. The shapes *are referred to from a function existing elsewhere*, namely, the area function. In contrast, in Figure 2.2, the notation for use appears in line 26 as s.area(), which means that the *shape* s *calls the in-class function* area, which belongs to the class.

The first program, in Haskell, was written using a paradigm called *functional programming* (Bird, 1998; Hudak, 1989). In languages using this paradigm, programs are described through functional expressions. A function is a mapping of an input set to an output set. In this paradigm, functions are considered the main entity;[9] therefore functions that apply to data are defined *outside* the data definitions. The use of data is not included in the data definitions, which thus remain *minimal.*

The second program, in Java, was written using another paradigm, *object-oriented programming* (Arnold *et al.*, 2000; Meyer, 2000). Programs are written and structured using objects, each of which models a concept consisting of functions and features. This programming paradigm enhances the packaging of data and functionality together into units: the object is the basis of modularity and structure. Therefore, the data definition *maximally* contains what is related to it. The calculation proceeds by calling what is *incorporated inside* the definition.

3.3.1 Dyadic/Triadic Identifiers

Now, let us consider the topic of the two sign models and see how the previously described difference between the programs is related to the dyadic and triadic models of signs.

There are two kinds of identifiers in the programs in Figures 2.1 and 2.2: one is dyadic and stands for either functions or data, whereas the other represents both functions and data. In functional programs all identifiers are dyadic, whereas in object-oriented programs dyadic and triadic identifiers are both seen. For example, in the Java program, the area identifiers in lines 4 and 13 are dyadic, in that each stands only for a procedure, whereas

---

[9] More technically, functions are considered first-order objects.

for the Shape, Rectangle, Ellipse, and Circle identifiers in lines 1, 7, 11, and 16, respectively, the class names are triadic in that they represent both data and functionalities. This mixture in object-oriented languages is a historical consequence of the fact that all identifiers were originally dyadic and the object-oriented paradigm was gradually incorporated into programming languages.

Since the theme of this chapter is the correspondence between dyadic and triadic modeling, from here on dyadic and triadic identifiers are distinguished as representing the functional paradigm and the object-oriented paradigm, respectively. This section gives further detail on this rough idea – that the dyadic sign model corresponds to the functional paradigm, whereas the triadic sign model corresponds to the object-oriented paradigm.

3.3.2 *The Functional Paradigm and the Dyadic Model*
A sign in the dyadic model has a signifier and a signified. Because all dyadic identifiers consist of a name and its content, the name is likely to correspond to the signifier and the content to the signified. For example, in Figure 2.1, the name Rectangle is deemed a signifier, standing for the data features of two Doubles, the signified. Through the name Rectangle, the set of features (i.e., the width and height) is collected. Such correspondence of the signifier and the signified also holds for identifiers that stand for functions: the function name area is a signifier representing a procedure of mapping as the signified.

These identifiers are used by other signs inside the program. For example, the shapes represented by the sign s are used by the function area. Note that this relation between Rectangle and area is not known from the Rectangle side (line 1). Rather, it is the function area that knows that it has a Rectangle as an argument (line 5). The fact adds a meaning to the sign Rectangle. Therefore, in the functional paradigm, identifiers acquire additional meanings by how they are used, but this is external to the representation of the identifier.

As in Saussure's theory, then, difference in use plays an important role. This can be seen from the fact that two identical definitions with different identifiers are not necessarily redundant or meaningless in the functional paradigm. For example, in Figure 3.5, data structures X and Y are identical but named differently. This does not make X and Y redundant, because they are used by functions in different ways, and this difference in use means that different meanings are given to X and Y; that is, X is used by funX (to increment X) but not by funY, whereas Y is used by funY (to decrement Y) but not by funX. Thus, X and Y are distinguished through their use difference. In other

```
data X = X Int
data Y = Y Int

funX (X i) = i + 1
funY (Y i) = i - 1
```

FIGURE 3.5. Additional meanings are applied to two identical data structures through the structures' use in the functional paradigm.

words, dyadic identifiers acquire meaning from use, which is located external to their content.

3.3.3 The Object-Oriented Paradigm and the Triadic Model

A sign in the triadic model has a representamen, an object, and an interpretant. Since all triadic identifiers in the object-oriented paradigm consist of a name, data, and functionalities, these lend themselves respectively to comparison with the relata of the triadic sign model. For example, in Figure 2.2, a Shape as the representamen represents two doubles (decimals), height and width, and the function area, which applies to the data. The data part makes up a concept of what a shape is, in terms of having a width and height, so the part is likely to constitute an immediate object in Peirce's term. This part cannot be an interpretant because it does not evoke any semiosis. Instead, semiosis is evoked by the functions that belong to each class. The function area utilizes multiplication in its calculation, thereby generating a further sign process. Also, the application of a function is analogous to interpretation because the area of a rectangle can be regarded as one interpretation of the rectangle. Thus, the functions defined within a class are deemed interpretants. This fits with semiosis generation in Peirce's model, which requires only local information incorporated inside the sign model and does not require the whole language system. The fact that each class has information about its functionality differs from the dyadic case, where it is the function that knows which data to handle.

In the dyadic model, different uses attribute additional meanings to dyadic identifiers. In contrast, in the object-oriented paradigm such meanings should be incorporated within the identifier definition from the beginning. Everything that adds meaning to an identifier must form part of its definition; therefore if two sets of data are to be used differently, they must appear as *two different structures*. The previous example of X and Y in Figure 3.5 is expressed using the object-oriented paradigm as shown in Figure 3.6. Here, the increment function is included in class X and the decrement function in class Y. Hence, X and Y are different data structures. That is, a triadic identifier

```
class X{                        class Y{

  int i;                          int i;

  X(int ii){                      Y(int ii){
    i = ii;                         i = ii;
  }                               }

  int fun(){                      int fun(){
    return i + 1;                   return i - 1;
  }                               }

}                               }
```

FIGURE 3.6. Meanings acquired via use in the functional paradigm are encapsulated within different classes in the object-oriented paradigm.

has its meaning described within its class. If two triadic identifiers' meanings differ in some aspect, then the difference must be visible within the identifiers' classes.

Note that this condition of putting *all class-related functions into the class* is actually applied, albeit in a limited manner, in a number of the most popular object-oriented programming languages. For example, consider the following functional program:

$$k \ (X \ i) \ (Y \ j) = i + j, \tag{3.1}$$

where k is the function and X and Y denote data types defined similarly to those defined in lines 1 to 3 of Figure 2.2. If this function is to be genuinely expressed in an object-oriented manner, the function k should belong to both classes, X and Y, because k uses both X and Y. This limitation, however, is not met in many actual object-oriented programming languages because of its technical difficulty.

3.4   The Babylonian Confusion Revisited

Finally, let us revisit the correspondence between the dyadic and triadic models. The two previous sections discussed which identifiers in the Haskell and Java shape programs correspond to each of the relata within Saussure's and Peirce's sign models. In the correspondence of the dyadic model and functional programming, signifiers and signifieds correspond to the names and content, respectively, of data and functions. However, in the correspondence of the triadic model and object-oriented programming, the representamen

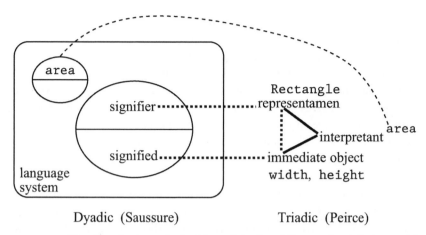

Dyadic (Saussure) Triadic (Peirce)

FIGURE 3.7. New hypothesis synthesized from Peirce's and Saussure's original material and verified through the correspondences of identifiers in the functional and object-oriented programming paradigms.

corresponds to class names, the object to the data structures that classes represent, and the interpretant to the functions that use these data. This implies the following correspondence between the dyadic and triadic models:

- Saussure's signifier corresponds to Peirce's representamen.
- Saussure's signified corresponds to Peirce's immediate object.
- Peirce's interpretant is located in the *use* that appears in Saussure's difference as another meaning of a sign. In Peirce's model, a use of a sign is represented as an interpretant, and semiosis is generated by calling an interpretant attached to the sign itself. In Saussure's model, however, semiosis is generated by a sign being used by another sign, which is used by another sign, and so on.

This correspondence is illustrated in Figure 3.7 following the hypothesis given in Section 3.2.2. In the dyadic model, meaning as use is distributed inside the language system as a holistic value, so that a sign sequence appears as a result of a sign being used by some other sign located in the system; in the triadic model, meaning as use is embedded inside the sign's definition, so that semiosis is generated through uses readily belonging to the sign.

If this hypothetical conclusion is applied to the two paintings discussed at the beginning of this chapter, Saussure's signifier and Peirce's representamen can be considered to correspond to the two tableaux; Saussure's signified and Peirce's immediate object correspond to the intuitive notions signified by each object; and Saussure's difference through sign use and Peirce's interpretant correspond to the conceptual interpretation associated with each. As a whole, Chardin's painting in Figure 3.1 is relatively dyadic and lends itself to the Saussurian sign model by excluding any obvious subtext from each object's representation. The interpretation evoked by the relation of objects, such as it is, is more concerned with composition and differences in texture. Such effects appear not through each object but rather through comparison among objects and through the relations in the placement of objects. In contrast, Baugin's painting lends itself to an understanding of the triadic sign model, evoking a literary interpretation in each object. Its interpretation relates the objects to the whole, together forming a higher significance.

Returning to programming, there is no definitive answer to the question of which model is better. Functional programming minimizes the target concept by excluding use from definition and instead distributing use throughout the system. This could raise the question of modularity, because much of the meaning of an identifier becomes holistic. However, the object-oriented model provides a rich, complete concept of the target, which enables modularity and encapsulation. Modeling and description of a target maximally for all entities, however, technically remains an open problem. Object-oriented languages still incorporate many dyadic uses of signs as illustrated in the sample program in Figure 2.2.

Assuming correspondence of the two models as hypothesized in this chapter, one important understanding gained is that the dyadic and triadic models are compatible: that neither model lacks or ignores components existing in some part of the other model. Although various software specifications might be better suited to one or the other of the two programming paradigms depending on the purpose of calculation, programs can be written using either paradigm for a given specification. For example, in the two program examples given in Chapter 2, the functional and object-oriented programs both give exactly the same output, as seen in Section 2.3. This is natural, because the difference between the two models lies only in where to situate the *use* of signs: inside or outside the sign model. Then, to the extent that my hypothesis is correct, Peirce's model is compatible with Saussure's model, and Saussure's model can be obtained when Peirce's interpretant is located outside the sign model but within the language system. Consequently, the dyadic and triadic models are compatible, both appearing in the artificial sign systems of computer programs.

3.5 Summary

The correspondence between the dyadic sign model proposed by Saussure and the triadic sign model proposed by Peirce was examined. Traditionally,

TABLE 3.1. Terms for each sign relatum given by two major semioticians discussed in this book, and the terms representing each relatum throughout the remainder of this book

Saussure (dyadic)	signifier	signified	holistic value
Peirce (triadic)	representamen	immediate object	interpretant
Terms in this book	signifier	content	use

it had been thought that Peirce's interpretant corresponded to Saussure's signified and that Saussure's model lacked Peirce's object. A novel hypothesis was developed by returning to Saussure's and Peirce's original definitions. That is, Peirce considered his object as a two-layered, dynamical object – the real-world object, exterior to the sign – and an immediate object – the concept of the object in the mind, interior to the sign. The immediate object was deemed to correspond to Saussure's signified, and Peirce's interpretant seems to be located in the *use* that appears in Saussure's difference as another meaning of a sign. The hypothesis suggests that Saussure's sign model is obtained when Peirce's interpretant is located outside his model but within the language system and that the two models are compatible. The hypothesis was thus verified through semiotic analysis of dyadic and triadic computer signs. The correspondence of program samples in each paradigm supports the newly proposed hypothesis. The contrast between dyadic and triadic sign modeling hence appears through the two computer paradigms of functional and object-oriented programming.

This newer hypothesis, as a potential solution for the Babylonian confusion, is summarized in Table 3.1, which might be of some help later in overcoming confusion about the correspondences among terms in the dyadic and triadic sign models. This table first includes the terms used by Saussure and Peirce. Hereafter, whenever Peirce's object is of concern the term indicates his immediate object, without being modified every time by *immediate*. The last line of the table also defines my own terminology for the relata of computer signs, which is used throughout the remainder of the book. There are two contexts in which I refer to the sign relata. The first context occurs when considering the thoughts of a semiotician (for either a dyadic or a triadic sign model). In this case, I will use the terms used by the semiotician in question. For example, I used both Saussurian terms and Peircian terms in discussing correspondences in this chapter. The second context occurs when considering the sign relata more generally according to the hypothetical correspondence obtained in this chapter. In the latter case, I will use the terms signifier, content, and use, as given in the table. These choices derive from the overlap of technical terms in semiotics and computer science.[10] Such names for sign relata indicate the nature of a sign in this book. The content concerns the *what*, or the semantics, of a sign, whereas the use concerns the *how*, or the pragmatics, of a sign. In other words, a sign is a medium for stipulating semantics and pragmatics.

Although the last row of the table contains three entries, this is not meant to imply that I am a partisan of the triadic model. As has been seen in this chapter and will be seen more extensively later in this book, the distinction between the two models can be made trivial as they are *equivalent* models under certain conditions. We pick up this train of thought in the next chapter.

Because I introduce a number of paintings in each chapter, I must briefly explain how I consider relata in terms of paintings as well, although they are meant only to provide intuitive introductions and the discussion of art in this book is not formal. Every work of art shown in this book forms a sign consisting of a visual graphic representing content or a subject interpreted by the painter. The dimension of the signifier corresponds to the visual/graphic representation of the artwork. The content can be considered to define the dimension of *what* is portrayed, and there are, briefly, two levels, as with Peirce's immediate/dynamical objects: the image of the content evoked in the painter's and the viewers' minds by the visual image, and the real-world object. The content of the paintings is considered to be on the former level. Note how this differs from the case of computation: the place of content could exist explicitly within a program, depending on the interpretive level (see Section 2.4), whereas content is mental in the case of a painting. In other words, the semantic level cannot stay within the painting because the content always concerns concepts that do not explicitly appear on the canvas, as opposed to the computer programming case. This has to be so because programs are interpreted by machines, whereas art is for humans to interpret, although the pansemiotic approach considers even such content generated in the human brain by a painting to be a sign – but I do not want to go that far for a domain such as art.

Last, the interpretation is considered to define the dimension of *how* the work is painted for a subject or content, which can be compared to *interpretation*, or the *use* of the content. The interpretation of a painting involves multiple aspects: linguistic interpretation, as seen in Baugin's painting in this chapter, and visual interpretation of the content, including composition,

---

[10] For example, the term *expression*, proposed by Hjelmslev, has a special signification in computer science, and the term *object* is the most ambiguous term in this book. The term *interpretation* also has a specific meaning in computer science, in terms of actual execution of program code. For the sake of clarity, I thus avoid using such terms, instead selecting the three terms given above.

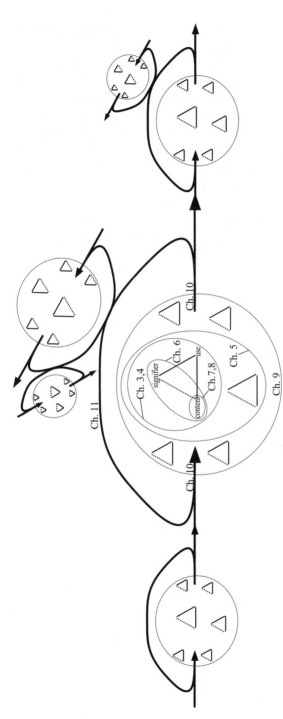

FIGURE 3.8. Map of this book. The first two chapters of Part I are dedicated to sign models, whereas Chapter 5 examines the ontology that appears when considering the relation of two signs. Part II covers the kinds of signs and content by looking more closely at the inner parts of signs. Chapter 6 considers the relation between sign and content, whereas Chapters 7 and 8 both analyze kinds of content. Part III is dedicated to a more global analysis of a sign system. Chapter 9 concerns the structure of the sign system, and Chapter 10 concerns the sign system's interaction. Chapter 11 analyzes the interaction among sign systems, including the system itself.

color, style, technique, and so on, or namely, everything that defines how the content should appear visually.

Consequently in this book, when I compare artworks to signs, the visual representation is considered to correspond to the signifier, the immediate object as the theme or subject of the painting to the content, and the stylistic/visual/linguistic interpretation of the content to the use, or interpretant. The difficulty in semiotic explanation of artwork as compared with programming lies in the mélange of all these relata, which appears as an essential problem for computer signs and also as the essential nature of a sign, as is discussed in the following chapters.

This chapter closes with a map of the themes appearing in the book, shown in Figure 3.8. Further ahead in this book, especially in Part II, some readers might get confused about what is of concern. In that case, this map might be of some help.

4

Marriage of Signifier and Signified

So it was that by frequently hearing words, in different phrases, I gradually identified the objects which the words stood for and, having formed my mouth to repeat these signs, I was thereby able to express my will.

From Confessions by Saint Augustine. Translated by Albert C. Outler.
Philadelphia: Westminster Press. Library of Christian Classics, Volume 7.
Original work published in 397. (Augustine, Saint, 1955, Book I, Chapter VIII)

4.1 Properties of Signs

The distinction between the two paintings shown in the last chapter might not be as clear cut as it might seem for many other paintings. Consider the two paintings shown in Figures 4.1 and 4.2. Each representation shows an interpretation of content, but given the marked modification of the content the interpretation itself might have been the content for the painter. The painter could have gone through a process of trial and error, looking for the right representation that best matched the visual image that he wanted to paint. When the work was completed, its content in turn must have expressed the interpretive intent of the painter. The representation thus prevents a clear distinction between content and interpretation. It is difficult to say whether the two paintings lend themselves to dyadic or triadic semiotic models, and the representation concerns the content and the interpretation at the same time.

This chapter further explores the coming together of the signifier, content, and use defined in the previous section, especially by examining the distinctions between the relata of signs. As a starting point, let us review in greater detail how Saussure viewed the association between the signifier and the signified.

FIGURE 4.1. Hasegawa Tohaku (1539–1610), *Pine Trees*, Tokyo National Museum. Image courtesy of Tokyo National Museum.

Saussure considered the signifier and the signified inseparable, such that "the association between the two should be maintained and considered together" (de Saussure, 1911, p. 79). Signifier and signified are two sides of a sign, rather than two separate entities such that each may exist without its counterpart. His thought is reflected in his metaphor of a sheet of paper, where the signifier is the front and the signified is the back (Nöth, 1990, p. 59).

FIGURE 4.2. Joseph Mallord William Turner (1775–1851), *Norham Castle, Sunrise*, Tate Gallery. Photo credit: Tate, London/Art Resource, NY.

This seems reasonable because the signifier and the signified are the two elements of a sign in his dyadic model.

Even in natural language, however, the content of a word changes, and the association between the signifier and the signified sometimes does not seem as intimate as the connection between the two sides of a sheet of paper. Indeed, such caveats are also present in Saussure's writings. He specifies the most important principle of the sign as follows: "the linguistic sign is arbitrary" (de Saussure, 1911, p. 76). Saussure mentions that "the connection between the signifier and signified elements is a radically arbitrary connection" (de Saussure, 1911, p. 93). This arbitrariness indicates that there is no essential necessity in association between the signifier and the signified. In the case of computing, as seen in Section 2.3, computer signs are indeed arbitrary, because they are specified by the programmer who introduces identifiers. The arbitrariness of signs is thus obvious within the context of programming. In natural language, in contrast, such arbitrariness had to be discovered, another important contribution made by Saussure. One reason for this lies in the fact that in natural language people have to use the same sign to mean (almost) the same thing to communicate with each other. Saussure calls this *social convention* and indicates how signs are arbitrary but bound. He also indicates that the arbitrariness is a matter of degree in natural language. He raises the concept of *absolute* and *relative* arbitrariness by using examples. The terms 'poire' (pear), 'vingt' (twenty), and 'neuf' (nine) are all absolutely arbitrary, but words derived from these words, such as 'poirier' (pear tree) or 'vingt-neuf' (twenty-nine) are relatively arbitrary (de Saussure, 1911, p. 85).

At first sight, it is not so obvious how the marriage between the signifier and the signified and the notion of arbitrariness may hold at the same time, because the former seems to unify the signifier and the signified, whereas the latter seems to separate them. Saussure further presents the following notion of *difference* that we saw in the previous section, which constituted the basis of structuralism (de Saussure, 1911, p. 141):

In the language there are only differences . . . there are only differences, without positive terms. . . . In the end, the principle it comes down to is the fundamental principle of the arbitrariness of the sign. It is only through the differences between signs that it will be possible to give them a function, a value.

Here, mention of both signifiers and signifieds disappears. A sign system is a system of relations, including that between the signifier and the signified, that among signifiers, and that among signifieds. To the extent that such a network of relations is formed, there is no necessity that a specific signifier be used to represent a signified.

Saussure himself seems to have questioned how all these go together: he frequently remarks how *paradoxical* the language system is regarding the nature of the signifier, arbitrariness, and difference (de Saussure, 1911, pp. 135 and 141). The questions underlying this paradox are the association between the signifier and the signified, whether or not they are separable, and, above all, the *role* of a signifier with respect to a signified. The aim of this chapter is to consider this role through computer signs. As was seen previously, computer signs are fundamentally arbitrary: in a compiled program there is neither social convention nor relative arbitrariness.[1] Therefore, the marriage of signifiers and signifieds in computer signs seems even less intimate than was previewed at the beginning of this chapter. By examining the signification of the association between the signifier and the signified this chapter attempts to clarify the paradox of this marriage and determine the nature of this association.

Thus far, I have considered high-level programming languages, which are elaborated with well-defined structures. These well-established programming languages have different kinds of signs, as will be seen in Part II. In contrast, this chapter examines the most minimal representation of computer language, called the lambda calculus, because the goal here is to consider the fundamental nature of signs, and the analysis must therefore remain as close as possible to the level of individual signs.

The lambda calculus has been widely adopted as a fundamental framework for describing languages in general, including both programming and natural languages. It was originally created to formulate problems in computability and is known as the smallest universal programming language. Being compact yet powerful, it is used as a metalanguage for analyzing programs. It has also been adopted in the domain of the formal semantics of natural language, as in the Montague grammar, where the lambda calculus is used as a metalanguage to formally describe the semantics of natural language discourse.

The extent of application of the lambda calculus as a formal language suggests that the key to what makes a language a language is embedded within the framework of the lambda calculus. If a language is formed of signs, each of which is a medium carrying meaning, then the lambda calculus should

---

[1]　This depends on the semantic level of interpretation, as introduced in Section 2.3. If a program is interpreted at the natural language level, social convention and relative arbitrariness are present in programming too. For example, identifiers are named conventionally to indicate certain data structures and functions. Social convention and arbitrariness are absent if a program is considered at the interpretive level of the programming language or the computer hardware (see Section 2.4).

consist of at least a relevant framework of signs. In my opinion, the lambda calculus does indeed consist of a systematic, uniform model of signs.

4.2 Lambda Calculus

The chapter starts by introducing the lambda calculus because some readers, even in computer science, might not be especially familiar with this fundamental theory. Readers who are familiar with the lambda calculus are invited to skip this section and proceed directly to the next section. The introductory section is very informal and limited, however, and is intended only to cover the basic theory necessary to explain the main theme of this chapter. For a more complete explanation of lambda calculus theory, see Barendregt (1984), Church (1941), Hindley and Seldin (2008), and other introductory books on the lambda calculus.

The lambda calculus was originally established by Alonzo Church and Stephen Kleene in the 1930s. It was created to formulate problems in computability, and since it is considered the smallest universal programming language, any computable function can in principle be expressed and evaluated using it. The lambda calculus has been mathematically proved to be equivalent to a Turing machine.[2]

Formally, the lambda calculus consists of (1) a function definition scheme and (2) variable substitution. Its complete grammar can be presented using a context-free rule set within only three lines, as follows:

$$<\text{expression}> ::= <\text{identifier}>$$
$$<\text{expression}> ::= \lambda <\text{identifier}> . <\text{expression}> \qquad (4.1)$$
$$<\text{expression}> ::= <\text{expression}> <\text{expression}>,$$

where <expression> and <identifier> denote the sets of expressions and identifiers, respectively, and the symbol ::= indicates the Chomskian recursive definition of a grammar by using rewrite rules (Chomsky, 1956).[3] As noted in Section 1.5, the composition of the following programs is often made explicit

---

[2] A Turing machine is an abstract computing machine proposed by Alan Turing to formally describe the computability of a function. A Turing machine is a triplet consisting of a tape of symbols, a head, and a transition table. Computing is described as a state transition using the transition table. The input consists of the symbol recorded on the tape at the place of the head, and the current state consisting of the content written on the tape and the location of the head. For every input, the transition table gives the machine movement (namely, the head movement and the read/write of symbols on the tape at the location of the head) and the next state.

[3] The notation here follows Backus–Naur Form from the computer science domain (Backus *et al.*, 1963).

by the use of additional parentheses, although parentheses are not defined in this grammar. In the rest of this chapter, the grammar and language derived from this three-line definition are denoted simply as LG.

Briefly, the first line of LG introduces identifiers and thus signs within a system. The second line expresses function definition as a composite of signs. The last line specifies how to use the function thus defined. First, to illustrate what the lambda calculus is, we assume the existence of numbers and a calculus for them even though they are not defined within LG. (This aspect is explained later in this section.)

An expression generated by the second line of LG is called a *lambda-term*. An example of a lambda-term is given by

$$\lambda x . x + 1. \tag{4.2}$$

This expression denotes a function that performs the addition of one to the variable x. In a lambda-term, the <identifier> located to the right of λ shows that the use of the identifier is limited to what is contained within the <expression> coming immediately afterward. This range, where the variable just after λ is valid, is called the *scope*. In the above example, the <identifier> to the right of λ is x, and the <expression> is x + 1. The scope of x is x + 1; that is, x is valid only within the expression x + 1. The variable x is arbitrary and can be replaced by any other identifier, such as ohDear, as long as all x are consistently modified within the scope, as in λ ohDear . ohDear + 1.

An identifier with a scope defined in an outer expression is also allowed in the lambda calculus. For example, in the expression

$$\lambda x . x + y, \tag{4.3}$$

x is bound within the lambda-term, but not y. This y is introduced by another lambda in an outer lambda-term starting with λ y, which restricts the scope of y. More precisely, expression (4.3) takes the form

$$\lambda y . (\cdots \ (\lambda x . x + y) \ \cdots), \tag{4.4}$$

where the first lambda defines the scope of y as being within the total expression coming after λ y, including the lambda-term for x.

A lambda-term thus defined can be juxtaposed with another expression, as expressed in the third line of LG. This evokes variable substitution, which is the semantics of the grammar of this third line. That is, calculation in LG proceeds by juxtaposition of two lambda-terms. The operation performed by this juxtaposition is called a β-reduction and is present in the system of the lambda calculus.

For example, in the composite expression $(\lambda x . x + 1)$ 2, the first <expression> in the third line of LG corresponds to $\lambda x . x + 1$, and the second <expression> corresponds to 2. Such juxtaposition triggers the β-reduction, which starts by substituting 2 for x, and the expression is further reduced as follows (where $\rightarrow$ denotes a *reduction*, a step in calculation):

$$
\begin{aligned}
&(\lambda x . x + 1) \ 2 \\
&\rightarrow 2 + 1 \\
&\rightarrow 3.
\end{aligned}
\tag{4.5}
$$

Another example of a β-reduction is the merging of two lambda-terms to obtain a simpler expression. For example, applying the function 'apply a function twice to 3' to another function 'add something to 1' is reduced to generate a simple expression of 5:

$$
\begin{aligned}
&(\lambda f . f \ (f \ 3)) \ (\lambda x . x + 1) \\
&\rightarrow (\lambda x . x + 1) \ ((\lambda x . x + 1) \ 3) \\
&\rightarrow (\lambda x . x + 1) \ (3 + 1) \\
&\rightarrow (\lambda x . x + 1) \ 4 \\
&\rightarrow 4 + 1 \\
&\rightarrow 5.
\end{aligned}
\tag{4.6}
$$

Various paths can be followed to reduce the juxtaposed lambda-terms. For example, by applying the β-reduction to the first lambda-term in the second line, the previous reduction could have proceeded as follows:

$$
\begin{aligned}
&(\lambda f . f \ (f \ 3)) \ (\lambda x . x + 1) \\
&\rightarrow (\lambda x . x + 1) \ ((\lambda x . x + 1) \ 3) \\
&\rightarrow ((\lambda x . x+1) \ 3) + 1 \\
&\rightarrow (3 + 1) + 1 \\
&\rightarrow 4 + 1 \\
&\rightarrow 5.
\end{aligned}
\tag{4.7}
$$

Church and Rosser mathematically proved that if an expression is reduced to another lambda-term by β-reductions and the resultant lambda-term is no longer reducible, then the expression will be unique, regardless of the path the reduction followed; this is the Church–Rosser theorem.

Returning now to the fact that numbers and addition are not defined within LG, Church formally showed that the numbers described as follows using only

LG (Church, 1936) are mathematically equivalent to the natural numbers.

$$
\begin{aligned}
\lambda f . \lambda x . x \quad & \text{signifies} \quad 0 , \\
\lambda f . \lambda x . f \ x \quad & \text{signifies} \quad 1 , \\
\lambda f . \lambda x . f \ (f \ x) \quad & \text{signifies} \quad 2 , \\
\lambda f . \lambda x . f \ (f \ (f \ x)) \quad & \text{signifies} \quad 3 , \cdots .
\end{aligned}
\tag{4.8}
$$

Hence, the number of times f appears within the expression indicates which number it represents. Also, the successor – the function to add one to a given natural number – is given as

$$
\lambda c . \lambda g . \lambda y . g \ ((c \ g) \ y) . \tag{4.9}
$$

Consider briefly how the addition of 1 to 2 is conducted. In the following, the substituted lambda-term is underlined.

the successor to 2 corresponds to
$(\lambda \underline{c} . \lambda g . \lambda y . g \ ((\underline{c} \ g) \ y)) \ \underline{(\lambda f . \lambda x . f \ (f \ x))}$
$\rightarrow \lambda g . \lambda y . g \ (((\lambda \underline{f} . \lambda x . \underline{f} \ (\underline{f} \ x)) \ g) \ y)$
$\rightarrow \lambda g . \lambda y . g \ ((\lambda \underline{x} . g \ (g \ \underline{x})) \ y)$
$\rightarrow \lambda g . \lambda y . g \ (g \ (g \ y))$
signifies 3

$$
\tag{4.10}
$$

Thus, the addition of 1 is expressed merely through substitution of identifiers, namely, through β-reductions. The addition of greater numbers is expressed as chains formed by applying the successor. Subtraction, multiplication, and division are expressed similarly to addition. Thus, the lambda calculus can fully express numbers and calculation on numbers. Similarly, functions such as if ... then ... else ... and comparison operators (such as the iszero function to determine whether an expression is equal to zero) are theoretically known to be expressible via lambda-terms (which are used in Section 4.4). In this chapter, for clarity of explanation, these basic functions and data are described in the usual way based on these previous formal studies. Also, an addition expression such as x + y is denoted by using the infix operator +, replacing a more formal expression, ((+ x) y).

Even within this small framework of the lambda calculus, the expressiveness of the language has been proved to be equal to that of a Turing machine (Rosser, 1939; Davis, 1965; Sipser, 2005, p. 160). This means that any computation can be described by chains of β-reductions through mere substitution of signs.

With this expressive power of the lambda calculus, its framework has often been used to describe both the semantics of a programming language and the formal semantics of natural languages. The formal semantics of natural language dates back to Gottlob Frege and Bertrand Russell, who denoted the semantics of language through logic (Lycan, 1999). The description later integrated the lambda calculus. Merging this trend with the formality of the *possible world* proposed by Rodolf Carnap and then established by Saul Kripke, Richard Montague developed a theory of semantics called the Montague grammar (Cann, 1993; Montague, 1974; Partee and Hendriks, 1997) based on the lambda calculus. Such use of the lambda calculus as the formal framework of natural language suggests the potential of natural language interpretation not being so far from that of computer languages: one essence of natural language interpretation might be substitution.

The widespread use of the lambda calculus as a fundamental framework for both natural and computer language is brought forth, I believe, through the uniform modeling and treatment of signs, which facilitates the interaction among expressions. This aspect is considered next from a more semiotic viewpoint.

4.3   The Lambda-Term as a Sign Model

The previous chapter presented the two kinds of sign models, dyadic and triadic. How these apply to LG is now considered. Since this chapter started with an introduction to Saussurian thought (Section 4.1), which is representative of dyadic modeling, the discussion now begins from the dyadic side. The relation between the lambda-term and the triadic model is discussed later in Section 4.5.

In any sign model, two different functions for sign generation are seen: one for articulation and the other for naming. The essence of Saussure's innovation lies above all in where to place the existence of the function of *articulation* within the sign model.

To *articulate* in this book means to construct a semiotic unit formed of signs. For example, the natural language term 'cold' usually is stipulated by people via relative temperature, but it can also be articulated by means of its definition in words, as in the Oxford English dictionary: "at or having a low temperature, especially when compared with the human body." Similarly, every lambda-term can be considered as an articulation. For example, the complex concept of adding one is articulated by $\lambda x . x + 1$. This definition of articulation means to situate the semantic level within LG (see Section 2.5). For example, the semantics of the sign f given a lambda expression $(\lambda f . f \ (f \ 3))(\lambda x . x + 1)$ is considered within the expression, such that the name f is introduced in $(\lambda f . f \ (f \ 3))$, set to $(\lambda x . x + 1)$, and used within the expression $f \ (f \ 3)$.

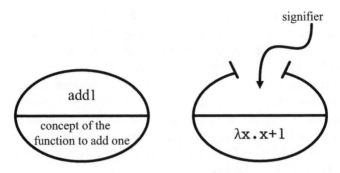

FIGURE 4.3. Modern dyadic sign model and the lambda-term.

Returning to Saussure's innovation, he elaborated his sign model, in a sense, by denying signs as *nomenclature*, or mere labels, applied to real-world objects (see also Section 3.1). Before Saussure, a sign was thought of as something that stands for something else. The function of articulation was considered to exist within the *content side*. Every real-world object was considered to have an essential (platonic) form (or *idea*) underlying it, which was necessarily articulated. This preexisting idea, the nature of a category of objects, emerged as each object's essence. The signifier's role was simply to attach a name to an idea, an essential name based on the content.

Saussure's innovation was to situate the articulation function on the signifier's side and consider these two processes to be tightly coupled. Within any dyadic model after Saussure, the signifier, or name, is a function to articulate the signified; that is, articulation is performed by the signifier.

A lambda-term such as $\lambda x . x + 1$ also has the two functions of articulation and naming. A lambda-term can thus be considered to possess the functions of a sign. In terms of articulation, every lambda-term articulates a unit. This articulation is not made by any signifier, because the lambda-term does not yet have a name, but rather is made by a special abstract entity provisionally called lambda. This lambda does not correspond to a signifier because a common λ is used for any articulation.

With regard to naming, the lambda calculus has a drastically different aspect with respect to both nomenclature and modern dyadic sign models. Naming occurs when two lambda-terms are juxtaposed for a β-reduction. The first expression then *names* the second expression. A lambda-term therefore has the function of naming, but this is to *provide* a signifier to others. For example, in the reduction of $(\lambda f . f \ (f \ 3)) \ (\lambda x . x + 1)$, the name f signifies the second expression $(\lambda x . x + 1)$. Thus, substitution of the identifier within the β-reduction is regarded as the action of naming the second expression.

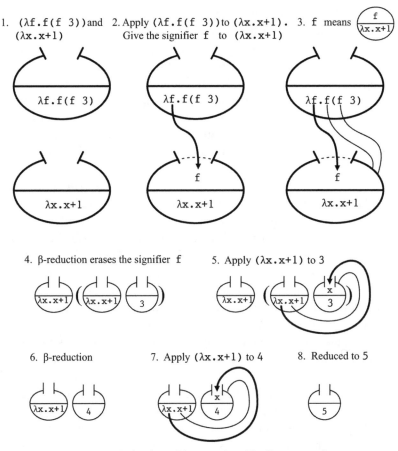

FIGURE 4.4. Reduction of $(\lambda f.f\ (f\ 3))\ (\lambda x.x\ +\ 1)$.

Within any dyadic sign model, the focus of discussion has been how a concept itself *acquires* a name. In contrast, in a lambda-term *A*, the naming process is modeled in terms of how to *provide* a name to an expression *B*, so that *B* is consumed within *A*.

An illustration of the difference between a modern dyadic sign and the corresponding lambda-term is shown in Figure 4.3. The left side shows the modern dyadic model for a sign with the signifier *add1* articulating the content of a function *to add one*. The corresponding sign model and lambda-term are shown on the right. As explained previously, the signified is $\lambda x.x + 1$, articulated by lambda, and a signifier is not yet given so the signifier part is shown as *open*.

Naming functions when two lambda-terms are juxtaposed. An illustration is given in Figure 4.4 for the example of $(\lambda f.f\ (f\ 3))\ (\lambda x.x + 1)$. In step 1, the two lambda-terms $(\lambda f . f \ (f \ 3))$ and $(\lambda x . x + 1)$ are juxtaposed. Then, in step 2, the first expression is applied to the second, providing the identifier f to the second expression. Step 3 shows how f consistently indicates the same expression. The β-reduction then proceeds, and the whole reaches the state shown in step 4, resulting in the number 3. Because two expressions juxtaposed within parentheses have higher priority for reduction, x is next provided by the second $\lambda x . x + 1$ to the number 3 for application in step 5. This β-reduction proceeds and the result is shown in step 6. In step 7, x is given to the number 4 this time and another reduction gives the resulting number 5.

Naming in the lambda calculus thus facilitates *interaction* between two lambda-terms through the substitution of β-reductions. In particular, a name is needed to consistently indicate a complex ensemble within a scope. As long as this purpose is met, the identifiers provided to lambda-terms are arbitrary. For example, even if $(\lambda f . f \ (f \ 3))$ were modified to $(\lambda \ ohLaLa . ohLaLa \ (ohLaLa \ 3))$, the reduction just seen would produce the same result of 5. This function of interaction among signs is not explicitly modeled within the modern dyadic sign model. Saussure further mentions interaction among signs under the name of syntagm (which developed into the concept of syntax in modern linguistics), but the syntagm is a mere juxtaposition of different signs and does not explain how signs actually interact by juxtaposition.

Another observation from the articulation and naming of lambda-terms is that a name is always given *dynamically* to something that has been previously articulated by λ. The name is thus always a *local* name provided by the first expression to the second, and it is only valid within the scope of the lambda-term. In contrast, in any dyadic model the sign model is not aware of the scope of the sign. All signs are considered global, then the names become static, because a global scope requires a large number of replacements in seeking to change a name. Even though the notions of local versus global and dynamic versus static are relative, modern dyadic models consider signs to be relatively *global* and *static*, in the sense that the scopes of signs are not considered.

Natural language, in fact, also has the notion of scope. For example, a research project usually acquires a name to which the researchers involved refer while the project exists. For those unrelated to the project, the name is meaningless. Thus, the project name remains local. Another example is the scope of a specific language, such as English or Japanese: words are used locally within a large scope. The locality of names – or social convention – forms a hierarchy, from a minimal scope of two people to scopes consisting of a family and then a community, within a more maximal unit consisting of an

TABLE 4.1. Contrast of three sign models: nomenclature, modern dyadic sign models, and lambda-terms

	Nomenclature	Saussurian Dyadic Models	Lambda-Term
Language	natural language	natural language	lambda calculus
Articulation by	signified	signifier	lambda-term
Naming	static	static	dynamic
Arbitrariness	not arbitrary	arbitrary	arbitrary
Name is given to	itself	itself	other
Scope	not considered	not considered	explicit

ethnicity, up to the whole human race, just as in the case of a lambda-term, as shown in expression (4.4) in Section 4.2. Therefore, there are different levels of scope even in natural language, although this notion has not been considered in the dyadic model.

Consequently, the lambda-term explains the various features of signs, such as sign interaction and scope, through the basic functionalities of articulation and naming. The argument thus far is summarized in Table 4.1. Before Saussure, a signifier was, in a sense, merely a name associated with some content, which was readily articulated by the content itself, and signs were not seen as truly arbitrary. The role of the signifier during this epoch was simply that of a *label*. Within the modern dyadic model, the main role of a signifier is articulation. Dyadic signifiers are relatively static and global, without the notion of scope. At the same time, these signifiers are arbitrary. The question of the role of the signifier in terms of how it functions for articulation while remaining arbitrary still has not been clarified at this point.

In the case of lambda-terms, articulation is made through an abstract function specially designed for articulation. A lambda-term has a mechanism to provide a name to another expression so that the expression interacts with the lambda-term. The name is the means of interaction to indicate identical content among communicators. Thus, the name suffices if it is a local name placed dynamically, being valid only within a certain scope. Under such circumstances, a signifier is by nature arbitrary because its role is to consistently indicate the same complex concept within an expression.

Such a view of the lambda calculus, however, shows that the name is introduced in a manner unrelated to the content.[4] For example, in $\lambda x . x + 1$, the content itself is already articulated before a name is given to it, and the

---

[4] In fact, to implement LG as a running system, a portion of memory space indicated by an address must be given to every lambda-term. At the level of implementation, therefore, it is always the case that a lambda-term is realized through an address that is, a signifier. A

name x is already present before some other content is signified. In contrast, for the dyadic model, Saussure says that the signifier articulates the signified; signifier and signified are inseparable two sides of a sign, and each side cannot exist without its counterpart.

If a sign consists of a signifier and a signified, there must be three cases of when to introduce each component: the signified first, then the signifier; the signifier first, then the signified; and both at the same time. Nomenclature follows the first case and the lambda-term follows either the first or the second case, whereas the Saussurian dyadic model follows the last case. The current LG is unable to introduce a pair consisting of a signifier and content at the same time. To observe the effect of simultaneous introduction, LG should be extended to allow such definition.

4.4   Definition of Signs by Self-Reference

Most practical languages, even programming languages, provide a mechanism to introduce a sign through definition. This allows introduction of a signifier to signify something articulated. In LG, too, this is enabled by adding another line to LG to allow introduction of identifiers whose content is readily defined. Inclusion of the following grammar adds the let-expression to LG.[5]

$$<\text{expression}> ::= \atop \texttt{let} <\text{identifier}> \ = \ <\text{expression}> \ \texttt{in} \ <\text{expression}> \tag{4.11}$$

The combination of LG with the let-expression and the language generated are denoted as LG–let from this point on. The let-expression means that the identifier is defined as the first expression, which is used within the two expressions, as is also seen in lines 9–15 in Figure 2.1. The scope of the <identifier> is thus limited to within the two <expressions>. For example,

$$\texttt{let} \ x \ = \ 3 \ \texttt{in} \ \lambda y \ . \ y \ + \ x \tag{4.12}$$

means adding y to x set to the value 3. With the scope being thus locally defined and any identifiers required to be consistent only within the scope, the identifiers are arbitrary even within this newly introduced let-expression.

As LG theoretically covers any computation, any expression described by LG–let can be transformed into an expression using LG. For example, the

---

general discussion with respect to the signifier and the content at the hardware level appears in Section 10.5 (also see Section 2.4).

[5]   Some functional languages such as Lisp and Scheme distinguish two let-expressions, namely `let` and `letrec`. The latter, `letrec`, is used when <identifier>=<expression> is recursively defined. Other languages such as Haskell do not make this distinction, so I do not in this book.

previous example can be rewritten as follows by removing the let-expression:

$$(\lambda x.(\lambda y.y + x)) \ 3, \qquad (4.13)$$

which in fact reduces to

$$(\lambda x.(\lambda y.y + x)) \ 3 \\ \rightarrow \lambda y.y + 3. \qquad (4.14)$$

Even though LG–let and LG are theoretically equivalent, the let-expression allows a different kind of expression that is unavailable in LG. An identifier defined in a let-expression can be used even in the *first* expression for which it is defined. For example,

```
let
 factorial = λ i. if (iszero i) then
                1
              else                        (4.15)
                i * (factorial (i-1))
   in
    factorial 5
```

is a let-expression in which the factorial function is defined in the first part and then applied to 5 in the second part. The identifier `factorial` is recursively defined by the use of `factorial` appearing in both sides of =. In other words, a let-expression allows definition of signs by *self-reference*, which means that an identifier is defined by referring to itself.

In the case of the factorial function, because this definition shows a mere recurrence, the function calculates the factorial value of 5 as follows:

```
factorial 5
 → (λ i. if (iszero i) then
            1
          else
            i * (factorial (i-1))) 5)
 →if (iszero 5) then
     1                                    (4.16)
   else
     5 * (factorial (5-1))
 → 5 * (factorial 4)
 → · · ·
 → 5 * 4 * 3 * 2 * 1 * 1
 → 120.
```

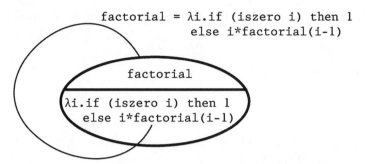

FIGURE 4.5. Self-reference for the function `factorial`.

Every time the expression is reduced, the problem is reduced to a subproblem of the original problem, and finally the recursive function halts.

Such a self-referentially defined sign for this case of the factorial function is illustrated in Figure 4.5. As the factorial is articulated through use of the signifier `factorial`, its upper part is not open, just as in a modern dyadic sign. The name `factorial` appearing within the signified part representing itself is shown by the curved line.

As definitions are not allowed under LG, lambda-terms are always given names after explicit articulation. In contrast, the let-expression introduces definitions which allow a sign to be articulated by using itself. To thus define a sign by self-reference, a signifier must be introduced so that it refers to the *self*, the content to be articulated. This means that a sign is speculatively introduced to allow self-referential expression. Speculative introduction means introduction of a sign before its content is consolidated. Introduction of a sign assigns a memory space for an identifier indicating some content. Note that any memory space always has some content in its bits, even though the content might be random. Thus, the signifier and the signified are indeed two inseparable sides of a sign. Nevertheless, a sign can be speculatively introduced to indicate content that has yet to be consolidated. Such speculative introduction enables self-referential description, by allowing reference to something not yet consolidated and defining this *something* in terms of itself.

Most importantly, in a self-referential sign, the signifier provides the means/functionality to articulate the content. Separation of the signifier and articulation then becomes impossible. At the same time, the effect of *use* on content is apparent in self-reference because the content of a self-referentially defined sign depends on its use. Note that the content in a non-self-referential expression is not affected by use. For example, in the expression $(\lambda x . x + 1)\ 2$, the content of x does not change because of the fact that x is used within the expression x + 1. The use attributes a further meaning to x, as seen in the previous chapter in Figure 3.5, that x is used in x + 1, but the content of x is 2 and is unaffected by its use in the expression x + 1. In contrast, when signs are allowed to be defined self-referentially, the use decides the content of a sign. In other words, the signifier articulates the content through use.

We see here how the signifier is still arbitrary: as long as it consistently refers to the self and all of its appearances are uniformly replaced, any signifier will be able to articulate identical content. Therefore, a sign defined by self-reference is articulated by a signifier, which is arbitrary.

This matches Saussure's sign model because the signifier articulates the content and the signifier is arbitrary. The question as to the role of the signifier lies in indicating the content defined through self-referential expression. In a self-reference, it is the signifier that articulates the content. At the same time, as far as the signifier refers to the complex self consistently, any signifier will do; therefore the signifier is arbitrary. The signifier and content forms two sides of a sign, but to the extent that content is articulated by means of a signifier, neither a signifier nor its content exist without its counterpart. Saussure's paradox is not a paradox at all, but is a necessity with self-referential signs, and as will be seen in Chapter 9, most natural language signs are self-referential.

Most recent programming languages allow for the definition of identifiers by self-reference, even though self-reference is generally ill-suited to computation. Introduction of self-reference is risky in that the content might not really exist or the expression might become contradictory. Introduction of definition inevitably introduces self-reference at the same time, which in turn leads to the risk of ambiguity and contradiction. Unlike in natural language, careless self-reference in programming languages can lead to nonhalting execution, as will be seen in Chapter 9. Programmers must therefore take the utmost care to avoid such errors. Moreover, recursive functions tend to be expensive in computation.[6] Despite this drawback, recursion is often the preferred approach, and many programming textbooks explain how definition by self-reference is natural, elegant, intuitive, and easy to understand. Thus, description by self-reference is frequently preferred by programmers, even when it is easily avoided. One reason for this preference is the reflexive nature of signs and sign systems, as will be discussed from now on in this book. Above all, computers are made to conform to self-reference by design; that is, the programs that drive computers are dynamically changeable by reinterpretation of the output, as will be seen in Chapter 11. Another intuitive reason might be that human language is founded on self-reference, as will be seen

---

[6] Not all recursive functions are expensive. For example, tail recursion (Clinger, 1998; Abelson *et al.*, 1998) has the same computational cost as a normal loop, where tail recursion refers to a procedure whose sole recursive call is at the end of the function. For a more detailed explanation, see Abelson *et al.* (1998).

in Chapter 9, and this characteristic also drives the artificial development of computer systems in a self-referential manner.

Before ending this section, the equivalence of LG–let and LG should be further examined. As seen in the previous discussion, specifically in expression (4.14), the transformation of an expression in LG–let to LG is trivial if there is no self-reference. Once self-reference appears, however, this transformation no longer seems trivial, because self-reference does not exist in LG. Nevertheless, through the use of a special function explained as follows, every self-reference can be expressed by LG. In other words, as mentioned already, LG and LG–let are equivalent.

Church showed theoretically that any recursive function can be transformed into a composition of the fixed-point function and a non-recursive function by transforming the recursion into an iteration (Church, 1941). Throughout the book, I refer to this as Church's transformation. First, a fixed point of a function f is a solution x for the equation x = f x. The calculation to obtain this fixed point of a function is expressed by the fixed-point function, defined as follows:

$$\lambda g.(\lambda x.g\ (x\ x))\ (\lambda x.g\ (x\ x)). \tag{4.17}$$

If this fixed-point function is applied to f, the function is reduced in the following way:

$$\begin{aligned}
&(\lambda g.(\lambda x.g\ (x\ x))\ (\lambda x.g\ (x\ x)))\ f \\
&\rightarrow (\lambda x.f\ (x\ x))\ (\lambda x.f\ (x\ x)) \\
&\rightarrow f\ ((\lambda x.f\ (x\ x))\ (\lambda x.f\ (x\ x))).
\end{aligned} \tag{4.18}$$

The application reduces to $(\lambda x.f\ (x\ x))\ (\lambda x.f\ (x\ x))$, which further reduces to f $(\lambda x.f\ (x\ x))\ (\lambda x.f\ (x\ x))$. That is, the second and third lines of expression (4.18) take the form of y $\rightarrow$ f y, and therefore, the function indeed calculates the fixed point of f. Continuing further, this reduction increases the number of f at the beginning as follows:

$$\begin{aligned}
&(4.18) \\
&\rightarrow \dots \\
&\rightarrow f\ (f\ \dots(f\ ((\lambda x.f\ (x\ x))\ (\lambda x.f\ (x\ x)))\ )\ \dots) \\
&\rightarrow \dots.
\end{aligned} \tag{4.19}$$

To give an idea of how the transformation from a recursive let-expression to a nonrecursive description by LG is carried out, the function factorial provides an example. For the sake of brevity, let h denote

$$(\lambda f.(\lambda i.if\ (iszero\ i)\ then\ 1\ else\ i * f\ (i-1))), \tag{4.20}$$

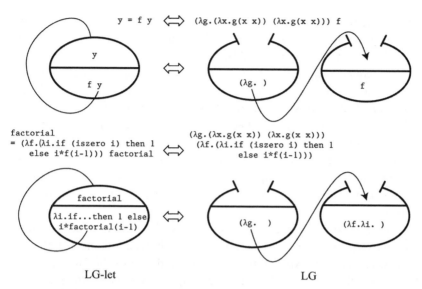

FIGURE 4.6. Relationship of the fixed point in LG–let (left) and the fixed-point function LG (right). An example of recursive function `factorial` and its version using fixed-point function.

then, from the first block of the let-expression of expression (4.18), the `factorial` function is rewritten as

$$\text{factorial} = \text{h factorial.} \qquad (4.21)$$

Therefore, `factorial` is the fixed point of h. Then it is transformed into

$$(\lambda g.(\lambda x.g\ (x\ x))\ (\lambda x.g\ (x\ x)))\ \text{h.} \qquad (4.22)$$

Because expression (4.22) has exactly the same form as that of expression (4.18), a self-referentially defined `factorial` is obtained through reflexive application of formula (4.20), that is, through h.

The relationship between a fixed point and the fixed-point function, and the two definitions of the factorial function in LG–let and LG, are shown in Figure 4.6. The upper block shows the general relationship for the expression using self-reference and that using the fixed-point function, whereas the lower block shows the corresponding relations for `factorial`. Note the correspondence between the left and right sides of the two blocks. The essence of this transformation is to modify the calculation of self-reference into calculation through a reflexive procedure, which is expressed by the fixed-point function. Church's transformation intuitively means squeezing the recursion into a fixed-point function and expressing the remaining functionality nonrecursively. Similarly, any recursive function can be generated through transformation of an expression in LG by using the fixed-point function. Hence, LG–let and LG are equivalent.

This equality suggests that reflexivity is readily present within LG, appearing in the reflexive form of the self-application x x, as seen in the fixed-point function. Reflexivity is visible in the reduction of expression (4.18), which took the form of y → f y. In other words, self-reference cannot be expressed directly in LG but is present in the form of the reduction process. Introduction of definition transforms this underlying reflexivity into self-reference. The relation between self-application and the dyadic sign model is not obvious, but upon transformation into self-reference, the relation becomes apparent.

This equivalence, however, is limited to cases in which both LG–let and LG are *untyped* (see Section 2.4.2 for a discussion of type) (Tennent, 1991). In a typed language, the expression x x is disallowed because the data types of the first x and the second x differ (the former applies, while the latter is applied). More precisely, the type of x in the expression x x becomes undeterminable. Therefore, a typed description of what is equivalent to the fixed-point function requires self-referential expression. In other words, to make a typed language as powerful as untyped LG, the lambda calculus necessarily requires the let-expression. We will see Church's transformation again for Haskell, a typed language, in Section 7.4.

The essence of *type* lies in the role of disambiguating the content of signs when they are *used*. When the type is known, then a function may acquire the same name for different content. For example, in Figure 2.1, the function area has the same name for calculations of three different shapes because the function is typed, indicating what to do according to the input data type. If there is no type, then the three functions must have different names, such as area_rectangle, area_ellipse, and area_circle. Introduction of type thus provides the capability to influence determination of the content of a sign when it is used.

We may recall here how self-reference also has the effect of defining content though use. LG is a sign system in which use and content are distinguished, whereas LG–let is a sign system in which use occasionally affects content.

Consequently, the introduction of definition induces self-referential definition of signs, which provides articulation of content through use. The signifier is indispensable yet arbitrary to the extent that it consistently refers to the complex self. Here appears the third relatum of the sign model, the use. For a proper marriage of the signifier and the signified, an intermediary 'priest', *use*, is necessary. This thought has always been present in triadic sign modeling, in that the *use* (interpretant) connects the signifier (representamen) and the content (signified) (see, for example, how the relation between the representamen and object is dashed in Figure 3.3). Since the questions regarding Saussure's model have been clarified and the concept of use has been introduced, we can now relate this discussion to triadic sign models.

4.5 Self-Reference and the Two Sign Models

Let us now recall the correspondence, illustrated in Figure 3.7, between the Saussure's dyadic and Peirce's triadic models. The key discussion lay in where to situate the *use* as regards the sign model. In the dyadic model, the use is situated outside the sign model as an underlying holistic value within the system. In the triadic model, in contrast, the use is situated *within* the sign model. This hypothesis is also consistent with two different views, as to how a chain of signs as language use is generated. In the dyadic model, a sign is used by some other sign, which is used by some other sign, and so on, such that the relations between signs do not exist in the sign model itself but in the language system. In the triadic model, however, it is thought that semiosis is generated successively by evoking an interpretant incorporated in a sign that relates itself to another sign, which evokes its own interpretant, and so on.

Let us consider applying this correspondence to the dyadic model of lambda-terms. Section 4.3 describes how an identifier provided by a first expression corresponds to a signifier and the second lambda-term corresponds to the content. The third relatum, the use, corresponds to the use in the expression of the *first* lambda-term, which is the one providing the signifier, because the first expression *uses* the second expression.

Both the dyadic and the triadic models apply to the lambda calculus. The difference lies in what is considered the unit of a sign. In a dyadic model, one lambda-term and the identifier provided to it are considered as a unit, and relations between signs are situated within the network of signs. In contrast, in a triadic model, the interaction between two lambda-terms as a whole is embedded within the sign model.

Within LG, where articulation and naming are completely separated, the content and the use are distinct. Thus, the two frameworks of the dyadic and triadic models remain distinct. Once a sign is able to be defined and self-reference is introduced, however, as was seen in the previous section, the content is affected by the use of the sign. The self-referential definition x = f x shows how the content is defined through the use and how the use is the content. Self-reference thus resolves the separation between content and use. Then, the distinction between the dyadic and triadic models is resolved too, and they become the same model. That is, in a self-referential sign, the dyadic and triadic models are equivalent.

In fact, in a computer language a large number of signs are defined non-self-referentially; thus, the dyadic and triadic frameworks are compatible yet distinct and form two different paradigms. The distinction typically appears in terms of where to situate the use of the sign: inside or outside, as seen in the previous chapter. This distinction dissolves with self-referential signs. In the case of natural signs, as will be seen in Chapter 9, most are defined self-referentially. No wonder, then, that the two models have existed for a long time: they are equivalent.

Recall the note in Section 3.5, indicating that within the sign model of this book the content accounts for the semantics of a sign, whereas the use accounts for the pragmatics. This mélange of content and use suggests that the semantics and pragmatics unify in self-referential signs. It recalls Harder's statement that "semantics is transparently a subdiscipline of pragmatics – frozen pragmatics" (Harder, 1996, p. 127). The opportunity for use to freeze into content is present in self-reference. Starting from using a sign, the sign's use freezes into its content.

Comparing these findings to the paintings shown in Figures 4.1 and 4.2, it is unclear whether the distinction presented in the previous chapter applies. In each case, the painting seems to represent the content and its interpretation as a whole, and the distinction between the representation and content is not obvious. To reach this visual representation, the painter must have sought it by changing the image of the content to match his painting technique and style and his linguistic interpretation of the content. The painter must have gone through a trial-and-error process to transfer the visual image to the canvas, which articulates the content through interpretation.

Similar thoughts then apply to the first two paintings in the book, Figures 3.1 and 3.2. Did Chardin and Baugin not both seek the best visual representation of the content through their interpretation? Visual representation concerns content and interpretation at the same time, which are often difficult to distinguish, and dyadic and triadic natures often both apply. Probably, the two models are equivalent in the majority of representations, except for a rare case such as computer programming, in which the distinction appears clearly because of its formality.

4.6 The Saussurian Difference

Finally, *difference* is considered, as mentioned in Section 4.1, in terms of its significance in computing. Because signs are arbitrary and replaceable as long as their consistent use is maintained, the remaining essence of a sign system is the relationships among signs. Saussure's difference is motivated by Saussure's direct observation of *equivalence*, or the *identity* of a sign, in his terms for signs as follows (de Saussure, 1911, p. 82):

The problem of identities can be raised in these terms. What form do identities take in the language? Just as we have found difficulty in recognizing what an entity is, it is likewise difficult to recognize an identity.

The difficulty in judging the equivalence of signs is readily formalized within LG. It has theoretically been proved that given any two lambda-terms, there is no computational procedure to judge their equality within LG (Cutland, 1980). In other words, a procedure to judge the equality of any two arbitrary lambda-terms cannot be expressed by a lambda-term. Similarly, it is known that the equivalence of two arbitrary expressions in a programming language (or of two Turing machines) cannot be judged through the use of a program (or a Turing machine) (Sipser, 2005).

In the computer science domain, it is often necessary to judge the equivalence of two arbitrary programs through another program. In such a case, the programs' equivalence is considered in other, more limited ways. One of the basic ways is to take an operational approach and judge the equivalence from the input and output sets (Gunter, 1962). When the inputs and outputs of two expressions are different, then they are considered different expressions. This operational way of judging the equivalence of two expressions within the computer science domain is analogous to Saussure's statement: there is only difference among signs.

These facts suggest that such difficulty is inherent to sign systems. As natural language is more expressive than LG, it might be more capable of describing a procedure to judge the equivalence of two lambda-terms. In analogy to the case in LG, however, given two expressions in natural language, a procedure to judge their equivalence might be impossible to describe through the use of natural language. In a general sign world like natural language, where signs are commonly defined by self-reference, it is even more difficult to judge the equivalence of two expressions. Generally, both the content and the use of a sign evolve dynamically, depending on the historical background. The meaning of a sign becomes impossible to explicitly articulate and can only float in a network of signs that have been juxtaposed and related. Just as Saussure says, then, the meaning of a sign must be this relational structure, generated through repetition and reflexive use among related signs.

4.7 Summary

The main goal of this chapter has been to argue the role of the signifier within a sign through consideration of a minimal computer language framework, the lambda calculus. A lambda-term has the two basic properties of a sign: articulation and naming. In the framework of a minimal lambda-term, the signifier is arbitrarily given to another lambda-term, used locally within the scope, thus serving for two lambda-terms to interact. Here, the functionalities of articulation and naming are separated. Still, reflexivity is readily present in its most primitive form of self-application within the reduction process.

When definition was introduced, however, this reflexivity appeared in the form of self-referential definition of signs. In a self-referential sign, the sign acquires its content through the use of itself. Thus, content and use become tightly coupled, and moreover, articulation and naming become tightly coupled because articulation requires reference to a complex unit operating as the *self* through a signifier. The signifier is indispensable yet remains arbitrary as long as it consistently refers to the complex self. Moreover, considering the correspondences between the dyadic and triadic sign models presented in Chapter 3, these models become equivalent for a self-referential sign because the content is defined through its use.

Examination of the lambda calculus has also illustrated signification as conceived in Saussurian thought, in which a sign system only has difference: it was proved by Church that the equivalence of two lambda-terms cannot be judged by a function described as a lambda-term. Thus, equivalence is often judged operationally, which is analogous to the notion of difference in Saussurian structuralism.

5

Being and Doing in Programs

The contrasts between the logic of 'doing' and that of 'being', and between the culture of 'doing' and that of 'being', come from the difference between putting emphasis on the status of the target or on the action or process.

From *Nihon no Shiso* by Masao Maruyama © 1961 by Yukari Maruyama. First published in 1961 by Iwanami Shoten, Publishers, Tokyo. Reprinted by permission of the proprietor c/o Iwanami Shoten, Publishers, Tokyo.

(Maruyama, 1961, p. 168)

5.1   The Antithesis of Being and Doing

The previous two chapters show the hypothetical relation of two sign models and the relations among the relata of the sign models. This chapter shows the degree to which sign models specify the design of a computer program ontology. In programming, an ontology must be described within a program. An example can be seen in Figure 2.2, where an ontology of shapes was constructed from the viewpoint of mathematical sets. Some readers might consider ontology as something definite and absolute if they have in mind a typical ontology, such as a phylogeny. This chapter questions this absolute view of ontology; or rather, the standpoint of this chapter is to consider the extent to which an ontology is stipulated by a sign model. This is similar to how Saussure reversed the order of the signifier and the signified; that is, it is not that a label is attached to content, but rather that the signifier articulates the signified.

The starting point of this type of discussion on ontological frameworks can be intuitively shown through the following examples. Figure 5.1 shows a painting of ice by Maruyama Oukyo. The particularity of this painting is obvious, in that he represented ice by using a number of lines. If one was asked to find other, similar paintings, two types would likely emerge. One is

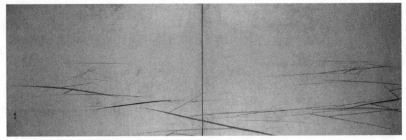

FIGURE 5.1. Maruyama Oukyo (1733–1795), *Cracked Ice*, British Museum. © Trustees of the British Museum.

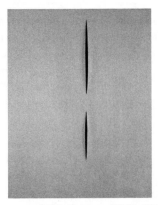

FIGURE 5.2. Caspar David Friedrich (1774–1840), *The Polar Sea*, Hamburger Kunsthalle. Photo credit: Bildarchiv Preussischer Kulturbesitz/Art Resource, NY.

FIGURE 5.3. Lucio Fontana (1899–1968), *Spatial Concepts*, Fondazione Lucio Fontana. © 2009 Artists Rights Society (ARS), New York/SIAE, Rome. Photo credit: CNAC/MNAM/ Dist. Réunion des Musés Nationaux/Art Resource, NY.

a painting of ice, such as that shown in Figure 5.2, in which the ice is painted with realism. The other is a painting based on the expression of some content by means of linear drawing. Among many similar examples within modern art, here I raise an example by Lucio Fontana, shown in Figure 5.3.

The relation between the paintings shown in Figures 5.1 and 5.2 is constructed through *what* is drawn, a relation based on 'being', whereas the relation between the paintings shown in Figure 5.1 and Figure 5.3 is constructed through *how* the content is represented, a relation based on 'doing'. Intuitive analogies to this antithesis can be seen in various domains besides painting, such as narratology. Todorov (1977) distinguishes between the 'being' and 'doing' motivations underlying the actant in a narrative. In a murder story, for instance, the 'being' motivation takes the form 'he kills because he is a killer', whereas the 'doing' motivation takes the form 'he is a killer because he kills'(Marsen, 2004).

Hence, the focus of this chapter is the ontological dichotomy between 'being' and 'doing'. *'Being'*, in this chapter, refers to the ontological status of an entity whose ontic character is established by what it is, while *'doing'* denotes that of an entity whose ontic character is specified by what it does and by what can be done to it.

The distinction between 'being' and 'doing' is seen also in computer programming. The computer programming domain is unique in that it may be seen as a complete world consisting only of signs, and yet even here the same contrasting paradigms of 'being' and 'doing' coexist. Curiously, among the various computer programming paradigms, this contrast is especially prominent in object-oriented programming. This fact suggests that the emergence of the 'being'/'doing' schism is a result of the way in which entities are described. Within the object-oriented paradigm, as seen in Chapter 3, a computational entity is modeled by a triple consisting of its name, its features, and its functions. I argue that an ontology of either 'being' or 'doing' must arise as a direct result of this triadic modeling of the entity: an emphasis on features leads to the 'being' ontology, whereas an emphasis on functions leads to the 'doing' ontology. I draw a more general hypothesis, namely, that the 'being'/'doing' antithesis emerges in any domain where entities are described according to triadic sign modeling. The 'being' ontology emerges when relations are constructed according to signs' content, whereas the 'doing' ontology emerges when relations are constructed according to signs' uses. The conclusion reached at the end of this chapter might well be readily predictable from the discussion so far that the content of a sign governs semantics, or *what*, while the use of a sign governs pragmatics, or *how*. Further, the conclusion of Chapter 3 suggests that such contrast does not occur when applying dyadic modeling, where the ontology always takes the 'being' form.

The beginning of the main argument is framed first by describing the 'being'/'doing' dichotomy existing within the object-oriented paradigm.

5.2   Class and Abstract Data Type

In object-oriented computer programs, entities are modeled and described by a data structure. The design of this data structure is critical because it determines the comprehensiveness, the ease of maintenance, the extensibility, and, above all, the reliability of programs incorporating the data structure.

TABLE 5.1. Contrast between 'Being' and 'Doing' in computing

	'Being'	'Doing'
Typology by Meyer (2000)	Class	Abstract data type
Java (Sections 5.3 and 5.4)	Class	Interface
Code sharing	Yes	No
Task sharing	Hard	Easy

Badly designed structures make errors and bugs difficult to identify and hinder cooperative development by a group of programmers. A bad data structure often requires rewriting an entire program from scratch.

Conflicts between 'being' and 'doing' ontologies are especially likely to occur within the object-oriented programming paradigm. Under this paradigm, programs are based on the interaction of units called *objects*,[1] where each entity is described by an abstract construct that models the entity in terms of functions and features (Meyer, 2000; Snyder, 1986). Using objects as units makes it easier to package data and functionality together. This packaging functionality is usually called *encapsulation* and represents the fundamental philosophy underlying the object-oriented paradigm. Objects are thus the basis of modularity and structure in an object-oriented computer program.

According to Meyer (2000), a set of objects can be described in one of two ways: by *class* or by *abstract data type*.

- A class is a collection of objects that have exactly the same internal structure; that is, they have the same instance variables, the same body, and the same functions.
- An abstract data type is a collection of objects that have the same functionality. An abstract data type provides an interface describing what actions can be applied to objects.

These two conceptions of a set of objects lead to completely different notions of the underlying ontological constructs, as compared in Table 5.1 and briefly explained here; detailed explanations using sample programs are given in the next two sections.

In programs based on classes every object deriving from a class has the same internal structure (i.e., features and functions); that is, code is shared.

---

[1] Note that the term *object* here has a meaning different from that seen in Peircian philosophy, which was mentioned in Chapter 3. In the present chapter, the term *object* denotes an object in the sense of the object-oriented programming paradigm (cf. Glossary), while an object in the Peircian sense – *Peirce's object* – is consistently referred to as such. Peirce's object appears only once in Section 5.5, however, so for the time being any use of *object* refers to the current programming definition.

Thus, a programmer using a class is assumed to be well acquainted with its internal structure. This assumption increases the programmer's responsibility to know about objects with respect to 'what they are' and how to use them consistently. Under such circumstances it is difficult for many programmers to work cooperatively, resulting in limited possibility of task sharing ('Task sharing' row, 'Being' column of the table). This is a 'being' sort of object construction, in which the ontological relation is formed according to what the object *is* ('Being' column of Table 5.1).

Programs based on abstract data types have exactly the opposite property. An abstract data type is a set of declarations of functionalities for a collection of objects. The declaration does not include the actual definitions of the function procedures because the procedures are supposed to differ depending on the object type; the actual definitions of functionality are provided in the class that implements the abstract data type. Therefore, code is not shared by objects of an abstract data type. The abstract data type instead provides a protocol for another object as a user, explicitly showing what can be done to an object of the abstract data type, and objects are thus typed only according to which abstract data type is adopted. All communication with such objects is conducted via this interface. Under such circumstances cooperative programming is relatively easy and task sharing is enhanced because the knowledge needed by a programmer is limited to knowledge of the abstract data type. This is a 'doing' kind of object construction, in which the ontological relation is formed according to what the object can do or what can be done to the object ('Doing' column of the Table 5.1).

The object-oriented paradigm initially accommodated only the 'being' concept but then gradually incorporated the 'doing' functionality in response to needs for more complex, larger-scale programs. The first successful object-oriented languages, such as Simula (Dahl and Nygaard, 1966; Pooley, 1987) and Smalltalk (Goldberg and Kay, 1976), allowed object design only via a class. The more recent C++ language has the implicit/limited functionality of the abstract data type (Stroustrup, 1986, 1994a). Recent languages, such as Java (Arnold *et al.*, 2000), incorporate the abstract data type as a major part of the language's design.

This historical development does not imply that 'being'-type paradigms are no longer used. In current programming language design, the 'being' and 'doing' approaches are balanced between code sharing and task sharing. Usually, criteria are drawn up concerning separation requirements in design and implementation. In actual coding, when a single programmer develops a small-scale program, the 'being' ontological framework is preferred. In contrast, the 'doing' framework is adopted when the scale is large and the project involves many different programmers and multiple tasks (such as when building a language library). Still, the question of which ontological framework should be used in various situations is controversial, and there is an ongoing argument on a fundamental level as to how to incorporate the 'doing' concept into programming language design (Arnold *et al.*, 2000).

This is confirmed by the fact that the term *abstract data type*, which has been used thus far to indicate the 'doing' construct, has yet to become well established. America and van der Linden (1990) use another, simpler term, *type*, defined as "a collection of objects that share the same externally observable behavior", but the usual meaning of the term *type* is different. Snyder (1986) uses the term *deferred class*, which is again ambiguous within the context of this chapter because here the term *class* has been consistently used to represent the implementation of 'being'. Again, in this study the term *abstract data type* is used following its use in Meyer (2000).

Classes and abstract data types, as defined here, are implemented as classes and interfaces, respectively, in Java. In the next two sections, two actual examples are considered to examine the above pros and cons in more detail: one of the 'being' type and one of the 'doing' type.

5.3   A Being Program Example

Let us recall the simple example of shapes given in Chapter 2. The purpose of the computation is to calculate the areas of simple shapes and print the area of each instance of a shape. The shapes are modeled by their width and height.

The class hierarchy used in this example is shown in Figure 5.4. All shapes are placed under the class named Shape, with features of width and height as well as a function to calculate the area. The ontology according to classes is constructed as class B being the parent of A when the relationship 'A is a B' holds (Meyer, 2000). For example, a circle *is a*n ellipse, but 'an ellipse *is not* necessarily a circle'; therefore the class Ellipse is placed as a parent of the class Circle. Similarly, a rectangle *is a* shape, and an ellipse *is a* shape; therefore the class Shape is placed as a parent of the classes Rectangle and Ellipse. More formally, the *is a* relationship can be mathematically interpreted as a set-theoretic relationship, with all instances of class A being included in class B. Such an interclass relationship of A with B, made by 'A is a B,' is called *inheritance* (Meyer, 2000); it guarantees that classes A and B have the same features and functions, whereas the child can have additional features. For example, a circle has the additional feature of its width equaling its height.

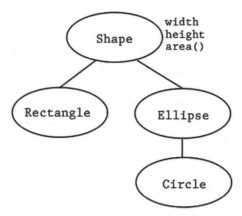

FIGURE 5.4. An object hierarchy of simple shapes.

This type of object design can be applied to generate the program in Figure 2.2. The four classes of Shape, Rectangle, Ellipse, and Circle are connected by the keyword extends, which establishes the *is a* relationship among the classes. In Java, the connection of classes A and B by 'A extends B' introduces the following two effects.

- Instances of class A have the same extended internal structure (features and functions) as instances of class B.
- Instances of class A can be handled as if they belong to class B.

The first effect means that instances of class A have all of the same features (called member variables) and functions (called member functions or methods) as those of any instance of class B. Therefore, in the sample program, classes that extend the class Shape inherit the features of width and height and the function of area(). This means that program code is shared by inheritance. This is an important feature in programming: if the same sequence of code is reproduced throughout a program, its creator must modify each part of that same code when a bug is found within it; with inheritance, the code is kept in a unique location, so errors are easily fixed.

Although inheritance enhances code sharing, it can also lead to chains of redefinitions within a class hierarchy. The member function area is defined to calculate the area as the width multiplied by the height (line 4). This *default* way of calculating the area does not apply for classes such as Ellipse and Circle. The function area is thus redefined (or overridden) as seen in line 13 in the class Ellipse, and this redefinition is further inherited by the class Circle.

The second effect of the Java keyword extends is that all instances deriving from the class Shape can be handled as instances of the same type. This is possible because instances deriving from the class are guaranteed to share the same features. An array of type Shape is allocated in line 25. Shape instances r, u, and v are inserted into this array in the same line and their areas are printed in line 26, all together in a uniform manner.

Classes and their relations defined by extends enhance code sharing through the inheritance feature. The relationships created among classes by inheritance are strict, however, since all structural information is shared among the classes. Such strict relationships can create difficulties. First, when one is required to add a new class to a previously developed program, the means to do so under such strict organization is often not so obvious. The sample program is able to describe new shapes, such as trapezoids or rhombuses, but first the complete structural design deriving from Shape would have to be clarified and understood to determine where to add the new shapes. Second, such strict sharing of the internal structure also makes it difficult to know which feature is declared where, especially when code is overridden. For example, the complete structure of the class Circle is unclear until we move up the class hierarchy as far as Shape: the function area is declared in the class Ellipse and the features width and height are declared in the class Shape. Because of these strict relations among classes, extending two classes to a single class is disallowed (i.e., multiple inheritance prohibition) in many object-oriented programming languages. This is because multiple inheritance amalgamates all features and functions, which can lead to inheritance of certain unwanted features or even to confusion like that caused by a feature being adopted from different parents.

Under such circumstances it is difficult for many programmers to work cooperatively because it is impossible to share the class design, especially when the class hierarchy becomes deep. Thus, class-based object-oriented programs are often unsuitable for task sharing. Consequently, class-based programming is used to describe objects according to what an object *is*. Referring to a class hierarchy based on applying extends to an *is a* relationship also demonstrates the way in which class design can be based on the 'being' concept.

Such 'being' constructs are essentially based on primordially having common features rather than common functions. A similar, but more primitive, 'being'-type program in Java is shown in Figure 5.5.[2] Here, the objects are related only by features, and functions are placed outside the classes (lines

---

[2] This program can be made executable by placing it within the code fragment in footnote 4 of Section 2.2.

```
 1: abstract class Shape {
 2:   double width, height;
 3:   Shape(double w, double h) { width=w; height=h; }
 4: }
 5:
 6: class Rectangle extends Shape{
 7:   Rectangle(double w, double h) { super(w,h); }
 8: }
 9:
10: class Ellipse extends Shape{
11:   Ellipse(double w, double h) { super(w,h); }
12: }
13:
14: class Circle extends Ellipse{
15:   Circle(double r) { super(r*2.0,r*2.0); }
16: }
17:
18: double area(Rectangle f)  { return f.width*f.height; }
19: double area(Ellipse f) { return Math.PI*f.width*f.height/4.0; }
20: double area(Circle f) { return Math.PI*f.width*f.height/4.0; }
21:
22: void run() {
23:   Rectangle r = new Rectangle(5.0,8.0);
24:   Ellipse   u = new Ellipse(3.0,4.0);
25:   Circle    v = new Circle(3.0);
26:
27:   putStr("area: " + area(r) + "\n");
28:   putStr("area: " + area(u) + "\n");
29:   putStr("area: " + area(v) + "\n");
30: }
```

FIGURE 5.5. Example program based on the 'being' ontology, modifying the program in Figure 2.2.

18 to 20). Note that the opposite approach – that of leaving functions inside the class and placing features outside – is not possible for a class because an object can only exist by first initializing its features, and then functions can be applied.

Even when functions are placed outside classes, the ontological relations are still based on 'being' and the discussion thus far holds in exactly the same way. Here we must notice how the class names in this example are degraded to dyadic identifiers and how the program structure is very similar to that of the Haskell program shown in Figure 2.1. Indeed, lines 1 to 16 of Figure 5.5 correspond to the first block of Figure 2.1, lines 18 to 20 correspond to the second block, and lines 22 to 30 correspond to the third block. Moreover, in this program, the function side defines which functions apply to which class

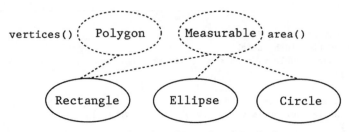

FIGURE 5.6. Another object hierarchy of simple shapes.

of objects, similarly to the Haskell program. For instance, the function that applies to instances of `Rectangle` has the form of `double area(Rectangle f) {...}` (line 18 of Figure 5.5), indicating that this function is uniquely defined for instances of the class `Rectangle`. Dyadic computer signs, therefore, in general constitute a 'being' ontology. This is because features are primordial with respect to the being of an object; that is, an object can only exist by first initializing its features, and then functions can be applied. When such a primordial, essential structure is shared by using the keyword `extends`, objects naturally become tightly related, which prevents task sharing by multiple programmers. Thus, 'being' refers to a way of being in which an ontological relation is established essentially according to features.

5.4   A Doing Program Example

Programming can be approached in a completely different manner by designing objects through the use of abstract data types. This structural design is illustrated in Figure 5.6.

Unlike Figure 5.4, this figure shows two *interfaces*, indicated by the dashed ellipses. An interface declares a set of functions, which only indicate how objects are accessed. The interfaces are implemented by classes, indicated by the solid ellipses. The functionality of a class is of the 'being' kind, but implementing an interface changes the functionality into the 'doing' kind by having a protocol declared within the interface. An interface only *declares* functions, indicating the function name to be applied to the instances, but the actual implementation of each function is up to each class. The interface `Measurable` declares the function `area()`, while the interface `Polygon` declares the function `vertices()`, a function that returns the number of vertices in a polygon. All three shapes (i.e., rectangles, ellipses, and circles) are measurable, but among them, only rectangles qualify as polygons.

```
 1: interface Measurable{
 2:   double area();
 3: }
 4:
 5: interface Polygon{
 6:   int vertices();
 7: }
 8:
 9: class Rectangle implements Measurable, Polygon{
10:   double width, height;
11:   Rectangle(double w, double h){ width = w; height = h; }
12:   public double area(){ return width*height; }
13:   public int vertices(){ return 4; }
14: }
15:
16: class Ellipse implements Measurable{
17:   double width, height;
18:   Ellipse(double w, double h){ width = w; height = h; }
19:   public double area(){ return Math.PI*width*height/4.0; }
20: }
21:
22: class Circle implements Measurable{
23:   double radius;
24:   Circle(double r){ radius = r; }
25:   public double area(){ return Math.PI*radius*radius; }
26: }
27:
28: void run(){
29:   Rectangle r = new Rectangle(5.0,8.0);
30:   Ellipse   u = new Ellipse(3.0,4.0);
31:   Circle    v = new Circle(3.0);
32:
33:   Measurable[] ms = new Measurable[]{r, u, v};
34:   for (Measurable m : ms){ putStr("area: "+m.area()+"\n"); }
35:
36:   Polygon[] ps = new Polygon[]{r};
37:   for (Polygon p : ps) { putStr("vertices: "+p.vertices()+"\n");}
38: }
```

FIGURE 5.7. Example program based on the 'doing' ontology.

This approach can be represented in another sample program, shown in Figure 5.7.[3] First, there are two interfaces, Measurable and Polygon, in which functions are declared (lines 1 and 5). Interfaces may include multiple function definitions but *not* their actual implementations. This differs from

---

[3] This program can be made executable by placing it within the code fragment in footnote 4 of Section 2.2.

the previous program, in which the `area` function of the `Shape` class was included at the place of declaration. Also, features are part of the implementation; therefore they cannot be described within the interface. All such actual implementation occurs inside classes.[4]

There are three classes, as in the previous program. Here, the functionality of a class is the same as that described in the previous section; therefore it is inherently of the 'being' type. When classes implement interfaces by using the Java definition 'A `implements` B', however, with A being a class and B being an interface, instances of class A are treated as the 'doing' type. Precisely, 'A `implements` B' has the following effects.

- A must define the functions declared in B.
- Instances of A can be handled as instances of B.

Regarding the first effect, objects that implement an interface are guaranteed to have the functionalities declared in the interface. Since an interface only declares functions without providing their implementations, the actual procedures must be implemented in classes. In our example, `Rectangle` alone implements `Polygon`, so the function `vertices` is implemented only in this class (line 13), whereas all classes implement the interface `Measurable`, so each class includes the function `area` within the actual code for the class (lines 12, 19, and 25).

The second effect is shared with the case of `extends`. The actual use of the objects is illustrated by the function `run` from lines 28 to 38. Instances of the three shape types are allocated in lines 29 to 31 and put in an array of type `Measurable` in line 33, and the instances' areas are printed together in line 34 by using the `area`. Similarly, the number of vertices of the rectangle, being a polygon, is printed by using an array of type `Polygon` in lines 36 and 37.

Such programming based on abstract data types has the following advantages and disadvantages. First, note how the class `Rectangle` implements two interfaces at the same time. This is enabled by the fact that the relation between the interfaces and the classes is loose, concerning no actual program code. Second, if another object type, such as a rhombus, is to be added to the program, the code can be designed by looking *only* at the two interfaces and can be added without reading the code for the other classes of `Rectangle`, `Ellipse`, and `Circle`. This is possible because the interface does not include any code. However, because of this, even if the function `area` is similar for `Ellipse` and `Circle`, the code cannot be shared through only the use of

---

[4] In Java, some limited features, such as constants, can be included in interfaces.

implements. In other words, programming only with implements tends to result in the same code being scattered in different parts of the program.

Programming based on implements has the advantage of separating the design and the implementation. The interface only provides the design by declaring what actions can be applied to objects. This allows implementation of two interfaces at the same time and task sharing becomes easy. The separation has the disadvantage, however, that the actual implementation is left to the actual classes, producing copies of the same code scattered within the program.

Consequently, a class that implements an abstract data type is treated as the 'doing' type; again, an abstract data type represents an object by means of what can be *done* to it. A frequent classroom metaphor used in teaching programming languages is that classes connected by extends create a family system, whereas abstract data types defined by implements create a license system (Arnold *et al.*, 2000). This metaphor provides an intuitive contrast similar to that between 'being' and 'doing', as illustrated by the analogical contrast of 'being', for 'he kills because he is a killer', and 'doing', for 'he is a killer because he kills'.

5.5   Being versus Doing and the Two Sign Models

So far, we have seen how the contrast between 'being' and 'doing' ontology arises in the world of computer signs. Let us now examine how such a 'being'/'doing' relationship can be related to sign models, continuing from the previous two chapters. As mentioned at the beginning of this chapter, the ontological framework and sign models are usually considered as issues on different levels. Usually, people tend to consider the ontology as something definite, absolute, and grounded by essential relationships of real-world objects. From this view, the ontological distinction of 'being' and 'doing' seems to be located at the real-world level, not at the level of description. The distinction still arises, however, in a world of only signs. Hence, the nature of the contrast could be located at the level of description.

The contraposition of 'being' and 'doing' is prominent in object-oriented programming. There must be a key to explain why this contrast occurs in terms of how objects are described within object-oriented programming. In Chapter 3, we examined how the object-oriented programming paradigm is particular in its triadic modeling of signs, analogous to Peirce's model. Here, the class name corresponds to the representamen, features correspond to Peirce's object, and functions correspond to the interpretant. Following

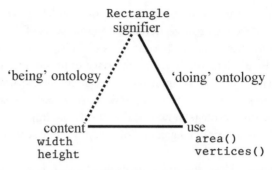

FIGURE 5.8. 'Being', 'doing', and the triadic sign model.

the terminology used in this book for sign relata, the class name corresponds to the signifier, the features correspond to the content, and the functions correspond to the use. For example, the signifier corresponds to names such as Shape, Rectangle, and Circle; the content corresponds to features such as width and height; and the use corresponds to functions such as area() and vertices(). These correspondences are illustrated in Figure 5.8.

We now have the following two correspondences:

- Between the focus on features/functions and that on 'being'/'doing' ontologies (Sections 5.3 and 5.4);
- Between the signifier, content, and use of the triadic sign model, on the one hand and the name, features, and functions of a class, on the other (Chapter 3).

Hence, the following hypotheses can be derived.

- 'Being' is an ontic state in which the ontological relation is established based on what is comparable to content in the sign model.
- 'Doing' is a state in which the ontological relation is established based on what is comparable to use in the sign model.

In other words, the hypothesis of this chapter is that the ontological difference between 'being' and 'doing' emerges depending on which side of the triadic sign model is emphasized in constructing an ontology, just as when Saussure and Peirce reversed 'aliquid stat pro aliquo'. Before Peirce or Saussure, signs were thought to be names attached to objects, but Peirce and Saussure reversed this so that the signifier defines the content. Similarly, an ontological hierarchy is thought of as being defined by actual relations existing between entities. The discussion here shows, however, that it is actually the other way around: the sign model is what defines the ontological framework. This is also seen from the fact that in computer programming the contrast of 'being' and 'doing' is remarkable when applying triadic modeling of signs but not when applying dyadic modeling. In other domains where objects are described by a triadic sign model, the same contrast of 'being' and 'doing' will emerge, as in object-oriented programming.

It is important to remark that the hypothesis in this chapter does not imply that both 'being' and 'doing' are dyadic ways of being. The ontology is formed through the relation of entities; the question is what is utilized to form the relation. The 'being' design approach could arise from both dyadic and triadic modeling. Recalling the correspondences between the dyadic and triadic sign models and the nature of each relatum presented in Chapter 3, when objects are represented by dyadic signs, the ontological relation is established based only on the relation of content, namely, in terms of 'being'. Evidence of this was given through the sample program in Figure 5.5, examined as taking the ontology of 'being', which had the same structure as that of the program in Figure 2.1, based on the dyadic sign model. Thus, the ontological relation with the dyadic model is that of 'being'. The 'doing' design approach, however, is solely triadic. Moreover, the 'being' and 'doing' contrast only appears under the triadic view, which generates a choice as to which part of the sign is used to establish the relation among signs. The argument is simply that 'being' is a way of being whose ontological relation is constructed from a relation among units of content, whereas 'doing' is a way of being whose ontological relation is constructed from a relation among uses.

This difference in focus for relation construction in 'being' and 'doing', in my opinion, derives from a difference in regarding an object from an interior or an exterior view. 'Being' takes the interior view, stipulating an object from what it is, whereas 'doing' takes the exterior view, stipulating an object from how it looks from the outside and how it can be used. The difference lies in the position of the focus vis à vis an object – inside or outside. There are two such views in object-oriented programming as well. When defining classes using inheritance, the programmer has to take the interior view by describing the whole being of an object. In contrast, it often happens that a programmer just wants to *use* predefined objects, such as those provided in a library. In this case, the programmer takes the exterior view.

Naturally, then, the dyadic model takes the viewpoint of considering an object from within or, more precisely, only from within, completely excluding how the object is used by other objects and instead regarding use as a holistic value in the sign system, as seen in Chapter 3. Since the dyadic model excludes use from the sign model, there is no exterior standpoint for the dyadic model, whereas the triadic model has an exterior standpoint within the sign model and this is the reason why the two standpoints of interior view and exterior view appear. Consequently we have seen three ways of viewing objects so far: one for the dyadic model, from the inside, and the two standpoints of interior and exterior consideration for triadic sign models.

Recalling the intimacy of Peirce's triadic sign modeling and object-oriented programs, how do such differences in viewpoint appear in Peirce's thought? Peirce seems to have taken the interior view: his stance favored 'being'. Peirce possessed his own methodology of considering any entity in terms of the universal categories of firstness, secondness, and thirdness, with firstness being primordial to secondness and secondness being primordial to thirdness. The details of the universal categories are introduced in Part II, but for now it is sufficient to note that Peirce considered the representamen as firstness, the object as secondness, and the interpretant as thirdness (Peirce, 1931, 2.274). That is, Peirce considered his object to be more primordial than his interpretant. This reveals that Peirce considered objects from the interior view.

Is there any thought corresponding to 'doing' in the humanities that takes the exterior view regarding objects? A philosopher who took the exterior view of 'doing' was Martin Heidegger. He suggested that the 'doing' relation is primordial with respect to the 'being' relation (Heidegger, 1927, Sections 15, 16, H.74). Michael Gelven summarizes this view as follows (Gelven, 1989, p. 61):

Our primordial relation with the world is to *use* it: i.e., the world for us is available – 'ready-at-hand' (zuhanden). To think of the world as made up of things independent of their function or use (i.e., to see the world as 'present-at-hand': vorhanden) is not our primordial relationship with the world, but a *derived* relationship.

Note how Heidegger's notions of ready-at-hand/present-at-hand correspond with 'doing'/'being'. As Gelven summarizes, Heidegger regarded ready-at-hand as more primordial than present-at-hand, meaning that 'doing' is more primordial than 'being'. Heidegger's primordiality derives from *outside* the object. When there exists one object and another object wanting to use the first object, to the extent that its use is known, then it is unnecessary that the actual content be known. As one continues to use the object, one will gradually understand what it really *is*.

5.6   To Be or To Do

The notion, taken by the 'doing' view, that use enables gradual understanding of content reminds us of what we saw in the previous section: use freezes into meaning (Harder, 1996, p. 127). We also saw how content and use melt into one whole under self-reference. Applying this discussion of the previous chapter, we see that the distinction between 'being' and 'doing' is likely to disappear for self-referential signs. For example, consider constructing the ontological relation between x of x = f x and y of y = f y, where f for x and f for y are two distinct functions of the same name and similar nature (such as area). The following two relations are equivalent: grouping x and y by the 'being' relation (in other words, through x and y being the fixed point of the function f) and grouping them under the 'doing' relation (namely through a functional viewpoint of obtaining the fixed point of f through its reflexive application). In Section 4.5, this was seen as the moment when the distinction between pragmatics and semantics dissolves, and so the distinction between 'being' and 'doing' dissolves.

The same consideration applies to painting. The contrast between 'being' and 'doing' was illustrated for the three paintings shown at the beginning of this chapter. The relation between the paintings in Figures 5.1 and 5.2 is established based on 'being', through the content of 'ice', whereas the relation between the paintings in Figures 5.1 and 5.3 is established based on 'doing', through the common interpretation of the paintings' content. Nobody, however, can say that Fontana had certain content in mind and that its interpretation took the form of lines: it might have been the case that he wanted to engrave the lines themselves. Since the same applies for Oukyo, the relationship between the paintings in Figures 5.1 and 5.3 can also be considered in terms of 'being'. This dissolution of 'being' and 'doing' is due to the dissolution of the two sign models, as seen in the previous chapter. Although I have chosen three paintings whose relations of 'being' and 'doing' seem relatively clear, such distinctions are usually not so obvious for humanistic signs such as those in art.

The contraposition of 'being' and 'doing' is yet present as a matter of fact, as in the case of computer programming discussed in this chapter. As mentioned in the previous section, a computer language is a formal, well-defined language, and the signs within are not always self-referential. This must be one reason why the contraposition of 'being' and 'doing' appears as a distinction. One common problem among programmers is how to integrate and balance the 'being' and 'doing' approaches to simultaneously maximize the advantages of code sharing and task sharing.

Masao Maruyama, a political scientist, has identified the shift from 'being' to 'doing' as a symbol of modernity (Maruyama, 1961). According to Maruyama, the dynamic of modernity is deconstruction of the social hierarchy rooted in 'being', the result of filtering away all kinds of ineffective dogma and authority. Such deconstruction was generated by a shift of value from 'being' to 'doing', which occurred because of the increased social *complexity* resulting from advances in communication and transportation technologies. According to Maruyama, the question for the modern world is 'to do or not to do', rather than the question of 'to be or not to be' in Shakespeare's *Hamlet*.

In programming languages, too, the abstract data type has become more important as software complexity has increased. This shift is indeed related to complexity because when many different objects are needed they can no longer be understood through deep knowledge of what they are. The solution is instead to define a simple interface, or communication protocol, and then to limit the relations among objects according to that interface. Under the 'being' ontology a programmer has the total responsibility to know what is going on; today, under the 'doing' ontology, the programmer's knowledge can be limited to the predefined communication protocol, or the interface.

The 'being' relation has not been entirely replaced, however, by 'doing'. Given today's complexity in computers, the question of 'being or doing' arises. Maruyama warns that the distinction between 'being' and 'doing' is poorly understood on a widespread scale. Domains of knowledge that should be evaluated in terms of 'how is' are often evaluated in terms of 'what is', and vice versa. Similarly, in programming the proper balancing of 'being' and 'doing' is nontrivial. In the future, appropriate criteria for deciding between these ontologies might emerge as it becomes more clear how to properly incorporate 'doing' into programming languages. One key strategy is to achieve a balance between task sharing and code sharing. To answer the question, 'to be or to do', it is important to investigate the nature of the contrast between 'being' and 'doing'.

5.7 Summary

The argument put forward in this chapter suggests that an ontology based upon either 'being' or 'doing' will emerge depending on which aspect of the triadic sign model is emphasized: content or use. The argument is based on an analysis of the two types of ontological constructs used in object-oriented computer programming: the class, which relates data structures according to features, thus taking a 'being' ontology, and the abstract data type, which relates data structures according to functions, taking a 'doing' ontology. The findings here include the observation that the ontology is specified by the sign model, as opposed to the inverse situation of a preexisting ontology defining the sign model.

Up to this point, Part I has considered models of signs, the relations among sign relata, and the resulting influences on the structure of description. In Part II, based on the findings discussed in Part I, the kinds of signs and content are considered.

PART 2

KINDS OF SIGNS AND CONTENT

6

The Statement `x := x + 1`

...we must bear in mind that the neatly differentiated categories which...seem to indicate three independent spheres of meaning, refer in reality to aspects of one phenomenon, namely the work of art as a whole. So that, in actual work, the methods of approach which here appear as three unrelated operations of research merge with each other into one organic and indivisible process.

From *Studies in Iconology* by Erwin Panofsky. Reprinted by permission of Oxford University Press. (Panofsky, 1939, pp. 16–17)

6.1 Different Kinds of Signs

Let us consider the three works of art shown in Figures 6.1, 6.2, and 6.3. All three paintings are related to birds but use different styles of representation. In Figure 6.1, the representation is realistic and shows a pair of birds. In Figure 6.2, there is not a bird but rather the blue sky in the form of a bird. In Figure 6.3, Constantin Brancusi sought the ultimate, essential form of what a bird is. The representation is made at an abstract level, as if it represents all forms of being that could be called a bird. These representations signify a bird at three different levels:

- a bird as an instance,
- a representation (unrelated to a bird) suggesting a bird, and
- an abstracted bird.

The same phenomenon appearing in these paintings – different levels of representation for content – exists in computer programs as well. For example, statements of the following kind often appears in programs:

$$\text{int x = 32.} \tag{6.1}$$

Here, the content 32 is represented by three different signs: 32, x, and `int`. The first sign, 32, is a literal (see Section 2.3) indicating the *value* 32. The value is

91

FIGURE 6.1. Ito Jakuchu (1716–1800), *The Large Cock and Hen*, Sannomaru Shozoukan. © The Imperial Household Agency, Sannnomaru Shozoukan, Tokyo.

FIGURE 6.2. René Magritte (1898–1967), *La Grande Famille*, Private Collection. © 2009 C. Herscovici, London/Artists Rights Society (ARS), New York. Photo credit: Banque d'Images, ADAGP/Art Resource, NY.

FIGURE 6.3. Constantin Brancusi (1876–1957), *Bird in Space*, The Metropolitan Museum of Art. © 2009 Artists Rights Society (ARS), New York/ADAGP, Paris Image Copyright © The Metropolitan Museum of Art/Art Resource, NY.

represented by an identifier x, which corresponds to a memory *address* where the value 32 is stored, as explained in Section 2.4. The sign int indicates the data *type* of the value 32 as an integer, a representation at the most abstract level. A statement similar to this one is also present in the program shown in Figure 2.2 (line 21):

$$\text{Rectangle r = new Rectangle(5.0,8.0).} \qquad (6.2)$$

Here, the right-hand side represents the value of a rectangle of width 5.0 and height 8.0, r corresponds to an address where the value is located, and Rectangle on the left-hand side indicates the value's type. Similar statements also appear in the same program in lines 22 and 23.

A value is thus represented on three different levels: value, address, and type. Such stratification generates the following ambiguity problem for the user:

Given a sign, does it indicate the value, the address, or the type?

Since a programming language is a language without ambiguity, any such problem can be disambiguated by using certain syntactic or pragmatic clues defined within the language specification. For the user, however, such disambiguation occasionally turns out not to be so obvious.

For example, the following statement often appears, especially in the traditional imperative programming paradigm in which programs are written in a state-transitive manner (see Chapter 10):

$$\text{x := x + 1.} \qquad (6.3)$$

This statement looks like a self-referential definition, as introduced in Chapter 4, but here := represents *assignment*, which is different from definition (represented by =).[1] Assignment denotes the action of first calculating the value represented by the expression on the right side of := and then assigning the value to the identifier on the left side. In a self-referential expression like x = f x, the statement must be true in the mathematical sense, but with :=, there is a time lag between the right and left sides. This expression is an instruction to increment the value of x by 1 and is executed as follows:

1. Get the value of x.
2. Add 1 to that value.
3. Store the resulting value at the memory address of x.

---

[1] In a language where self-referential definition through the use of = is disallowed but must instead be made in another form, assignment is often described by = instead of :=. Java is one such language.

The point here is that the two signs x in this one statement do not have the same signification (Barron *et al.*, 1963; Stroustrup, 1994b). The x on the right side means the value, or content, of x, whereas x on the left side means the address (see Section 2.4). This ambiguity of x can be compared to whether the painting shown in Figure 6.2 represents a bird or the sky.

Such ambiguity of interpretation puzzles novice programmers and has been controversial among programming language designers. At the computer hardware level, since an identifier denotes both the address and the value stored there at the same time, as explained in Section 2.3, the identifier x is inevitably ambiguous as to which of these it represents.

Such ambiguities as to the level of representation are present, in general, in signs. This problem forms a theme readily formulated in semiotics. The second part of this book is dedicated to an examination of various kinds of signs and content. This chapter concerns different levels of sign representation for content (see Figure 3.8). The discussion consists of considering the correspondence between the sign classifications proposed in dyadic and triadic sign modeling, as a continuation of Chapter 3. Each sign modeling framework, dyadic and triadic, led to an original classification. For the dyadic framework, Louis Hjelmslev, a successor to Saussure, proposed a way to classify signs, whereas for the triadic framework Peirce himself proposed a classification method. This chapter considers the correspondence between these two sign classifications.

Dyadic and triadic sign models have independently been developed in different cultures and applied to semiotic objects. The consequence was the Babylonian confusion already discussed at the level of sign models, as seen in Chapter 3. Further consideration of correspondence at this level of sign classification has hardly been attempted. One exceptional investigation is that of Parret, who compared Hjelmslev's and Peirce's theories (Parret, 1983, Chapter 2). His discussion, however, is more or less of a juxtaposition of the two theories from an abstract viewpoint, without proposing any concrete correspondence between the classifications.

If there are two relevant frameworks for modeling the same target in different ways and each framework has a relevant theory, then a corresponding theory should exist in the other framework as well. Since an approach to correspondence of sign models is hypothesized in the previous part of this book, then why not look for further correspondence in classification too? In Chapter 3, the confusion is tackled by looking at computer programs and trying to map the sign theories onto them. When two models are mapped onto the same target, the correspondence is understood via that target. This chapter applies the same tactic by considering the ambiguities of computer

```
1: var dw  1234          ;;   allocate one word memory space, name it
                              var, set value 1234
2:      mov ax,var       ;;   store the value of var in ax
3:      mov ax,offset var ;;  store the address of var in ax
4:      lea ax,var       ;;   store the address of var in ax
```

FIGURE 6.4. Example program in 8086 assembly language.

signs appearing in programs and applying the sign classification approaches of Hjelmslev and Peirce. Through this line of reasoning, the ambiguity presented above is formalized under the two frameworks and a hypothesis is raised regarding the correspondence of the two approaches. The argument starts with an overview of sign ambiguity problems in computer programs.

6.2 Semiotic Ambiguity of Identifiers

The ambiguity between value and address, as in the previous example of x, simply lies in what identifiers really are and thus cannot be avoided. A computer is a state transition machine in which temporary calculation results are stored in memory and the calculation itself proceeds simply by referring to these results. These temporarily stored data are called values, and they are referred to by indicating their respective memory addresses in programs (see Section 2.4).

The problem concerning the two x's seen in the previous section occurs more explicitly at a lower level of program description, in assembly language. An assembly language is designed to control a computer's central processing unit (CPU), and its design directly reflects the CPU design. An example of a description in Intel 8086 assembly language (Rector and Alexy, 1982) is given in Figure 6.4.[2]

This program does nothing remarkable: it simply allocates a one-word memory space named var and stores the value 1234 there (line 1); then it stores the value of var in a register, called ax, which is a special memory space used for calculation by the CPU (line 2). The program then stores the address of var in the register in each of lines 3 and 4, whose actions are exactly the same in this example. Here, mov and lea represent two different CPU operations of storing,[3] whereas var is an identifier representing an address. In

---

[2] Any text following ;; in a line is merely a comment intended for human consumption.

[3] The two operations lea and mov are different in that the former is for acquiring an address, whereas the latter is for assignment. Since the operation expressed in this example is to assign an address, it can be expressed using either mov or lea.

addition, `dw` and `offset` are called pseudo-operations and specify to the assembler how the program should be translated into binary machine language, the lowest level of program description.

Note how `var` is used in two ways:

- as the value stored in the memory space named `var`, and
- as the address of the memory space named `var`.

In line 2, for example, `var` means the value stored at the memory space, whereas in lines 3 and 4 `var` means the address of this memory space. This ambiguity between value and an address cannot be avoided, since any value is stored at a memory space having an address: a memory address can thus mean the address itself or the value stored there.

Contextual information provides the only means of resolving this ambiguity. Here, the context consists of

- which operation is used (`lea` or `mov`), or
- whether the reserved word[4] `offset` exists before the identifier.

For example, lines 2 and 3 have the same operation, `mov`, but `var` denotes the value in line 2, whereas it denotes the address in line 3 because of the presence of `offset`. This shows that identifiers are disambiguated pragmatically through their use within a context.

Such ambiguity between value and address at the assembly language level cannot be resolved in higher-level languages and often appears, as in the example given in the previous section. In the expression

$$x := x + 1, \qquad\qquad (6.4)$$

x is the identifier, like `var` in the assembly language example. An identifier in a program is translated into an actual memory address by the language system, so the same ambiguity problem arises as to whether the identifier should be denoted as a value or as an address. This ambiguity is also resolved pragmatically through the context. In the case of x, the context is the *side* of the assignment operation indicated by `:=`. Although the precise definitions and implementations are given within the language specification, typically, the x on the left side indicates an address, while that on the right side indicates a value. To highlight these differences, Stroustrup (1994b) and Barron *et al.* (1963) distinguished these different interpretations by using the term *l-value* for an identifier on the left side and the term *r-value* for an identifier on the right side.

---

[4] For the term *reserved word*, see Section 2.3.

```
1: void noset(int b) {
2:    b = 123;
3: }
4:
5: void set(int[ ] a, int i) {
6:    a[i] = 123;
7: }
8:
9: void test() {
10:    int x = 456;    // x is set to 456
11:    noset(x);       // x is not set to 123
12:    int[ ] v = new int[100];
13:    v[0] = 789;     // v[0] is set to 789
14:    set(v, 0);      // v[0] is set to 123
15: }
```

FIGURE 6.5. Call by value and call by reference.

The same ambiguity occurs every time a program refers to an identifier. A significant example of this within programming languages is the contrast between *call by value* and *call by reference* (Aho *et al.*, 1986), an important concept that all good programmers understand. Let us consider the example Java program in Figure 6.5.[5] There are three functions: noset, set, and test. The noset function receives b as input and sets its value to 123. This is called from line 11 of the program, where x is handed to noset as input after its value is set to 456 in line 10. The same action is done by the function set, which receives an array[6] a and sets the value of the ith element of the array to 123. The set function is called at line 14, with the argument being array v, whose 0th element was previously set to 789 in line 13. Basically, set and noset perform similar actions: both simply assign 123 to the target identifier.

When these functions are called, though, their results are totally distinct, as illustrated in Figure 6.6. The value of x remains unchanged, but the value of v[0] is changed to 123. This is because noset handles b by value, whereas set processes a by reference. When noset is called, a new space b is allocated inside memory, and the value is copied from x, so that b is initialized to the value 456. In the function body, the value of b is changed to 123, but the original value of x does not change because b and x represent different

---

[5] In Java, whatever comes after // in a line is a comment. Moreover, as noted in footnote 1 of this chapter, = in Java may denote assignment, and lines 2, 6, and 13 of this program all show assignment.

[6] An *array* is a data structure consisting of an ordered set of data of the same type. An array appeared in the program shown in Figure 2.2.

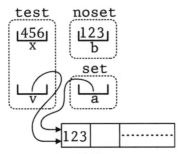

FIGURE 6.6. The memory usage for the program shown in Figure 6.5.

memory spaces. However, the value of v denotes the address of the memory space where the array is stored. When set is called, a is newly allocated and the address of v is copied. Thus, a and v represent identical content. When the first element of array a is changed to 123, the value of array v also changes. In other words, when an argument is given to a function, a copy of it is made in terms of value or address. The former is a call by value, whereas the latter is a call by reference.

The signification of these identifiers is again disambiguated pragmatically by the notion of type. As noted in Section 2.4.2, types in Java are classified into two categories: basic types, those predefined within the language design; and complex types, defined in libraries or by programmers as a combination of basic types. Java specifies that the values of basic types are processed directly by value, whereas the values of complex types are processed indirectly by reference. This aspect of the language design applies to function calls. Since b is of a basic type, the call to noset uses a call by value, whereas a is an array and an array is a complex type, so the function call to set uses a call by reference.

Programmers should understand such language design characteristics before they start writing programs, and this includes the disambiguation of the meanings of identifiers. The question of when to use call by reference or call by value depends on the language. Such concepts as value and address can be confusing for beginners since disambiguation requires a simulation of how computers run. This can sometimes even be confusing for professionals because what a sign indicates is not shown explicitly within the sign itself.

So far, we have considered the sign ambiguity between value and address, which is rooted in computer semantics at the hardware level and appears at the programming language level (see Section 2.4 for the semantic level of identifiers). Another ambiguity can be seen between type and value at the semantic level of the programming language.

Recall the following expression examined at the beginning of the chapter:

$$\text{Rectangle r = new Rectangle(5.0,8.0)}. \qquad (6.5)$$

This statement allocates a data structure of type `Rectangle` and represents it by an identifier `r`. On the left side, `Rectangle` means that the identifier `r` is of data type `Rectangle`, defined in lines 7–9 of the program shown in Figure 2.2, whereas on the right side `Rectangle` means that an actual instance is allocated by calling the initialization function defined in line 8. In natural language, the left `Rectangle` corresponds to an expression such as 'Rectangles include squares', indicating the rectangle as a *kind*, whereas the right `Rectangle` specifies an instance of a rectangle, as in the sentence '*The* rectangle has width 5.0 and height 8.0.'

Thus, the sole identifier `Rectangle` can mean either a type or a kind of value.[7] The same ambiguity is also seen for instantiation of the other shapes, of type `Ellipse` represented by u, and of type `Circle` represented by v (lines 22 and 23). This can only be disambiguated by the context, such as the existence of the reserved word `new`.

Much effort has been made within programming language design to distinguish what exactly an identifier denotes (Meyer, 2000). This includes attempts to avoid address-value and type-value ambiguities. For example, in Simula (Dahl *et al.*, 1970; Dahl and Nygaard, 1966), identifiers are declared as follows.

$$\begin{array}{l} \text{x : ref Rectangle} \\ \text{m,n : INTEGER} \end{array} \qquad (6.6)$$

The declaration thus specifies whether an identifier represents an address or a value. This complicates the representation, however, since addresses themselves must sometimes be handled as values through computation.

As for the type-value ambiguity, some languages give the initialization function a different name. In Ruby (Thomas and Hunt, 2000),[8] instance constructors should be named `initialize`, and expression (6.5) is instead given as follows:

$$\text{r = Rectangle.new(5.0,8.0)}, \qquad (6.7)$$

---

[7] Some readers might question whether the `Rectangle` on the right-hand side could be considered a value. Precisely, this `Rectangle` is a constructor, a function to construct a value. Since a Java constructor always belongs to a class, it may be considered equivalent to a type. Nevertheless, `Rectangle` is used ambiguously as either a class name or a constructor, and as a constructor, it does generate a return value. This section considers such ambiguity underlying signification.

[8] Ruby is a dynamically typed language in which types are considered dynamically at execution time.

where new calls the function initialize. The type name Rectangle always signifies a *type*. Although this solution in Ruby seems simple and relevant, the type and the instantiation function, whose output is a value, have the same identifier in many object-oriented languages.

The ambiguity is caused by a value being represented by a sign in a stratified manner: a value is represented by a bit pattern stored at a memory space location specified by an address, which is represented by an identifier, which in turn is typed. Given content, therefore, there are multiple levels on which an identifier represents it. Such variety of representation of content is formalized in semiotics as sign classification. Every sign is ambiguous as to what it signifies among the relata of the sign model, and in addition, since every relatum is reciprocally represented by another sign, this mashes up different signs so that the original sign signifies derived content. Focusing on sign classification in relation to content, we next look at how the sign ambiguity presented so far fits into the dyadic and triadic sign classifications.

6.3   Hjelmslev's Connotation and Metalanguage

In dyadic modeling, it was, a successor of Saussure, who considered this problem of sign types. Hjelmslev extended Saussure's dyadic framework and called it glossematics (Hjelmslev, 1943).[9] Hjelmslev renamed the two relata of a sign, namely the signifier and the signified, as the *expression* and the *content*, respectively, to distinguish his signification of two sides of a sign from that of Saussure. In this section, however, the two sides of a sign are denoted as the signifier and the content, adopting the terms of this book, since the term *expression* is used ambiguously throughout and also to facilitate further explanation in correspondence with the triadic model. The introduction of Hjelmslev's theory in this section is based on an interpretation using a graphic formulation that was devised by Roland Barthes through his studies on applying Hjelmslev's sign classification to various targets (Barthes, 1970, 1983).

Hjelmslev considered that the dimension of either signifier or content could further form a sign, as shown in Figure 6.7. The upper part of the figure shows the case in which the content forms another sign, whereas the lower part of the

---

[9]   According to (Nöth, 1990), glossematics is the study of the sign, or *glosseme*, as the basic unit or component carrying meaning in language. The term glossematics combines glossary with mathematics, which represents the underlying philosophy of the field of study. It takes a formalized approach to sign systems, as in mathematics, by attempting to describe a sign system through a framework of axioms and principles of the functional relationships among glossemes. For example, the explanation of connotation and denotation presented here attempts to explain their formation from the dyadic nature of signs.

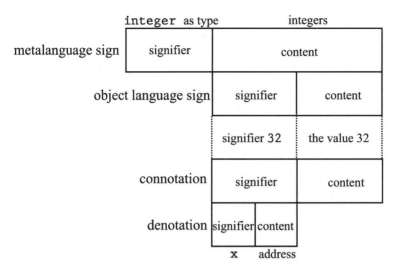

FIGURE 6.7. Hjelmslev's connotation and metalanguage.

figure shows the case in which the signifier forms another sign. Hjelmslev said that the former case establishes the relation between the two signs as *object language* and *metalanguage*, whereas the latter case establishes the relation between the two signs as *denotation* and *connotation*.[10]

According to Hjelmslev, a connotation is a semiotic layer whose signifier plane consists of the denotative elements of the language and whose content plane consists of stylistic values (Nöth, 1990, pp. 71–72). Here, two completely unrelated signs combine so that the signifier of the denotation signifies the content of the connotation. Taking an example given in Hjelmslev (1943, p. 105), the signifier 'green-eyed monster' connotes 'jealousy' in terms of content. At the same time, for the denotative sign 'green-eyed monster', its content corresponds to the literal signification of a 'monster'. The derived meaning of 'jealousy' is located as the content in the connotative layer for the dennotation layer whose direct content is the 'monster'. Another example is that of (Nöth, 1990, p. 310). The photo shows "a black African in a French uniform saluting a French flag". In the denotative layer, the photo forms the signifier, and the literal meaning of the photo forms its content. From this denotative sign derives a connotative layer whose content is "France is a great colonial Empire with loyal black citizens in its army, etc."

---

[10] The terms denotation and connotation are used according to Hjelmslev's dyadic formulation only, and this differs from the typical sense related to materiality and subjectivity. See glossary.

On the other hand, the metalanguage concept corresponds to the logical definition of the term as a language about language. The target language to be explained is called the object language. A metasign is a sign of metalanguage.[11] The content part of a metasign covers the signifier and the content of the corresponding object language signs at the same time. For example, a part of speech is a metasign (Nöth, 1990, p. 311) in the case of signs in natural language as the object language. The metasign is obtained through abstraction of several different signs, just as Hjelmslev denotes the metasign as *science* (Hjelmslev, 1943, pp. 100–101).

Let us now apply Hjelmslev's sign classification to identifiers in programs. All information handled by computers ultimately consists of zeros and ones, which are actually composed of electric signals passing through circuits. These bit patterns are the ultimate values, the content, inside a computer. Correspondingly, in higher-level programming languages, literals[12] that represent values only as values represent the actual content, such as integers appearing simply as numbers like 123 and 456.

Such values are represented by identifiers, where an identifier is a sign whose signifier corresponds to the identifier's name and whose content corresponds to its address. This signifier, however, refers to the content stored at the address. For example, given a program statement x = 32, the direct content as an address is unrelated to the value of 32. The layer consisting of x as a signifier and its address forms a denotational layer, and the layer consisting of the value indicated by x is deemed to form the connotational layer. In other words, the signifier x connotes the content 32.[13]

On the other hand, a metasign is deemed to correspond to the type, which is an abstraction of data instances. For example, in int x = 32, the declaration of the type of the value 32 as int is likely to be the signifier in the metasign, and its content would then be integers inclusively of the data 32,

---

[11] This metasign and metalanguage are Hjelmslev's terminology and differ from metalanguage in the computational sense, which appears in Chapter 11 (cf. Glossary).

[12] See Section 2.3.

[13] Considering sign classes as in Hjelmslev and Barthes's formulation, so that the dimension of either signifier or content recursively forms a sign, there are only two possibilities, as indicated in Figure 6.7. It is certain that the value/address relation does not correspond to the object language/metalanguage relation, which leaves one sole candidate for its correspondence with denotation/connotation. This seems relevant since the layers suggest the combination of two unrelated signs (such as monster and jealousy). Which layer corresponds to denotation is still a question. Nevertheless, since the signifier consisting of the value 32 *cannot* connote anything in a program, but x can, it has to be the case that x forms the denotational layer and the value forms the connotational layer. This in fact conforms with further consideration of ambiguity and also with the correspondence to Peirce's triadic sign modeling.

which is deemed the object language sign of the instance. An overview of this hypothetical correspondence with Hjelmslev's scheme and this example signifier is shown in Figure 6.7, where the relation between int and 32 appears in the upper part for the metasign and object language sign, while the relation of x and 32 appears in the lower part for the denotation and connotation.

Another example is demonstrated by the following expression, also shown earlier:

$$\texttt{Rectangle r = new Rectangle(5.0,8.0).} \qquad (6.8)$$

Here, the left Rectangle is likely the metasign, whose signifier is the Rectangle as type, while the content is the set of instances of Rectangle, including the instance allocated as Rectangle(5.0,8.0). Naturally, this Rectangle(5.0,8.0) seems to correspond to an object language sign. The address-value contrast appears here, as well, in that the signifier r is a denotation of an address, which connotatively signifies the content represented as Rectangle(5.0,8.0).

How, then, can the sign ambiguity problem be explained according to this correspondence? In Hjelmslev's model, a sign is allowed to signify the content of another sign in relation with itself, as in the cases for a denotation and a metasign. Then, a sign becomes ambiguous in one of the following two cases:

- when a signifier signifies its own content, or
- when a signifier signifies the content of another sign.

For example, Rectangle is a type but is ambiguously used, indicating a value. Moreover, x connotatively signifies a value but may ambiguously signify the denotational address itself. In other words, the ambiguity within Hjelmslev's model arises when the signs are layered and one signifier signifies multiple content, that of itself and that of another sign.

6.4   Peirce's Icon, Index, and Symbol

Within the triadic framework, Peirce himself provides a theory of sign classification. This is based on his universal categories, in which any logical form is classified by the number of forms in relation, namely, one, two, or three forms. Forms related to more than three forms are reduced to combinations of relations among three or fewer forms. There are thus only three categories among forms, defined as follows by (Peirce, 1931, 8.328):

Firstness is the mode of being of that which is such as it is, positively and without reference to anything else

Secondness is the mode of being of that which is such as it is, with respect to a second but regardless of any third.

Thirdness is the mode of being of that which is such as it is, in bringing a second and third into relation to each other.

The significance of these universal categories is reconsidered in the next chapter. For now, note that in Peirce's universal categories classification is made by counting how many items of content are involved. Moreover, the universal categories are *not* categories of signs but rather categories of forms and content. As is explained further in the introduction to the next chapter, the question of how a sign represents given content is different from what form the content itself takes, although any content can be perceived only via signs by applying the pansemiotic view presented in Section 2.5. A universal category concerns the properties of a form, whereas the theme of this chapter is the means of representation, considering the possible relation between a sign and its content.

According to Peirce, a typical example of a form of thirdness is the sign. Therefore, for Peirce, a sign has three relata, and he favors the triadic model. Since a sign has three relata, there are three relations operating as forms between the sign and each relatum. Peirce's basic typology of signs is obtained by classifying these forms (relations) in terms of the universal categories. Such a scheme thus gives three relations (between the sign and each of the representamen, the object, and the interpretant) classified into three categories (firstness, secondness, and thirdness).

Since our focus is the level at which content is represented by a sign, we examine the sign classification with respect to the content. Peirce (1931) himself refers to this classification as "the most fundamental division of signs" [2.275]. Applying the universal categories to the relation between a sign and its content gives three kinds of signs – icon, index, and symbol. Peirce's definitions of the icon, index, and symbol are as follows (Peirce, 1931):

- An *icon* is "a sign which stands for something merely because it resembles it" [3.362], "partaking in the characters of the object" [4.531]. For example, a portrait of a person or a color sample of paint is an icon since it stands for something merely because it resembles the original.
- An *index* is "physically connected with its object; they make an organic pair, but the interpreting mind has nothing to do with this connection"

[2.299]; "it is a 'reference'" [2.283]. According to Peirce, clocks, sundials, and door knocks are example of indexes, since each makes an organic pair with another fact. Moreover, uses of signs A, B, and C in a formal statement such as 'A and B are married and C is their child' are indexes [2.285].

- A *symbol* is a sign that "refers to the object that it denotes by virtue of law, usually an association of general ideas" [2.249]; "Any ordinary word as 'give', 'bird', 'marriage', is an example of a symbol" [2.298].

Therefore, the universal category of a sign in relation to its content describes the abstraction level to which the sign refers. The reason why the icon and index correspond to firstness and secondness, respectively, is intuitively comprehensible in that the icon represents the content as it is, whereas the index represents the content by means of another term referencing the original. The reason why the symbol corresponds to thirdness, however, depends on the essence of thirdness, which is discussed in the following chapter.

Now let us consider applying this trichotomy to the computer signs. The most primitive entities are zeros and ones, and the bit patterns representing values are icons. A bit pattern has the ultimate resemblance to the data partaking of the object's character. Similarly, literals denoting these values in digits and instance constructors within programs could be considered icons. An index naturally corresponds to a reference to the value located at the address represented by x, since data are physically stored in computer memory and form an organic pair with the value, and the address has nothing to do with the value. Moreover, the previous example of the notation of people by A, B, and C shows how such representation is similar to the use of identifiers. As for the symbol, a type seems to be a sign that embeds a general idea about a value. As a consequence, in the following example expression,

$$\text{int x = 32,} \tag{6.9}$$

int seems to correspond to the symbol, x to the index, and the value 32 to the icon. The following expression also demonstrates this hierarchical representation of signs:

$$\text{Rectangle r = new Rectangle(5.0,8.0),} \tag{6.10}$$

where the left Rectangle may be thought to correspond to the symbol, r to the index, and Rectangle(5.0,8.0) to the icon denoting the value. Consequently, correspondences can be hypothetically established such that a value is viewed as an icon, an address as an index, and a type as a symbol.

How, then, can the sign ambiguity problem seen in Section 6.2 be explained according to this correspondence? There are multiple ways to formulate the

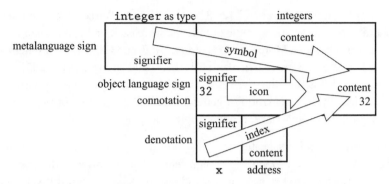

FIGURE 6.8. The correspondence of the two sign classifications.

ambiguity by using Peirce's sign categorization framework. One possibility is to use a detailed sign categorization, which is briefly introduced in Section 7.5. Here, however, another possibility for this formulation is presented. Peirce considered a higher-order category to include a lower-order category (Peirce, 1931, 1.365–366, 1.521–529). For example, thirdness includes secondness, and secondness includes firstness. Peirce also indicates that such degeneration occurs with indexes and symbols (Peirce, 1931, 2.283, 2.293). Applying this way of thought to the relation between the sign and the content, the symbol and index include signification as an icon. For example, it could be considered that Rectangle as a value occurs when Rectangle as a symbol is degeneratively used as an icon. Moreover, x as an index represents an address when it is considered to be used degeneratively as firstness. In other words, one way to formulate ambiguity in Peirce's framework is to consider it to occur when the universal category of the relation of a sign with its content degenerates.

6.5   Correspondence of the Two Sign Classifications

The sign classifications proposed within the dyadic and triadic frameworks were each examined to see how they apply to computer signs. Moreover, the cause of ambiguity was analyzed through these correspondences. The two correspondences suggest how the two sign classifications themselves could correspond, as summarized in Figure 6.8. This figure is similar to Figure 6.7, but here the layers of connotation and object language overlap since they indicate the same sign. In Figure 6.8, the large arrows indicate Peirce's three sign classes. Remember that the subject of this section is the classes of how a signifier indicates content; thus the three arrows are directed toward the content consisting of the value.

This layer consisting of a value whose signifier is 32 and whose content is 32 forms an icon within Peirce's classification. In the dyadic model, this layer is the layer of the object language sign, overlapping a connotative layer for the denotative layer of identifier x. In the expression x = 32, x's direct content is the address, forming the denotative layer, but it connotes the value. This notion of a signifier of the denotative layer indicating the content of the connotative layer corresponds to Peirce's index. On the other hand, when the sign integer signifies the value 32, the value 32 forms the layer of object language and the notion of integer forms the layer of metalanguage. This indication of the signifier of a metasign indicating the value 32 corresponds to Peirce's symbol.[14]

The ambiguities appear because the signifiers of the index and the metasign indicate the content of another sign as the content of their own. The index x has denotational content consisting of the address and connotational content consisting of the value, and the symbol integer indicates the content of the class or a specific value.

The concepts of icon/index/symbol and denotation/connotation plus object language/metalanguage correspond within the context of application to programming languages. Similar concepts have been developed within both the dyadic and the triadic frameworks, and the resulting correspondences validate each framework. This correspondence is deemed to stipulate universal kinds of signs. At first sight, the dyadic and triadic frameworks seem very different. By composing two dyadic signs in a layered manner, however, as Hjelmslev did, a triadic relationship is obtained. At the same time, from the triadic side, a dyadic relationship is readily embedded within a triadic sign system.

When a semiotic phenomenon is described by two different explanations, a question arises as to which is the better explanation. In short, the triadic sign tradition is better when the purpose is to view sign levels within the sole axis of the universal categories. The dyadic tradition is superior when the purpose is to examine the different significations of signs from the relation between two signs. The dyadic framework might also be more flexible because there are other possibilities for composing the two layers of denotation/connotation and object language/metalanguage. If such composition is genuinely important, however, what corresponds to it should also exist within the triadic framework.

---

[14] I referred to the relation of the interpretant and the connotation in footnote 7 of Chapter 3. Under the hypothetical conclusion presented in this chapter, which is based on Hjelmslev's framework, the connotation represents the *content* that derives from the original sign. Therefore, the connotation is considered to be the relation between the signifier and the content, not the signifier and the use. For a self-referential sign, however, since content and use are unified according to the observations of Chapters 4 and 5, the connotation also concerns the use. In any case, the notion of connotation varies and depends on the definition. The question of where to situate connotation within the sign model must be considered according to the definition.

Looking back to the three works of art shown at the beginning of this chapter, the representation of birds in Figure 6.1 seems to function as the icon, that of Figure 6.2 as the index, and that of Figure 6.3 as the symbol, in Peirce's terminology. Correspondingly, the second painting can be considered to connote a bird, with its denotation being the sky, and the third painting can be considered to represent an abstract bird as a metasign, with its object language sign being a bird, in Hjelmslev's terminology. Thus, what we have seen so far seems to also apply to artwork. In art, however, such clear distinctions are a matter of degree, as has been the case in each chapter. The cock and hen in Jakuchu's drawing might not be based on exact bird instances; rather, they might represent the core essences of cocks and hens for Jakuchu as the forms of the birds.[15]

6.6 Summary

This chapter has examined the correspondence of sign classification schemes proposed within the dyadic and triadic frameworks. In computer programs, a value is represented by a sign in a stratified manner: a value, an address, and/or a type. This causes ambiguities as to what a sign signifies. The three representation levels were formulated by applying Hjelmslev's connotative and metasemiotics from the dyadic framework and Peirce's sign classification from the triadic framework. Through this application, the ambiguity problem was interpreted in each framework. By comparison of the application of the two frameworks, the correspondence between the two frameworks was hypothesized. The index corresponds to the case where the signifier of the denotational layer signifies the content of the connotative layer, whereas the symbol corresponds to the case where the signifier of the metasign signifies the content of the object language.

---

[15] Jakuchu is known to have observed multiple cocks and hens in his garden for years before he actually painted them.

7

Three Kinds of Content in Programs

These days we make an idea out of the precipitation of everything into its opposite and the solution of both into a single category, which is itself reconcilable with the initial term, and so on until the mind attains the absolute idea, the reconciliation of every opposition and the unity of every category.

From *The Lost Steps*, an English-language translation of *Les Pas Perdus*, by André Breton, translated by Mark Polizzotti. Reprinted by permission of the University of Nebraska Press. © 1996 by Mark Polizzotti. © Éditions Gallimard, 1924, 1969.

(Breton, 1924, pp. 77–79)

7.1 Thirdness

The previous chapter was dedicated to an analysis of the different levels of representation of content (see Figure 3.8). This chapter, in contrast, considers the various kinds of represented content and examines how signs are involved in such representation.

As usual, we consider a selection of paintings, shown in Figures 7.1, 7.2, and 7.3. Figure 7.1 represents the imaginary world of Paul Klee, Figure 7.2 represents a real-world flower assembled through a painter's interpretation, and Figure 7.3 represents the painter Rembrandt himself, another real-world subject. The first differs from the other two in that the content is not based on a real-world entity. Among real-world themes, the third has a particularity in that the painter himself forms the subject.

In terms of how many forms constitute the content of the painting, the first painting has only one, the painter's imaginary world. The second involves two, the image of real-world flowers in the painter's mind and their visual interpretation as expressed by the painter. In the third painting, in addition to forms of the two types, there is a special hidden form – the constraint that the content of the painting and the subject of the interpretation should be

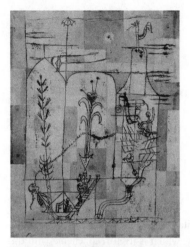

FIGURE 7.1. Paul Klee (1879–1940), *Tale à la Hoffmann*, The Metropolitan Museum of Art. © 2009 Artists Rights Society (ARS), New York/VG Bild-Kunst, Bonn. Image copyright © The Metropolitan Museum of Art/Art Resource, NY.

FIGURE 7.2. Suzuki Kiitsu (1796–1858), *Morning Glories*, The Metropolitan Museum of Art. Image © The Metropolitan Museum of Art.

FIGURE 7.3. Rembrandt Harmensz van Rijn (1606–1669), *Self-Portrait*, Wallraf-Richartz-Museum. Photo credit: Bildarchiv Preussischer Kulturbesitz/Art Resource, NY.

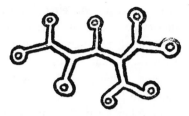

FIGURE 7.4. Peirce's intuitive explanation of the the universal categories. Reprinted by permission of the publisher from The COLLECTED PAPERS OF CHARLES SANDERS PIERCE, VOLUME I – PRINCIPLES OF PHILOSOPHY, edited by Charles Hartshorne and Paul Weiss, p. 196, Cambridge, Mass.: The Belknap Press of Harvard University Press, Copyright © 1931, 1959 by the President and Fellows of Harvard College.

equal. In other words, the first, second, and third paintings involve one, two, and three forms, respectively.

Peirce provided a way to classify different types of forms in terms of the number of forms involved. This classification is called *the universal categories* and was introduced briefly in Section 6.4. The underlying question of the universal categories is to seek the minimal basic forms from among all forms. In the universal categories, the form of firstness essentially involves only one form, that of secondness involves two forms, and that of thirdness involves three forms. Peirce makes two assertions about the the universal categories:

- Firstness, secondness, and thirdness are essentially different forms.
- Firstness, secondness, and thirdness are sufficient as forms. All multiple-term relations involving more than three terms can be decomposed into relationships of at most three terms; therefore, there is no need for another form involving four or more terms.

It is abundantly clear that firstness and secondness are different. A form without any relationship is essentially different from two forms in relation. It is less clear, however, what essentially distinguishes secondness from thirdness. Why not decompose thirdness into secondness and firstness? Why is it possible to say that three is necessary and sufficient?

Peirce (1931, 1.370, 1.371) himself gives an intuitive answer to these questions by using the drawing shown in Figure 7.4. This figure shows that it is essential to have three-term relationships to relate any number of forms freely to each other. According to Peirce, if there are only two-term relationships, they only form a chain without branches, but with three-term relationships any two forms can become connected in various ways. A three-term relationship thus provides a sufficient number of forms for any two forms to be freely related; additional forms are not required. Peirce thus reasons about the universal categories from the viewpoint of connectivity of forms. I consider that this argument does not sufficiently represent the nature of forms in the universal categories. To start with, consider firstness. Peirce (1931) claims that firstness "is the mode of being of that which is . . . without reference to anything else" [8.328] (as noted in Section 6.4). At the same time, if firstness cannot *be referenced by* any other form, then its signification as a form is doubtful, since it will not have any relation with any other form. Hence, it must be the case that the universal categories stipulate forms from a *functional* viewpoint; that is, there must be a distinction between a form *referring to* another and a form *being referred to* by another. In other words, firstness itself does not refer to any other forms, but it can *be referred to* by other forms. If so, a similar functional view must apply to secondness and thirdness. Considering secondness, a form of secondness can be referred to by any other form of secondness, and also, forms that are referred to by secondness can be referred to by any other forms of secondness. In other words, various relations can be constructed only from firstness and secondness, by connecting forms in various manners. Then, the validity of Peirce's explanation from the viewpoint of connectivity of forms becomes questionable, and it is also questionable why thirdness is necessary, in addition to secondness and firstness.

It was not only Peirce, however, who presented this idea that there are only three forms. Historically, similar reduction of any form into one of three forms predates Peirce. For example, John Locke (1690, p. 159, Book II, Chapter XII, Of Complex Ideas) wrote as follows according to a trichotomy regarding the number of other terms involved:

The acts of the mind, wherein it exerts its power over simple ideas, are chiefly these three: 1. Combining several simple ideas into one compound one, and thus all complex ideas are made. 2. The second is bringing two ideas, whether simple or complex, together, and setting them by one another so as to take a view of them at once, without uniting them into one, by which it gets all its ideas of relations. 3. The third is separating them from all other ideas that accompany them in their real existence: this is called abstraction, and thus all its general ideas are made.

Peirce considered Georg Hegel's study of dialectics to be related to his universal categories, and it is referenced in Peirce's explanation of the universal categories (Peirce, 1931, 1.368, 5.38). Hence, influential thinkers have contemplated the notion that any form can be classified into one of three kinds, according to the number of other forms that are essentially involved.

The criteria that distinguish thirdness from secondness must be clarified to gain a better understanding of the way of thinking that any form is one of only three types. If thirdness is essentially different from secondness, it should be impossible to decompose a form of thirdness into forms of firstness and secondness. At the same time, if every relation that concerns more than three forms can be decomposed into forms of firstness, secondness, and thirdness, then the universal categories can be considered to represent the minimal basic forms from among all forms.

In this chapter, these questions of the universal categories are considered in the functional programming paradigm by examining the functional language Haskell. This paradigm was chosen because I consider Peirce's universal categories to have a functional nature, as mentioned previously. Moreover, every item of content – the implementation of the computational form – in the functional paradigm is considered functionally, whereas all other paradigms offer multiple kinds of computational content. This does not mean that the argument of this chapter does not apply to other programming languages, since the differences among paradigms are differences in their ways of description and the paradigms are compatible, as is seen in Chapter 3. Therefore, consideration of the universal categories in the functional paradigm accounts for the other paradigms. In other words, the theme of this chapter is to consider how many forms appear in computation in general.

In this functional paradigm, all functional forms are decomposed by using Church's transformation (Church, 1941) and *currying* (explained in Sections 7.3 and 7.4) (Bird and Wadler, 1988). Analysis of the result of the transformation shows that thirdness is essentially different from secondness and cannot be decomposed into firstness and secondness. This chapter demonstrates this decomposition scheme and examines the essence underlying thirdness. Note also that the argument of this chapter assumes *referential transparency* – a restriction applied to a programming language system that requires that every expression must have a unique value (Bird, 1998); the notion is explained in detail in Chapter 10. This assumption does not decrease the generality of the discussion, however, since any program without referential transparency can be transformed into a transparent one, as is also shown in Chapter 10.

The theme of this chapter (and the next) is an examination of the kinds of *content*, as opposed to the last chapter where the question was the kinds of signs, or more precisely, the *relationship* between a sign and its content. The questions of how a sign represents content and of what properties the form has are different. It is true, though, that categories of forms are only considered via signs under the pansemiotic view (as explained in Section 2.5). It might be the case that the forms of a category are systematically represented by signs of certain categories. Although I do not go as far as to attempt to solve this question of the correspondence of the form category and its sign category, it is briefly revisited at the end of Section 7.5, after covering the main thrust of this chapter.

Fortunately, any confusion of focus between sign classification and the universal category of a form is eliminated by choosing the functional paradigm, since the signs appearing in this discussion are all indexes in Peirce's classification, as introduced in the previous chapter. As classified in the previous chapter, literals are icons, but once these values are represented by identifiers, they become indexes. Haskell is a typed language, and types are represented by symbols in Peirce's categories, but the main point of the argument can be discussed without considering types. Therefore, the signs appearing in this chapter are all indexes. Under this uniform condition, the question of the universal categories is considered.

7.2　Definitions and Expressions

Since the universal categories concern the number of essentially related items of content, the categories can be analyzed in a functional program by considering how functions are related. As explained in Section 2.2, a program consists of two parts: the definition part, in which identifiers are defined in terms of their content, and the use part, in which identifiers are used through expressions. Signs are related through these definitions and expressions. The objective of this chapter is therefore to see how many signs are essentially involved in a definition and an expression.

In Haskell, the definition of an identifier y takes the syntax of y = *an expression*, and the defined signs are used in an expression. An expression has the syntax of a functional application, $f\ x_1 \cdots x_n$, or simply f, where f is either a data constructor, a function defined elsewhere, or a lambda-term as seen in Chapter 4. As is noted in Chapter 2, definitions and expressions are interrelated. A definition includes an expression, usually on the right-hand side of =. Conversely, an expression may include a local definition, as seen for the let-expression in Figure 2.1 and also in Section 4.4.

Putting aside its local definition, the expression at first glance seems to consist of $n + 1$ terms, as it includes f and a total of n terms of x_i at maximum. Similarly, a definition seems to consist of $n + 2$ terms, since it includes y in addition to f and its n arguments. The functional paradigm possesses ways to transform expressions and definitions so that a large relation of multiple items of content is decomposed into combinations of a small number of relations. More precisely, through *currying*, the maximum number of terms involved in an expression can be transformed exactly into a combination of relations of two terms, provided that the expression does not include or is not included in a self-referential definition. Moreover, Church showed that any self-referential definition can be transformed into a composition of a special function and non-self-referential parts. Application of Church's transformation and then currying will therefore decompose functional relations into minimal relations, as is shown in more detail in the following sections.

Such transformations of a program involve the program's semantics. The transformed program should be equivalent to the original. At the same time, however, verification of the equivalence of programs involves an essential difficulty, as introduced in Section 4.6. Here, currying and Church's transformation, described in the following two sections, are typical transformations known to preserve the formal semantics of a program. Formal semantics defines the semantics of a program on the basis of an abstract mathematical object (Tennent, 1991). Given program code f with the same semantics as f', it is guaranteed that f' is mathematically equivalent to f. The transformations described here are thus guaranteed to transform one program into another that is equivalent with respect to formal semantics.

7.3 Currying

Currying is a transformation that applies to expressions. A functional application to multiple arguments can be reduced to multiple applications of *one-argument* functions (Bird and Wadler, 1988).[1]

An expression of a two-argument function is reduced to that of a one-argument function as follows:[2]

$$f \ x \ y \Rightarrow g \ y \ \text{where} \ g = (f \ x), \qquad (7.1)$$

---

[1] According to Bird and Wadler (1988), currying is a transformation of a functional application to arguments with a structure into a chain of functional applications to simple arguments.

[2] This where-expression using **where** syntax corresponds to the let-expression seen in Chapter 4. For example,

$$g \ y \ \text{where} \ g = f \ x$$

equals

$$\text{let} \ g = f \ x \ \text{in} \ g \ y \ .$$

Haskell also has a let-expression, but since the referenced textbook on currying was written using **where**, and since some of the programs in this chapter are much more comprehensible with the where-expression than with the let-expression, these programs are written using the where-expression.

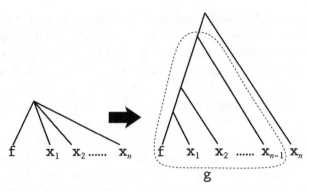

FIGURE 7.5. Currying: A multiple-argument function (left) is transformed into chains of one-argument functions (right).

where => indicates a transformation. This transformation in fact does not need to use the where-expression and g; it is no more than transforming f x y into the following:

$$(f\ x)\ y. \tag{7.2}$$

Here, $(f\ x)$ is regarded as a one-argument function, with its argument being y. Similarly, an expression of a function with n arguments can be regarded as a chain of one-argument functional applications by currying multiple times as follows.

$$\begin{aligned} &f\ x_1\ x_2 \ldots x_{n-1}\ x_n \\ &\Rightarrow g\ x_n \text{ where } g = (f\ x_1\ x_2 \cdots x_{n-1}). \end{aligned} \tag{7.3}$$

The consequence of this repetitive application of the transformation is illustrated in Figure 7.5. On the left side, f applies to the arguments $x_1 \cdots x_n$. In contrast, on the right, a new function g is constructed and applied to x_n. This g is further decomposed similarly using (7.3), generating a new function that is applied to x_{n-1}, and so on, thus creating a chain of one-argument function applications. Without using a where-expression and g, the result of this transformation is no more than the following:

$$\begin{aligned} &f\ x_1\ x_2 \ldots x_{n-1}\ x_n \\ &\Rightarrow ((\ldots((f\ x_1)\ x_2)\ldots)\ x_{n-1})\ x_n. \end{aligned} \tag{7.4}$$

Consequently, by currying, functions of at most one argument suffice to provide the expression of a function with multiple arguments.

Currying thus applies to expressions, but expressions appear in definitions. Suppose that definitions are self-referential as follows:

$$x = f\ y_1 \ldots y_i\ x\ y_{i+1} \ldots y_n. \tag{7.5}$$

Then, even if the expression of the right-hand side is curried, the x can be reciprocally replaced by the whole of the right-hand side. Currying does not easily apply in such a case.

Moreover, expressions can include local definitions. When these definitions are non-self-referential, they can be eliminated using parenthesis, like in the previous cases we saw for g and the where-expression. For example, the local definition of x in

$$f \ x \ \text{where} \ x = g \ z \ y \tag{7.6}$$

can be eliminated to give a simple expression as follows:

$$f \ (g \ z \ y). \tag{7.7}$$

Such an elimination is similarly made when f is locally defined, or even when there are multiple local definitions, as long as the signs to be replaced are defined non-self-referentially. The elimination is nonobvious only when the local definitions include self-referential definitions.

Before one applies currying to expressions, therefore, all self-referential definitions should be transformed into compositions of the special function fix and non-self-referential parts. This is done by using Church's transformation, which was introduced in Chapter 4. The following section explains Church's transformation again but in the context of Haskell.

7.4 Church's Transformation

Church's transformation applies to definitions. A self-referential function is characterized as a function that is defined by its use of itself, as explained in Chapter 4. It has the characteristic that the function name appears on the right side of its definition, thus making the function *recursively* defined.

The transformation described in this section is almost the same as the removal of self-reference by the use of the fixed-point function, shown in Section 4.4, except for the difference between Haskell and the lambda calculus. The difference lies not only in the language syntax but also in the fact that Haskell is typed, whereas the lambda calculus as introduced in Chapter 4 is untyped. This requires that the definition of the function fix be different from that of the fixed-point operator introduced in Chapter 4. Therefore, I repeat the explanation of this type of transformation, but this time I use Haskell syntax. As is the case in Chapter 4, this is an informal introduction through examples only; for a more thorough understanding of Church's transformation, see Gunter (1962) and Church (1941).

Haskell has two kinds of definitions: those of functions and those of data. The two definitions require different syntaxes, as shown by lines 1–3 and lines 5–7 in the Haskell program in Figure 2.1. The definition of data is also considered functional in the functional paradigm, as seen from Church's study demonstrating a way to express data in the form of functions (Church, 1936) and from the example of expressing numbers by lambda-terms in Chapter 4. The discussion in this chapter is therefore given only in terms of function definition, but the same discussion also applies to data definition.

The transformation is shown through two examples. The first is the function `factorial`, introduced in Section 4.4, which calculates the factorial of a given input positive integer n and is defined as follows:[3]

$$\text{factorial n =}$$
$$\text{if (n==0) then 1 else n * factorial (n-1).} \qquad (7.8)$$

Note that the function name `factorial` recursively appears on both the left and the right side of the definition. Given an integer, this function calculates its factorial value in the same manner as that shown in Section 4.4.

We may also note that in Section 7.2 a definition was shown to be reducible to a syntax of $y = f\ x_1\ \cdots\ x_n$, but here there is an argument after the sign `factorial`, namely n. This definition, however, can be written as follows by applying Haskell's lambda expression, introduced in Chapter 4:

$$\text{factorial =}$$
$$\text{\textbackslash n -> (if (n==0) then 1 else n * factorial (n-1)),} \qquad (7.9)$$

where λ n. of Chapter 4 corresponds to `\n ->`. Note that this syntax also appeared in Figure 2.1 (line 15). We may remark here how the part of the expression to the right of = of expression (7.9) remains the same as in expression (7.8), other than the addition of `\n ->`. Similarly, any functional definition with arguments can be described in the form of $y = f$ by making f a lambda-term.

Our second example is the `map` function. It applies a function f to each element of a list[4] denoted as (x:xs). The definition is self-referential as follows:

$$\text{map f [] = []}$$
$$\text{map f (x:xs) = (f x):(map f xs).} \qquad (7.10)$$

---

[3] Here, the expression n==0 means to verify whether n equals zero.

[4] A list also appears in the program shown in Figure 2.1 (line 13) and is a data structure designed to handle multiple data items, one after another.

Here, (x:xs) denotes that the first element of the list matches x and the rest of the list matches xs. Also, ':' denotes the conjunction of an element with a list. The execution example given here maps the function factorial to each of the numbers [1,3,5] and outputs the result as a list, thus calculating the factorial of each number. The execution proceeds as follows, with → indicating a reduction step.

Note that underlining indicates an expression that is expanded in the successive calculation.

$$
\begin{aligned}
&\underline{\text{map factorial [1,3,5]}} \\
&\rightarrow (\text{factorial 1}):\underline{\text{map factorial [3,5]}} \\
&\rightarrow 1:(\text{factorial 3}):\underline{\text{map factorial [5]}} \\
&\rightarrow 1:6:(\text{factorial 5}):\underline{\text{map factorial []}} \\
&\rightarrow 1:6:120:[] \\
&\rightarrow [1,6,120]
\end{aligned}
\tag{7.11}
$$

Church mathematically proved that any recursion can be transformed into a composition of nonrecursive parts and a special function fix, given in Haskell (Jones and Lester, 1992, p. 115) as follows:

$$
\text{fix f = x where x = f x.} \tag{7.12}
$$

The expression fix f outputs the fixed point of a function f, namely, x such that x = f x. Therefore, this definition includes a self-reference of x. fix corresponds to the fixed-point function introduced in Section 4.4. As mentioned in Chapter 4, since Haskell is typed, the definition is made using the local definition x = f x. Versions of the fix function were proposed by Turing (1936–1937), Curry, and others, as well as by Church; one of these versions is the fixed-point operator shown in Chapter 4 for the untyped case.

The function factorial can be rewritten through the use of the fix function as

```
factorial' = fix nonrec
  where
  nonrec f n = (if (n==0) then 1 else n * f (n-1)).
```
(7.13)

Note how the function factorial' itself is not recursively defined, as the right side of its definition does not contain factorial'. Neither is nonrec recursive, since it only appears once, on the left-hand side of =. The recursion is instead embedded in `fix`. The execution of `factorial'` then proceeds as follows when applied to 5:

```
factorial' 5
→ fix nonrec 5
→ (x 5) where x=nonrec x
→ (nonrec x 5) where x=nonrec x
→ (if 5==0 then 1 else 5 * x (5-1)) where x=nonrec x
→ 5 * (x 4) where x=nonrec x
→ 5 * (nonrec x 4) where x=nonrec x
→ 5 * (if 4==0 then 1 else 4 * x (4-1)) where x=nonrec x
→ 5 * 4 * (x 3) where x=nonrec x
...
→ 5 * 4 * 3 * 2 * 1 * 1
→ 120.
```
$$(7.14)$$

In other words, the calculation of `factorial` becomes a reflexive application of `nonrec` defined inside `factorial'`.

The following is another example of Church's transformation, for `map`:

$$\begin{aligned}
&\texttt{map' = fix nonrec}\\
&\texttt{where}\\
&\texttt{nonrec m f [] = []}\\
&\texttt{nonrec m f (x:xs) = f x:m f xs.}
\end{aligned}$$
$$(7.15)$$

Here too, `map` is decomposed to consist of `fix` and nonrecursive parts. Again, as noted above, Church proved that any self-referential function can be transformed similarly through the use of `fix`. The significance of this transformation is that it allows us to separate the recursive part of a definition from the non-recursive part.

The result of such a transformation shows how a term can actually be hidden in a self-referential function. In the transformed results for `factorial'` and `map'`, the number of arguments of the `nonrec` function is increased by one as compared to the number for the original function: `nonrec` in `factorial'` has two arguments and `nonrec` in `map'` has three arguments, whereas the original functions `factorial` and `map` had one and two arguments, respectively. This increase shows that a self-referential function *inherently* includes a hidden argument, which appears upon transformation into `fix` and nonrecursive parts. Therefore, the calculation of `f x` as a fixed point is affected by another implicit input, which is the *constraint* that the final execution `f x` should fulfill `x = f x`.

A program of
-recursive and nonrecursive definitions
-functional expressions with multiple arguments

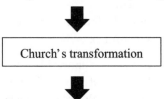

A program of
-nonrecursive definitions+fix
-functional expressions with multiple arguments

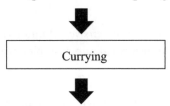

A program of
-nonrecursive definitions+fix
-functional expressions with one argument

FIGURE 7.6. Program transformation scheme given in this chapter.

7.5 Thirdness in Programs

Definitions and expressions are decomposed using currying and Church's transformation so that the results can be analyzed in terms of the universal categories. A proposed scheme with three stages is illustrated in Figure 7.6. The original program generally includes both self-referential and non-self-referential definitions and expressions with multiple arguments. Among the self-referential definitions could be an indirect self-reference – for example, a function A defined in terms of B, with B defined in terms of A – but such an indirect self-reference can easily be rewritten into a direct self-reference, say, by eliminating either A or B. First, by applying Church's transformation, all self-referential definitions are transformed into compositions of fix and non-self-referential parts. This requires adding the definition of the self-referential function fix. Then, all self-referential definitions, inclusively of local self-referential definitions within expressions, are eliminated, except for the x = f x within fix. Second, by currying, all multiple-argument functional applications are turned into one-argument applications.

The resulting program consists of the following three components:

- functional one-argument expressions of the form `f x`, where `f` is either `fix` or a nonrecursively defined `f`,
- nonrecursive definitions of the form `y = f x` or `y = x`, and
- the definition of the function `fix`.

In the case of the second component above, identifiers introduced in the nonrecursive definitions can be removed because they are unnecessary, temporary definitions. For example, consider the following program.

$$
\begin{aligned}
&x = g\ z \\
&y = x \\
&h\ y
\end{aligned}
\tag{7.16}
$$

This program includes two nonrecursive definitions and the expression `h y`. The three lines can be transformed into a simpler program as follows.

$$
h\ (g\ z)
\tag{7.17}
$$

This single line is obtained by removing the temporary signs y and x. Since they are nonrecursive, the definition `y = f x` is essentially no more than the expression `f x`, and `y = x` is no more than the expression x. By removing all such unnecessary temporary signs appearing in definitions, a program finally consists only of

- functional one-argument expressions of the form `f x`, where `f` is either `fix` or a nonrecursively defined `f`, and
- the definition of `fix`.

Now, let us consider how many terms are involved in this resulting program. In the expression `f x`, x is a term without an argument, placing it in the category of firstness, while the function `f`, which is not `fix`, represents a two-term relationship: secondness, applied to x. The `fix` function is essentially a three-term relationship, as it involves `fix`, `f`, and its resulting solution x. Here, the solution x is not a mere output of `fix f`, because the calculation of `fix f` requires x. The three terms here are inseparable during the calculation of x, so this expression cannot be broken down into smaller parts. The thirdness of the fixed-point operator is visible from the use of the operator in formula (4.17), defined in Chapter 4 within untyped LG. Here, since self-reference is disallowed, the number of arguments of `fix` is two.

Consequently, the remaining program has the term x having firstness, the function `f` having secondness, and the function `fix` having thirdness. This result is summarized in Table 7.1. A program essentially consists at most of

TABLE 7.1. Universal categories in computing

Firstness	x of the expression f x
Secondness	f of the expression f x, where f is nonrecursive
Thirdness	fix

a number of three-term relationships. The function fix represents genuine thirdness, whereas the other components can be transformed into relations of secondness and firstness. This indicates that the essence of thirdness is fix, the self-reference.

Thirdness is a kind of content. Self-reference as thirdness means that something is stipulated by means of itself in relation with some other content. Articulation of content as such requires a means to refer to the content. Moreover, this means must be speculative, since the target to be stipulated will be defined by means of itself. In other words, signs and a sign system play a crucial role in realizing content of thirdness. They provide a means to articulate thirdness, as we saw in Chapter 4 for the situation in which speculative introduction of a sign allows description of self-reference.

Moreover, once the description is obtained by the use of signs, it applies to any content that fulfills the description. A description using signs in this sense involves an abstraction. This way of considering thirdness as an abstraction explains why Peirce considered a sign as representative of thirdness (introduced in Section 6.4), since the abstraction consists of reflexively reconsidering content in comparison with similar content. Moreover, the reason why Peirce's symbol is considered as thirdness with respect to the relation between the sign and the content must be clear now. This line of thought also matches with Locke's and Hegel's remarks about what corresponds to thirdness.

Computer science includes another domain in which researchers attempt to describe the minimal forms underlying calculation. This domain is combinatorial logic (Curry and Feys, 1968; Smullyan, 1985), which is based on combinators that describe the relations among terms. Combinatorial logic is a variant of the lambda calculus, and a typical set of combinators that is equivalent to the lambda calculus consists of the following SKI combinators:

$$\mathbf{I}\,x \to x$$
$$\mathbf{K}\,x\,y \to x$$
$$\mathbf{S}\,x\,y\,z \to x\,z\,(y\,z).$$

Note how the **I** combinator represents the term itself. In contrast, **K** and **S** represent the relations between two terms and among three terms, respectively, thus giving a hint of their relations with the universal categories. The relation to the universal categories is not immediately obvious, however, from the right sides of → of each combinator. Neither is it obvious how to count the combinator itself when counting the number of forms in a relation. There are variants consisting of sets of other combinators (Smullyan, 1985), and none of them shows a trivial relationship with the universal categories. I presume that further studies on the relation of combinatorial logic with the universal categories will illuminate its correspondence with the universal categories, but this remains to be attempted.

Another issue that should be considered before proceeding further is the relationship between sign classification and the universal categories. As emphasized in Section 7.1, the universal categories are categories concerning forms, and the notion of how a sign represents a form of a category is a different issue. Still, it is natural to raise the question of how the category of a form corresponds with sign classifications, since every form is represented by a sign. Peirce made no argument about this. Moreover, this question is not easy, since the forms compared here are of different categories and for each form there are multiple means of representation via signs, as seen in the previous chapter.

A contemplation of this question could start by considering the sign classification of x, f, and fix, representing firstness, secondness, and thirdness, respectively. In Section 6.4, it is explained that the relation between the sign and the object is classified by the universal categories. Similarly, the relations between the sign and the other two relata are also classified in terms of the universal categories. Such a scheme thus gives three relations (between the sign and each of the representamen, the object, and the interpretant) classified into three categories (firstness, secondness, and thirdness).[5] In other words, a sign's category can be represented by the triplet (n_1, n_2, n_3), where n_1 indicates the universal category for how the sign is, n_2 indicates the category of the relation to the object, and n_3 indicates the category of the relation to the interpretant. The triple parameters (n_1, n_2, n_3) all take a value of 1, 2, or 3, denoting firstness, secondness, or thirdness, respectively. There are theoretically $3^3 = 27$ types of signs. Peirce (1931), however, added a constraint that $n_1 \geq n_2 \geq n_3$, considering that a lower-order relatum could only have a category equal to or higher than that of a higher-order relatum (Peirce, 1931, 2.264).[6] Therefore, there are only ten sign categories in total.

[5] The relation between the sign and its representamen is considered in terms of how the sign is itself.

[6] The reason for this constraint comes from Peirce's notion of degenerated forms, which is briefly considered in Section 6.4 too. Since I do not address this in any further detail in this book, readers interested in a more thorough understanding of degenerated forms are invited to refer directly to Peirce (1931).

For x, f, and fix, since they are indexes, $n_2 = 2$. The constraint of inequality implies only four sign categories for $n_2 = 2$: (2,2,1), (2,2,2), (3,2,1), and (3,2,2). The correspondences of x, f, and fix might be examined with these four categories . . . but I stop here, since there would be no way to justify the obtained result in any case. Regardless of whether this result is correct, it does not seem to add anything general. The relationship between Peirce's fine sign classification and computer signs can probably be further considered, but this is difficult without sufficient motivation.

The answers to the questions raised in Section 7.1 can now be seen, at least for the case of computing. All relations can be decomposed into one-term, two-term, and three-term relationships; therefore, three categories are sufficient. In computing, forms are as Peirce suggested, with content classified into three categories according to how many items of content are involved. Moreover, the difference between secondness and thirdness lies in whether self-reference is involved. For expressing reflexivity, it is seen that three terms are required, and signs are an important means to realize reflexive being.

Our understanding so far can be compared to the contents of the three paintings introduced at the beginning of this chapter. Here we note again that the theme in this chapter is the *content* to be represented. The two levels of content and representation might not be considered to have such a distinction in painting, but for given content there are various representations, including the structure, the framing, and the level of abstraction, as seen in the previous chapter. In contrast, the theme of this chapter has been the nature of the content, or the subject. For the painting in Figure 7.1, the painter's concept constitutes the theme, and this is the imaginary image of the painter, constituting firstness. For the painting in Figure 7.2, real-world morning glories inspired a realistic image in the painter's mind, which was then deformed by the painter's imaginary reinterpretation. In this case, the imaginary interpretation, applied to the realistic image, would form the content as secondness. Finally, for the painting in Figure 7.3, the realistic image of the painter himself was interpreted by *disguising the subject as Zeuxis laughing*, under the constraint that the disguised person is reciprocally the painter himself. Self-portrait as such is deemed to form the content constituting thirdness.

7.6 Summary

The essence of thirdness in Peirce's universal categories has been discussed through its application to computer programming. The discussion was developed through the application of transformations known in the functional paradigm. All functional definitions and expressions can be decomposed into terms related with no other, one other, and two other terms, corresponding to firstness, secondness, and thirdness, respectively. Examining the difference between secondness and thirdness in functions reveals that the essence of thirdness lies in self-reference. Further, it was seen how a sign provides a means to stipulate thirdness.

8

An Instance versus The Instance

Because statements are rare, they are collected in unifying totalities, and the meanings to be found in them are multiplied.

From page 135 of Foucault, M. (2002). *Archaeology of Knowledge* (2nd edition). Routledge. Reprinted by permission of Taylor and Francis Books UK. (Foucault, 1969, p. 157) (Foucault, 2002)

8.1 Haecceity

Painting is, among other things, an act of instantiation. An artwork is instantiated from a creative mind through hard work, and the result, normally, is a unique instance. Artwork that calls this uniqueness into question was, however, first introduced in the twentieth century. Figure 8.1 shows a representative work of this approach, where the artist took a ready-made object and claimed it as an artwork. Such works raise a fundamental question of what art is. Mass production frames a class of instances that are exactly alike, each devoid of haecceity. This section considers the contraposition of *an* instance and *the* instance, which is a more serious issue in computation than in art because of the ease of perfect reproduction.

The term *haecceity* in this chapter signifies a property that *the* instance possesses but *an* instance does not, namely, something about the kind of a thing that makes it different from any other. The term has some relation to uniqueness – something is unique when it is the only one or the sole example. As will be seen further ahead, since computer instances are ultimately all completely reproducible, they can never be unique in the strictest sense. Still, even in computing, there are *the* instances. Namely, some important instances are *the* instances, with haecceity, yet reproducible.

Today's computers handle an immense variety of information, and the process is articulated in the form of a computer program. A program's aim

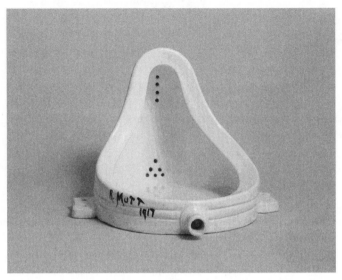

FIGURE 8.1. Marcel Duchamp (1887–1968), *The Fountain*. © 2009 Artists Rights Society (ARS), New York/ADAGP, Paris/Succession Marcel Duchamp. Photo credit: Jerry L. Thompson/Art Resource, NY.

is described at the level of a *class*,[1] through an inductive process of *modeling* the class's purpose. The actual information processing is then conducted through a deductive process using concrete objects called *instances*, which are generated through the process of *instantiation*.

In this chapter, instantiation means raising content through a sign. For example, in the deduction of 'Men are mortal; Socrates is a human; Therefore, Socrates is mortal', Socrates is instantiated representing the class of *men*, or raised through the sign 'Socrates', and then subjected to a deductive inference. Such class/instance contrast is clear in programs using the object-oriented paradigm. For example, in the case of the Java program for computing the areas of shapes, shown in Figure 2.2, the various shapes are modeled and described in the form of classes and then concrete rectangles and circles are instantiated for calculation of their areas. A block used for a class definition is indicated by the keyword `class`, and instantiation is signaled by the keyword `new` (lines 21–23). Though not as explicitly as with these keywords, functional programs also follow a similar abstraction and concretization process. For example, Figure 2.1 shows the corresponding Haskell program for calculating

---

[1]   So far, the term *class* has been used as a technical term specifically in object-oriented programming. In this chapter, the term is used in a more general sense indicating a collection of instances having similar features and functionalities (cf. Glossary).

the areas of shapes. Here, the abstraction process is described at the level of data types (lines 1–3), whereas the actual calculation is conducted through concrete instances (generated in lines 10–12).

Thus, computational description always concerns the human activity of modeling a purpose through inductive abstraction, generation of instances through instantiation, and calculation through deduction. Among the three processes of induction, instantiation, and deduction, the plausibility of the inductive process has been a philosophical problem, so many ways to justify and reinforce this weak form of inference have been elaborated. Deduction as a valid inference scheme is well established through mathematics and logic, which constitute the foundation of computation. In contrast, instantiation has been forgotten in the haecceity of the scholastics and has not received attention equal to that given to inference.

If the user of a program has a specific context in mind and knows exactly how to generate appropriate instances, then instantiation is not a problem. Moreover, if instantiation only concerns random selection from among a possible set of instances belonging to a class, then the process is trivial. In the previous example of Socrates, indeed, any other instance among human beings qualifies as an instance. Still, raising Socrates offers more signification here, in that he is widely familiar and also in that even a great mind such as Socrates cannot escape this fate. Just as people often talk about good and bad examples, a good example is no longer *an* example but rather becomes *the* salient example, representing a class. The choice could depend on the context, but even then generation of such an instance/example is not at all trivial, requiring a combinatorial search or human instinct: such an instance/example must be *found* among a vast range of possibilities. Upon facing a huge number of instances, the quest for *the* instance could be the objective of computation.

The theme of this last chapter of Part II is instantiation aimed at obtaining *the* instance, which is another problem having to do with types of content. In a manner similar to that of the previous chapter, therefore, the theme here lies in the very nature of content, and not in how a sign indicates content. The issues addressed here are how *the* instance differs from *an* instance and how to obtain *the* instance. The motivation for this discussion lies in the difficulty of obtaining *the* instance rather than *an* instance within computation.

The broadest scope of discussion should perhaps not assume the existence of a class. For example, a work of art as the instance does not usually assume the existence of a class when it is produced. Assumption of a class is probably rare in art, as in the case of the art example presented at the beginning of this chapter. Even in computer programming there is the programming language Self (Ungar and Smith, 1987), which was designed with the idea of removing the distinction between the class and the instance. Such languages, however, are rare, and the discussion in this chapter therefore mainly considers a narrower problem in which the class is present and the most plausible instance is selected from a set of instances as the representative of the class.

8.2   A Case Study of a Digital Narrative

Vladimir Propp constructed a narrative theory of Russian stories (Propp, 1968, 1984). He conducted a thorough analysis of Russian folk tales and obtained 31 basic narremes (narrative units) lying underneath. In Propp's model, any Russian story is generated through combination of these narremes by using a narrative syntax.

Reading Propp's writings, a programmer feels that he or she could write an automatic Russian story generator based on Propp's model. Indeed, in the domain of artificial intelligence some work has been done on automatic narrative generators based on Propp's framework (Lönneker *et al.*, 2005). Even if not based on Propp's work, most digital narrative software is likely to adopt a similar formulation based on a narrative unit and narrative syntax. Such commonality in the modeling of narratives shows how general and natural it is to model narratives with narremes and narrative syntax.

The challenge of these systems, however, does not really lie in the modeling. Rather, the problem lies in the generation of a significant narrative instance. An example is my experience in developing a narrative software program called Mike (André *et al.*, 2000). Mike generated automatic commentary in natural language and real time for soccer games played by autonomous robots and computer programs in a competition series called Robocup (Kitano *et al.*, 1995). The mission of the Mike software was to analyze input (consisting of raw data, provided every 100 milliseconds, for all players and the ball's position, direction, and so on) and create real-time commentary from the analysis (Tanaka-Ishii *et al.*, 1998). An example of Mike's output is shown in Figure 8.2. As with real-world commentary, two autonomous agents, an announcer and an analyst, communicated and generated comments on the matches, which were between red and yellow teams, with the players referred to by numbers. Although working on the Mike project was rewarding, a significant anticlimax occurred when Mike actually commented on soccer games in real time: the generated commentary was itself not very exciting to human audiences.

Mike generated its commentary as follows. The narremes and narrative syntax were modeled after a detailed analysis of actual, real-world soccer commentary (Tanaka-Ishii *et al.*, 2000), not unlike Propp's analysis of Russian

Announcer: Yellow 9, in the middle of the field, yellow team (*a set play happened here*). Any impressions, E-MIKE?
Analyzer: Well, here are statistics concerning possessions, left team has slightly smaller value of possession, it is 43 percent versus 56. Right team is ahead there. (*Score is currently 0-0. E-MIKE judges that red-team is doing better*).
Announcer: Really, dribble, yellow 3, on the left, great long pass made to yellow 1, for red 6, red 2's pass success rate is 100 percent. E-MIKE?
Analyzer: Looking at the dribbles and steals, red team was a little less successful in dribbling, red team has a lower value of dribble average length, left is 21 meters whereas right is 11, right team has a few less players making zero passes, yellow team has made slightly less stealing, . . .
Announcer: Wow (*interruption because red 11 made a shot*), red 11, goal, red 11, Goal! It was red 10, and a pass for red 11! The score is 0 1!

FIGURE 8.2. Output from an automatic commentator, Mike, used in Robocup (Tanaka-Ishii *et al.*, 2000).

folk tales. The narrative content was triggered by events occurring within a soccer game, and the commentary was further elaborated using a narrative syntax. To instantiate the actual output, random selection was used, since the final instance was not uniquely determinable. For example, the next narrative content to be spoken was randomly selected from among the possible narremes; the natural language wording for a narreme was also randomly selected. Broadly put, commentary was generated through random selection from a possible set of narratives under the constraints of the game and the context.

Further investigation of audience impressions of Mike's commentary revealed that people considered it repetitive and mechanical. Such shortcomings were largely the result of poor content planning, and further study on this theme would be worthwhile. The problem of how to instantiate good commentary at each point, however, is not at all trivial. Propp did not explain how to instantiate a story from his narrative framework either. An automatic narrative generator using only Propp's framework is likely to suffer from the same problem as Mike because that framework lacks a mechanism for quality instantiation, as do many narrative software applications based on random instantiation. The main reason for this is the lack of methodology for well-conceived instantiation.

There is, however, a related genre of narrative software that does not suffer from the same problem: computer games. Role-playing games are usually based on narratives. The players assume the roles of characters within a class of stories provided by the software creators. The story a player follows is chosen by the player. The basic structure of a role-playing game is broadly similar to that of the Mike commentary system with respect to the use of narremes and narrative syntax. Such games are developed through the use of descriptive software that provides the prototypes of a genre of role-playing games. Using one of these software applications, a designer's task is to feed a virtual world and characters into narremes and chain these narremes in the form of narrative syntax.

The automatic commentary system and role-playing games share the same architecture in that both systems define a class of narratives and generate a narrative instance belonging to the class. Still, the audience reactions have been opposite. The largest difference here lies in the difference between the instantiation processes used in each genre.

8.3   Levels of Instantiation

The opposition of form and matter is present in one of the oldest philosophical problems, called *the problem of universals*. The problem has its roots in ancient Greek philosophy. Opposite positions were taken by Plato and Aristotle, as illustrated in the famous painting of Raphael, where Plato points up, indicating that the universal exists as a form, and Aristotle gestures toward the ground, indicating that the universal exists in the individuum.

This contrast flowered into an academic controversy representing the epoch of the scholastics. Three parties, supporting realism, conceptualism, and nominalism, pondered the existence and location of *universals* vis-à-vis instances (Yamanouchi, 2008). During this period, the instantiation process was considered an important problem, denoted by using the term haecceity – a scholastic term expressing individuality or singleness. Duns Scotus considered every instance, in principle, to have what makes it unique, in addition to universal features. As this name of the problem shows, however, the central issue consisted of the universals, the abstract form, and the process of reaching this form.

The form is reached through induction, but inference through induction is much weaker than that through deduction: even if all blackbirds observed so far have all been black, it cannot be said that blackbirds are black in general, if speaking precisely. Therefore, the means to reinforce, justify, and systematize induction have been studied in philosophy. Deduction, on the other hand, has been considered a strong type of inference, and the means of deductive inference have been established through logic and mathematics. This pair of induction and deduction led to the hypothesis–test model within empiricism (Ben-Chaim, 2004; Popper, 1943).

This quest for universals, however, degraded the importance of instances. We can see how instances gradually lost value[2] over the course of a shift through three different methods of instantiation[3] as follows:

1. The instance is irreproducible or has limitations on reproduction. Instantiation in this case raises a real-world object.
2. The instance is generated by copying from an original real-world object. Such copies are reproducible. Instantiation in this case raises the original real-world object through a sign or by signs. An example is a picture or a recording of a musical performance.
3. Instances themselves are completely reproducible. Instantiation here raises a sign/signs through a sign/signs. An example is computer graphics generated by a program.

Originally, every instance was unique and existed for one period of time only. Since the technology of reproduction was limited, instances were essentially rare, and they were not replaceable. The production of an instance was limited to God or a genius, and originals had the aura of being unique. This aura in turn engendered universality, as Walter Benjamin (1935) indicates, explaining how universality was pursued in the ancient Greek era because of the limited technology for reproduction.

The second method of instantiation is related to technologies for making copies. Printing, photography, and the gramophone produced copies as instances. Once copied to a recording or a digital image, as a chain of bits, the copies become reproducible and thus are deprived of uniqueness. Consider photographs, however: simply taking a random picture is easy, but taking a good picture requires skill. The copy might remain a mere reproducible copy, but it can acquire haecceity thanks to the uniqueness of the photographed target or if the method of copying or representation is studied.

The third method of instantiation is to produce completely reproducible instances. Computational instances are often of this type. Computational

---

[2] This historical consequence seems deeply related to the virtualization of signs, as indicated in footnote 5 of Chapter 3.

[3] Baudrillard (1976) presents a related idea that there are three stages of simulation. The first level is an imitation, the second level is a reproduction of the original as a copy indistinguishable from the original, and the third level is a simulation, which has no grounding in the original. Baudrillard's interest lies in the copies, whereas the focus here is on the original.

representation is always grounded by a representation in digital bits, and instances composed of bits are all perfectly reproducible. If such an instance is generated only from a program, without taking after something unique in the real world, the instance is completely deprived of uniqueness. Instances thus seem to have completely lost the aura of uniqueness and seem to have been degraded to mere instances. Some particular instances, however, can still be *the* instance with haecceity, such as high-quality computer graphics that have been developed. These are *the* instances yet they are reproducible.

The key to this shift lies in reproducibility, which is founded, again, on technologies invented in the quest to make an ephemeral instance universal. Reproducibility highlights all the more the question of instantiation because improving reproducibility makes instantiation easier and degrades uniqueness. At first sight, haecceity might seem to be conditioned by uniqueness, but there are reproducible instances with haecceity. Then, the nature of haecceity must be considered. The question is how can such salient instances be obtained and what kind of content are they?

8.4   Restoring Haecceity

8.4.1 Optimization

Benjamin (1935, p. 26) described how modern technology "operates by means of experiments and endlessly varied test procedures." Computers can fit well with such trial-and-error experimentation by performing a systematic, exhaustive search among instances. A class defines a set of instances; therefore, all instances are considered and the best one can be chosen according to certain criteria. This exhaustiveness may restore the haecceity to the instance of *optimality* under certain criteria, attributing this signification to an instance. Since the instance obtained through optimization is the best among all other instances, it acquires the significance of representing the class.

This optimization is nontrivial in two ways. First, the procedure for solving the optimization problem is nontrivial. The number of possible instances is usually huge and could even be exponential with respect to the number of attributes and their possible values. The solution to optimization therefore requires scanning through a huge search space of class instances with different variable settings. Combinatorial problems often cannot be solved completely and are relaxed or approximated to produce an instance within a reasonable time. In such cases, the process can degrade into approximation, and the resulting instance might only acquire local optimality among the subclass instances. Second, optimization requires a global *evaluation function* – one

FIGURE 8.3. Examples of automatically synthesized Chinese calligraphy. From Xu, S., Lau, C.M.F., Cheung, W. K., and Pan, Y., "Automatic Generation of Artistic Chinese Calligraphy," *Journal of Intelligent Systems* © IEEE (Xu *et al.*, 2005)

judging the degree to which an instance can qualify as *the* instance – and the selection of such a function is nontrivial. Just as a good example requires human intuition, the evaluation function generally requires human judgment and creativity. Moreover, the evaluation function could depend on the context or need, and therefore it must be designed in consideration of such context. Without a good function, the resulting instance could be as bad as a random one and will not add any great significance to *the* instance.

Among various evaluation functions, a common approach is to *mirror nature*.[4] A typical evaluation function is formulated in the form of the probability of *naturalness*. The target phenomena are modeled as a composition of parts, and the overall probability is calculated as the product of the probabilities for each of the parts. The probability function is statistically estimated from a large body of learning data. Among a set of instances, the most probable instance is then obtained through maximization of the evaluation function.

Such procedures are common in various forms of synthesis using computers. For example, in the automatic synthesis of Chinese calligraphy (Xu *et al.*, 2005), a character is decomposed into components describing drawing styles, and the probability function is formulated as a combination of the probabilities of the component subproblems. A calligraphic character is then synthesized by maximizing the probability function. Some examples taken from Xu *et al.* (2005) are shown in Figure 8.3, where each character represents the instance obtained when using a different set of learning data based on different calligraphic styles.

---

[4] This term *mirror nature* comes from Rorty (1979).

In contrast, the digital narrative example of Mike introduced above was intended to synthesize commentary, but the evaluation function involved in content generation was not sufficiently elaborate. A good commentator does not randomly choose what could be said but rather produces anthropomorphically interesting commentary in the heat of the moment. Haecceity was not restored in Mike's output. The means of improving this performance, however, is not at all trivial, but one approach would be to apply probabilistic modeling of a large body of learning data consisting of commentaries, in the style of mirroring nature. Similar studies of mirroring nature have been presented in all computer science domains connected to human analysis – speech, natural language, image processing, and robotics – by designing the evaluation function to capture the characteristics of natural data as derived from a large body of natural data.

Consequently, once an evaluation function is defined, a machine provides the possibility of conducting an exhaustive search to reach the optimal instance. A path for future work on restoration of haecceity through optimization consists of categorically examining the kinds of optimization functions other than those mirroring nature. The impulse to mirror nature has overwhelmed computing because of the technological requirements to simulate the real world. As Benjamin (1935) indicates, however, reproducibility impelled humans to start keeping their distance from nature. It remains an open question as to whether there are other possible optimization approaches besides mirroring nature. Some related discussion is given in Chapter 11.

8.4.2 Interaction

Another possibility for haecceity restoration was already suggested in Section 8.2: *interaction*. If a user selects one instance from among many, this act attributes a special significance to the instance of *now* and *here* in the user's own personal record. Restoration of haecceity through interaction thus is limited to the party involved in instantiation. Computer games and interactive art make use of the special effect that whenever the user is involved in instantiation, the instance reacquires haecceity. For example, a role-playing game interactively generates the instance of a narrative through communication with the player. The instance is chosen by the player through interaction, and because of this the instance is significant to the player as an irreplaceable play record.

Interaction thus effectively assumes another evaluation function from the user's viewpoint, in addition to the one attributed to the class that stipulates instances. The two functions could cause a conflict between how the system is intended to behave and the choice of the user, since the user might not make a selection that conforms with that made by the system's evaluation function. In role-playing games, for example, the system usually has a global narrative and tries to guide the user along this, but the user might choose an unpredictable narreme that conflicts with this flow. Since this stalls the game, it should be designed to proceed by balancing two different intentions. Interaction can thus be considered the meeting point of two different evaluation functions.

A special case of interaction that avoids this conflict is *adaptation*. After a period of use, the instances generated by the system adapt to what the user prefers. Adaptation thus proceeds through collaboration between the system and the user by applying an evaluation function. This type of evaluation function optimizes *through* interaction. Such a procedure is conceptually based on replacing the large body of learning data for mirroring nature with data consisting of user actions. Moreover, since this learning process consists of chains of happenings of the moment and place, the resulting system becomes the instance of the system, generating what the user prefers as a holistic consequence of the user's personal record.

Adaptation is popular within the user interface domain. An example is text entry systems (MacKenzie and Tanaka-Ishii, 2007). Some recent entry systems suggest words, or instances, that the user might want to enter next, and these suggestions are adapted by the system. Upon initial use, the system suggests optimal words concerning the context entered thus far. At every word entry, the user agrees or disagrees with the system's suggestion. In the case of disagreement, the user enters his or her preferred word. Repetition of such training enables the parameters of the evaluation function to be adapted to the user, so that preferred words can be suggested.

8.4.3 Haecceity and Reflexivity

Consequently, the restoration of haecceity concerns some singularity, or rareness, of the instance derived by choice from some viewpoint among other instances belonging to the same class. Optimization chooses the best instance among other class instances, and interaction decides the special instance for the user among other class instances.

Both schemes are realized by computation, and as noted at the beginning of the section, computation is founded on induction and deduction through instances. The particularity of the two schemes of optimization and interaction is that they are attributed with test procedures. Usually an instance is input to a test procedure, and the evaluation is the output. This procedure can be used differently to obtain the best instance among instances. This works by starting from an input and then choosing the next input according to the evaluation result for the first instance. By repeating this process, *an* instance is gradually improved to obtain *the* instance. The test procedure is thus changed into a reflexive procedure to obtain the best instance.

So far, we have seen reflexivity of signs in the form of self-reference, typically denoted in the form of the statement x = f x. Such a procedure can be considered more broadly at a higher level of a sign system, where f is compared to a system. Here, the basic step of the procedure to obtain the fixed point of a system/function is to reinterpret the output of the self. Namely, reflexivity in this book is broadly considered as the capability of a function or system to reinterpret what it produces.

The procedure of optimization often parallels that used to obtain a fixed point. Theoretical computer science in fact formulates calculation as obtaining a fixed point in a solution space (Gunter, 1962). The majority of optimization procedures indeed can be transformed into a complex procedure to obtain such a point, and the solution can be obtained via recursion, where f is the transformed version of the evaluation function.

Interaction also has a relationship to reflexivity. Since two systems are involved, the user and the computer, both are influenced by the interaction. The user can evolve via interaction with the system, which changes the user in that the user learns about the system and modifies his or her behavior, which grounds the strategy of subsequent interactions. Conversely, the system's behavior can be modified incrementally, as in the case of adaptation, or through another means of modification. Each interaction modifies the system behavior, which constitutes the behavior of the next interaction.

Thus, a common scheme of reflexivity seems to lie behind the instantiation procedures restoring haecceity. An instance possibly gains singularity or rareness when it becomes the fixed point of some reflexive procedure. The intention of this section is *not* to say that reflexivity is the only scheme underlying all haecceity, nor is it to say that any instance that has gone through such a scheme attains haecceity. There might be other schemes for attaining haecceity, and an instance might not attain haecceity even by going through the scheme discussed here. Still, behind many instances having haecceity, reflexivity is often involved, occurring in various ways and at different levels. The fixed point as a singular point within the domain provides a possible rationale for haecceity. Reflexivity, in my opinion, is one means to transform *an* instance into *the instance.*

Moreover, as was seen in the previous section, a sign plays a crucial role in realizing such reflexive content. Through the use of a sign or a sign system, the signification is poured and frozen into the final instance with haecceity. Under the pansemiotic view, in particular, of a world consisting only of signs without basis, reflexivity could be one important means to generate such a basis.

8.5   The Kind of *The* Instance

So far the discussion has proceeded in a way that completely separates class and instance. The discussion, however, has revealed how the instance acquires signification of singularity at the higher level of the class. The evaluation function is attributed to the class; therefore, the resulting optimized instance has signification at the class level. It is not that the model is given first and the optimization function is considered after modeling, but rather that the model concerns the design of the global optimization and the instance. This raises the question as to what kind of action instantiation is and what kind of content *the* instance is as an outcome of the instantiation.

The last chapter introduced three types of content under the universal categories, namely, x as firstness, f as secondness, and fix as thirdness. It was seen in the previous section that an instance x can acquire haecceity if subjected to a reflexive process. The question to be considered here, then, is what kind of content is such an x under self-reference? In the previous chapter, the definition x = f x appeared as part of fix as thirdness, but the category of x in the definition was not considered.

Peirce denied the haecceity of the scholastics and instead distinguished the forms of class and instance as different existences (Peirce, 1931, 8.208). Even then, Peirce knew that there are cases in which different categories are folded into one. Accordingly, he proposed the notion of *degenerated forms* [1.365–366, 1.521–529], which is briefly introduced in Sections 6.4 and 7.5. For example, thirdness could appear as degenerated secondness. Then, perhaps, *the* instance x could be considered as a degenerated form of fix, that is, of thirdness. Verification of this has been limited though, because, as Yonemori (1981) explains, Peircian philosophy is unfinished with regard to this degenerated form and the notion lacks clear definition or reasoning. Another possibility along the line of Peirce's universal categories might be to consider the term x to be further classified recursively by the universal categories, like the recursive consideration of signs seen in Section 6.4. Neither of these ideas, of degenerated form or recursive classification, however, seems to adequately describe the category of x. The reason is that optimization can be approximate, and the degree, or quality, of approximation seems to range continuously from bad to good. On the other hand, the universal category is not continuous; rather, it is trichotomous. It is unknown how to situate such a continuation of x ranging from *an* instance up to *the* instance within the trichotomy of the universal categories.

Another approach for considering the nature of x might be from the viewpoint of inference, by analyzing the types of inference with which optimization and interaction are concerned. Peirce categorizes logical inference into three types: deduction, induction, and abduction.[5] Although he raises these three types of inference, Peirce did not show how they are categorized under his universal categories. Two possible categorizations have been proposed so far (Yonemori, 1981). The first regards abduction as firstness, since it requires instinctive human ideas, which are categorized as firstness. In this case, deduction and induction are considered secondness and thirdness, respectively. The second categorization regards deduction, induction, and abduction as firstness, secondness, and thirdness, respectively, situating abduction as the highest-level inference. This lack of mention of the universal categories in regard to inference might suggest that Peirce was not so certain about the categories for inference.

Moreover, the procedure of optimization and interaction is usually conducted as a mixture of different inferences. Starting from optimization, the computational scheme of optimization is implemented as deduction. At the same time, though, optimization requires an evaluation function attributed to a class generated through human inductive analysis of instances, as seen through the typical example of an evaluation function mirroring nature. Turning to interaction and adaptation, once a human is involved, instantiation cannot be situated as either strong or weak inference. The *now* and *here* are thus woven into the instance. The inference obtained through interaction is a mixture of different inferences.

The nature of the instances thus obtained through optimization and/or interaction is the melting point of class and instance, of strong and weak inference. Forms of different categories must be mixed within the content, as in the case of x in $x = f\ x$. That is, *the instance* is the point where the sheer distinction of class and instance dissolves. Haecceity had been considered as a sort of notion opposed to universality, but it is in fact the transformation of an instance to the instance, the deconstruction of form and matter.

Such thoughts regarding deconstruction of the sheer separation between binarily opposed concepts are attributed to postmodernist philosophy. For example, Jacques Derrida's deconstruction suggests how Western binary oppositions such as subject/object, form/matter, and universal/individuum are not as clear cut as had been long considered and are subject to deconstruction (Culler, 1982). The form $x = f\ x$ can be compared to his notion of *différance*,

---

5 Abduction is a kind of weak inference, based on observation, to hypothesize a general proposition from which the observation can be explained. For example, given a surprising event C (for example, fish fossils are found in the mountains), abduction gives a hypothesis A that explains C (e.g., the rocks composing the mountain were under the sea in prehistory). According to Peirce, abduction "is a weak kind of argument"(Peirce, 1931, 2.625).

where x is differentiated by f x and the differentiation is iterated to reach a fixed point as a deconstructive being.

The questions of what makes an instance into the instance and why the instance was chosen resurged with the prevalence of mechanical reproducibility, as represented by Duchamps' fountain shown in Figure 8.1. The underlying reflexivity has been highlighted in this chapter through an attempt to understand haecceity. Interestingly, reflexivity as such a deconstructive point seems to represent something essentially human, which cannot be easily transferred into mechanical sign systems like those used in computing. If haecceity could be explained by reflexivity, and the nature of humanistic value lies in reflexivity, then this requires further elaboration within computing. The next chapter examines the problem of reflexivity in computer systems and how it characterizes the structure of computer sign systems as different from human sign systems.

8.6 Summary

It has been argued how one important computing problem lies in instantiation, the procedure to produce a significant instance, given a class. Instances on computers are reproducible, being constructed of digital bits; therefore, instantiation has become all the more important for attaining signification. Analysis of a case study on digital narratives suggested two general processes for instantiating significant instances: optimization and interaction. It was argued how the two processes restore haecceity via a reflexive scheme derived from test procedures. The discussion hypothesized how reflexivity, which is realized through a sign system, is a possible key to attach haecceity to an instance. This chapter has further explained how the sheer separation of class and instance requires deconstruction when attempting to understand the nature of significant instances and the process of their instantiation.

PART 3

SYSTEMS OF SIGNS

9

Structural Humans versus Constructive Computers

Crab: HOLISM is the most natural thing in the world to grasp. It's simply the belief that "the whole is greater than the sum of its parts." No one in his right mind could reject holism.

Anteater: REDUCTIONISM is the most natural thing in the world to grasp. It's simply the belief that "a whole can be understood completely if you understand its parts, and the nature of their '*sum*'". No one in her left brain could reject reductionism.

From *Gödel, Escher, Bach: An Eternal Golden Braid* by Douglas R. Hofstadter
© 1979. Reprinted by permission of Basic Books, a member of Perseus
Books Group. (Hofstadter, 1979, p. 312)

9.1   Uncontrollable Computers

HAL 9000 in *2001: A Space Odyssey* and Speedy in *I Robot* are examples of computers that become uncontrollable. Such stories are fiction, but they are based on a real problem for many people. Becoming frustrated with the difficulty of controlling computers is a common experience for any computer user. Occasionally, your computer hangs up and ignores your commands. In such cases, you might have to reboot the computer. If it still fails to work correctly even then, you might have to refresh the whole computer system by reinstalling the operating system; you might feel like literally kicking the computer. Why are computers so cumbersome to control even after decades of research and development history?

Both machine calculation and human thinking are in a sense based on the processing of signs, according to the pansemiotic view introduced in Section 2.5. Some might argue that human thought also includes the processing of things apart from signs, such as emotions, but under logical circumstances like seeking to *control a computer* (until resorting to kicking it), human thought

FIGURE 9.1. Victor Vasarely (1908–1997), *Globe with Spheres*, Musée Vasarely. © 2009 Artists Rights Society (ARS), New York/ADAGP, Paris. Photo credit: Erich Lessing/Art Resource, NY.

can also be considered to be based on signs, usually the signs of a natural language. On the other hand, every calculation on a computer *is* controlled by signs, from the lowest level of bits consisting of zeros and ones to the higher level of the description of a calculation in a programming language. As a whole, both machine calculation and human thought are thus based on sign processing.

The structures of the sign worlds of computers and human beings in general are very different, however, which is deemed one reason why humans and computers sometimes fail to get along well with each other. This can be intuitively shown through a consideration of paintings, as we have been doing, before going on to the main discussion of the chapter. Figures 9.1 and 9.2 show two paintings formed only of squares, but the relations among the squares are totally different. In Figure 9.1, the squares are interconnected to produce an optical illusion. The illusion is produced as an effect of the holistic relation among interconnected squares. If one or two squares were randomly removed, the power of the effect would decrease but the optical illusion would remain. In contrast, in Figure 9.2, the squares are placed on top of one another; the fundamental relation among squares underlying this painting is placement of a square on top of another square.[1] Since there is a partial order of dependency among the squares, a square cannot be removed

---

[1] This minimal relation is seen in some of Malevich's minimalist paintings formed only of two
    squares: a background square and a foreground square.

FIGURE 9.2. Kazimir Malevich (1878–1935), Suprematist Painting, Stedelijk Museum. Photo credit: Art Resource, NY.

randomly (for example, the big black square at the bottom of the painting on the left cannot be removed). Even though both paintings contain only squares, the structures constituted from them are different. Human and computer sign systems seem to have similar structural differences.

One apparent cause of such structural differences is the difference in how people and computers handle reflexivity. Part III is dedicated to the analysis of sign systems. As noted at the beginning of this book, a sign system consists of a relation among signs and their interpretations. To begin with, this chapter discusses the structural differences between human and machine sign systems, highlighted through their handling of reflexivity. Recall that the focus of our discussion on the interpretative level has so far been limited to the level within programming language, in terms of its definition and use for computer signs, among the different levels of interpretation (see Section 2.3). In this chapter the same approach is taken, and correspondingly, the interpretive level of natural language signs is examined only at the level within language, disregarding external real-world objects, by considering the meanings of natural language signs to be constituted through their definitions and uses in the language.

9.2 Signs and Self-Reference

Language is used by means of linguistic expressions, which are considered interpretable in a system. Some linguistic expressions are situated at the margins of interpretability; among these are those exemplifying reflexivity.

As discussed in Chapters 4 and 7, self-reference is the definition of a sign referring to itself. An example in natural language is 'The goal is to realize the goal.' Here, the sign 'the goal' is introduced and defined self-referentially as 'to realize the goal'. Another self-referential sentence – this time, a famous one known as the Epimenides paradox – is 'This sentence is a lie.', where 'this sentence' refers to the whole sentence. In addition to such direct self-reference, this chapter also considers indirect self-reference, which entails multiple definitions that can be rewritten into a self-reference. For example, these two sentences – 'A chicken lays an egg. An egg hatches into a chicken.' – can be reduced to a direct sentence of self-reference: 'A chicken lays an egg that hatches into a chicken.'

Some reflexive expressions can be interpreted without any problem. For example, as seen in Chapters 4 and 7, the self-referential definition of the factorial function was no more than the recurrent definition of the factorial that one learns in junior high school. The example of the factorial also shows that some self-references can be transformed into a definition without self-reference. Such cases are limited, however, and the interpretation of self-reference in general is problematic because the content could be null or even contradictory. For example, the previous expression regarding a 'goal' is rather empty because what exactly is aimed at is not specified. Similarly, the subsequent expression 'This sentence is a lie.' is contradictory.

In Chapter 4, it was seen how self-reference is introduced when definition is introduced in LG. Such self-reference is made by using a speculatively introduced sign referring to content that will become consolidated in the future. This cannot avoid introducing uncertain content – which could even be void or contradictory – into the system as well. Such problems caused by speculative introduction of signs are present in both computer language and natural languages.

The rationale of Chapter 4 can be reconsidered through a more intuitive discussion, as follows, this time not only for computer language but also for natural language. Recalling that any sign involves an implied definition and use, as seen in Chapter 2, self-reference can be considered from both sides. As for definition, when a sign is newly introduced, it is defined by means of other signs. The sign 'A' is typically defined by another expression 'B', in the form 'A is B'. In natural language, such definitions by means of words are commonly presented in a dictionary or encyclopedia, whereas in programming language such definitions are made by statements like 'A = B'. Supposing that 'B' is another expression, say 'X Y A Z', the definition then becomes 'A is X Y A Z' or 'A = X Y A Z', and 'A' is self-referentially defined by means of 'A'. For example, if a chicken is described as 'a chicken is a bird that lays an egg that hatches into a chicken', then this has the corresponding form. The definition of factorial as 'the factorial of n is n times the factorial of n minus 1' also takes this form.

Nor is the mere use of signs immune to the pitfalls of self-reference. The self-referential signs in 'A is X Y A Z' stipulate the content of 'A' through this self-referential use. Similarly for computer signs, the exact content of a self-referentially defined sign depends on how it is used within the self-reference (see Section 4.4). For example, the content of 'A' in a self-reference 'A = X Y A Z' depends on the use of A within this statement. Moreover, natural language terms acquire additional meanings through their uses. When a sign 'A' is used in an expression 'A is C', the use restricts 'A' to be a sign such that 'A is used in *A is C*'. 'A' appears twice in this expression, before and after 'is used', so the use in general is self-referential. Some readers might consider that the use does not affect the meaning of a sign in computing, other than in self-reference. We previously saw, however, in the program example of Figure 3.5 in Section 3.3.2, how use adds meaning to a sign; this was also seen in Section 4.4, in particular, through the way in which the type disambiguates content by virtue of context.

Note how self-reference causes the definition and use to become mingled. 'A is X Y A Z' is another use of 'A', and 'A is used in *A is C*' is another definition of 'A', because the main sentence form consists of 'A is B', with 'B' being 'used in *A is C*'. In computer signs too, 'A = X Y A Z' gives the definition and use at the same time. This mingling aspect of content and use was seen through lambda expression in Chapter 4, in terms of how the use defines the content for self-referential signs. As a consequence, the dyadic and triadic sign models become equivalent when signs are self-referentially defined.

What we have seen here through an intuitive reconsideration of the concepts of Chapter 4 is that natural language also has reflexive signs and that their nature at the level of definition and use is shared with that seen in Chapter 4. In other words, to this point, there is no large difference between natural and computer signs. The interpretation strategies for reflexivity, however, are different in the two language systems, causing them to have totally different structures.

9.3   A Structural System

Given any expression, humans always have the choice of abandoning an attempt at interpretation if the interpretation process stalls. For example, the interpretation of 'The goal is to realize the goal.' is limited, but people do not stop thinking about all other things because they are stuck on an expression like this. Humans have the choice to give up, switch the context, or continue. Eventually, another expression will perhaps provide more information, such as 'The goal is related to my ambition.' One can then return to the problematic expression and continue with the interpretation process. This capability enables human beings to choose dynamically when to suspend and restart interpretation.

Such an interpretive strategy allows robust interpretation of problematic expressions with self-references; at the same time it generates a sign system in which much of the concrete content of signs is left ambiguous but still exists within the language system. This process can be expressed through a generative model as follows. A sign is speculatively introduced with its concrete content remaining ambiguous. This ambiguity is clarified through additional definition and use. For example, consider the introduction of the sign 'projectX' as the name of some research project. The actual content of a research project is initially defined in little detail because the project refers to future results. Yet, a name is needed for reference even if its content is not clear, because when a project is set up there is much discussion of it by many people. The project starts, runs, and ends, and at this ending point people (might) finally realize what the project really was. During the time the project runs, the sign 'projectX' is referred to through expressions such as 'projectX is not interesting' or 'projectX had its budget doubled'. Every time such an expression is made, the expressed fact adds meaning to the term 'projectX'. Every such statement attributes the term 'projectX' with meanings such that, in this example, people consider it an uninteresting project whose budget has been doubled. Such repeated reference between subsequent and antecedent occurrences of the term weaves the *now* and *here* into the term 'projectX'. Borrowing Harder's (1996) terms, the pragmatics thus freezes into semantics, as considered in Chapter 4. Every natural language sign is reciprocally defined every time it is referred to. Naturally, the whole natural sign system becomes self-referential.

In addition, the uses and content of a sign change over time, and the whole represented by the signifier evolves. It often happens, as seen in Chapter 6, that derived signification of a sign activates further, different uses of the sign. For example, the term 'spam' was once only the name of a processed meat product, but its content has changed to also signify unwanted, mass-generated e-mail. This use as spam e-mail was triggered from the analogy of genuine 'ham' versus 'spam'. How a sign is used in a conventional way activates changes in its uses and furthers the whole represented by the signifier.

As a result, it is often difficult to precisely define the concrete content and meaning of a natural language sign, even a simple one. The exact content of the sign is seldom explicitly obtained, which would require resolving self-references and obtaining an explicit value, as in the calculation of the factorial. For example, even for a simple term like 'water', the contour of its meaning is left inexplicit. *The Oxford English Dictionary* gives the definition as "a colorless odorless liquid that is a compound of oxygen and hydrogen," but the term 'water' has many further attributes with respect to usages that affect the content: the term can be modified by a limited number of terms such as 'hot', 'spring', and 'tap', but it cannot be modified by a vast range of other nouns and adjectives.

The meaning of a natural language sign thus exists floating among the network of signs that are used in expressions referring to the sign. In other words, a sign is referred to from an expression consisting of signs referred to from many other expressions, whose signs are likewise referred to, and so forth, so that the meaning of the first sign relates to the whole system. A signifier then represents everything that is related to the sign with respect to the content and uses. The signifier functions as the kernel onto which the uses and content accumulate. It is thus the signifier that articulates the meaning; the meaning is *not* named by the signifier a posteriori.[2]

The origin of this holistic view underlying the sign system lies in Saussurian structuralism (de Saussure, 1911). A language system is *structural* if the meaning of an element exists within a holistic system. Although the signification of the term *structuralism* has greatly diversified (Sturrock and Rabaté, 2003), the core concept is present in the following quotation from Saussure (1911, p. 134):

We must not begin with the word, the term, in order to construct the system. This would be to suppose that terms have an absolute value given in advance, and that you have only to pile them up one on top of the other in order to reach the system. On the contrary, one must start from the system, the interconnected whole; this may be decomposed into particular terms, although these are not as easily distinguished as it might seem.

---

[2] This function of the signifier might probably be understood as follows: it often happens that people cannot recall the correct term or name when exposed to an image or content. For example, we may consider trying to recall the name of a 'navigational instrument used for measuring angular distances, especially the altitude of the sun, moon, and stars at sea'. People typically have the name 'sextant' on the tips of their tongues, if they have any idea at all (Aitchison, 1994). Another example is the tantalizing experience of trying to recall a person's name while standing in front of the person. These cases are different from moments when the content should be brought forth given a signifier. The result is either knowing or not knowing the term. The reason for such experiences probably lies in the fact that the signifier functions as the trigger for every signified. Recalling the signifier is not about obtaining a mere association but rather it is about solving the inverse problem, searching for the optimal term in the vast sea that is the web of signs in the mind.

The generative model explains this structural aspect of the system in relation with how the signifier articulates the signified: the speculative introduction of a signifier generates a meaning consisting of an ensemble of content and uses, thus forming a structural system.

9.4   A Constructive System

Computers process self-referential definitions in a totally different manner from humans. Interpretation of the self-reference x = f x, in general, is made as follows. The final result to be obtained is x = f x. Considering the second x, since it is f x it is replaced accordingly, generating x = f (f x). Replacing this second x by f x generates x = f (f (f x)). Repeating this process generates x = f (f (f (f ...(f (f x)))))). Unless every recursive application of f converges, such as by handling a subproblem with respect to that given originally, as seen in the case of the factorial function, the application of f can form an infinite chain. A computer therefore risks falling into an infinite loop when interpreting self-reference.

Perhaps a computer could judge whether the processing of a program halts before it starts the actual calculation. It has been logically proved, however, that any computer based on a Turing machine is incapable of such a judgment procedure (Sipser, 2005), which is known as the halting problem. That is, a computer program capable of judging whether a given program halts is impossible. A computer thus cannot distinguish between a program that ends within one minute and one that will not end even after countless years of computation. Without the ability to judge whether a given program halts, once a computer starts running any calculation it risks falling into an endless cycle.

Programmers therefore have to write programs that will halt, by manipulating signs that might be self-referentially defined and thus might not be capable of halting. In this sense, programming languages contain an inherent flaw that may result in nonhalting computation. Programmers must take care to ensure that they avoid this flaw when writing programs. This underlies a fundamental attitude among programmers in generating programs: that they should be constructed in a bottom-up manner. Programmers define components by only using signs that are guaranteed to halt. These signs are provided primordially by the programming system, and further utilities are included in a library. Programmers write programs by composing these signs with the utmost care to ensure that the computation halts.

The halting problem is such a large issue that various ways to aid programmers in generating properly halting programs have been an important part of the history of programming language development. Recent programming language systems incorporate these techniques. First, theoretical support is provided by clarifying the general features that executable self-referential definitions possess (Gunter, 1962; Tennent, 1991). Second, various linguistic restrictions are introduced so as to better control the signs used in programs. One approach is to classify signs hierarchically by *type*. As seen in Chapter 4, the introduction of type disallows an expression such as x x, since the types of each x are different. Moreover, paradoxical descriptions, which usually form the source of infinite execution, are disallowed by typing. For example, considering a set of all sets as the member of a set is paradoxical, but since the typing system attributes the set of sets and the set as different types, this paradox is avoided.

Another aid is the notion of scope (see also Section 4.2), meaning the range of code within which a sign is valid. Programmers have to be cautious about signs with a global scope, since the definition and uses of such global signs may be scattered throughout the program text, making it difficult for the user to verify the uses of these signs at a glance, that is, to verify where in the program a sign is generated and destroyed. Suppose that at one place a sign x is defined in terms of y and that the programmer forgets this and defines a sign y in terms of x at another place; then, the program falls into an infinite loop. In most languages, a sign has the notion of scope, which aids programmers in determining the range within which a sign is valid. A sign defined within a smaller scope is usually prohibited from use within a larger scope that contains the smaller scope, thus encapsulating signs within a local area. It is much easier to control the uses of signs if their appearance is kept within a certain range of locations. If a sign's introduction, use, and destruction are properly and thoroughly administered, it is unlikely that a global sign will be freely used to generate an unexpected self-reference.

In fact, self-reference can be completely enclosed in the fixed-point function through the use of scope in a radical way, as introduced in Chapters 4 and 7. Such enclosure might at least prohibit many signs from being defined self-referentially, so that programmers could concentrate on examining whether the procedure halts only around places where the fixed-point function appears. A sign is by nature self-referential, however, as seen so far; therefore, the constraint of description with only the fixed-point function is too unnatural, in any case. The design of a programming language must still consider finding a balance between allowing free, natural manipulation of signs and restricting sign uses to help programmers to avoid producing nonhalting programs.

Design through such techniques and the bottom-up programming attitude generates *constructive* systems. A constructive system, in this book, means a system in which a larger element is generated as a composition of smaller components. Any computer sign system has a direction of construction, from signs representing small structures at the lower level toward signs representing large structures at the higher level. Any programming language system has basic data and functions, with values that are predefined within the system when it is designed. These values consist of numbers, characters, Boolean values, decimals, and the basic operations that are applicable. The programmer's responsibility is to write a program so that any content of a sign can be *reduced* to a combination of such basic data and operations. Such construction also applies to self-references, since halting self-references can always be reduced to basic data and functions. To write a program is thus to give a constructive view of the target calculation.

This term *constructive* is related to the philosophy underlying constructive logic, mathematics, and programming, which is based on the concept that if a mathematical object exists then it should be possible for it to be constructed (i.e., found or explicitly described). This philosophy was elaborated by Luitzen E. J. Brouwer through his intuitionistic logic (Brouwer 1923, 1927), which has developed into the form of the constructive mathematics of Errett Bishop (Bishop, 1967; Bishop and Bridges, 1985). Briefly, intuitionistic logic is a logical framework that does not rely upon *reductio ad absurdum*, thus eliminating indirect proofs that explicitly avoid showing the existence of mathematical formulas. The sophistication of this theory relates to the programming method called constructive programming, in which the specification of a software application is formally expressed and programs are developed as proofs.

9.5   Structure versus Construction

Here we must note how different a sign system formed as a natural language is from one formed as a computer language. The terms *structural* and *constructive* each contain the morpheme *struct*, but the underlying philosophies of each are opposites in terms of the relation between the system and its elements as signs. By analogy to Saussure's quotation displayed in Section 9.3, in a structural system, we *must not* begin with the word, or term, but we should instead begin from the system, whereas in a constructive system we *must* begin with the word, or term, in order to construct the system. The difference between these two kinds of systems is illustrated in an intuitive manner in Figure 9.3. The left side shows a holistic structural system in which the relations between signs are formed naturally, without any hierarchy. In contrast, the right side shows a constructive system in which the relations between signs are formed hierarchically in a bottom-up manner and every term is

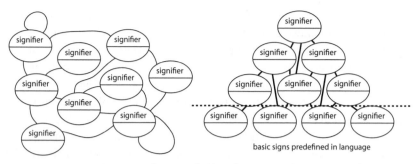

FIGURE 9.3. A structural system (left) and a constructive system (right).

reduced to grounding terms, which consist of the basic data and operations initially provided in the language system.

In a way, a structural system is naturally formed, without any formal requirements, so the signs connect with each other arbitrarily and freely. The resulting system is holistic, irreducible to a minimal core. Since such a system makes the best of reflexive signs, the sign system itself is reflexive. However, a constructive system is generated from a minimal core of signs guaranteed to halt, and the system must then be further constructed in a bottom-up manner to fulfill the formal requirement of halting. Connections among signs are made by necessity, and any system finally reduces to a small set of signs and their relations, representing the functions and data provided by the language system, which further reduce to CPU commands.

Such differences affect the robustness of a system. In a structural system, because any meaning of a sign is inexplicit, the sign is always ambiguous to some extent, so its meaning might overlap that of another sign. Thus, various expressions can signify almost identical content. Also, the elimination of one sign will not render the system dysfunctional, and it will continue to work somehow. In a constructive system, in contrast, even if a sign is introduced speculatively, it is defined so that its content becomes explicit after calculation. The content of one sign hardly overlaps that of another sign, and a single sign is introduced to represent a function, without substitution. The elimination of a sign could therefore be all the more disastrous, as compared with a structural system.

This difference was intuitively introduced at the beginning of this chapter through the contraposition of the paintings shown in Figures 9.1 and 9.2. The relation among squares is likely comparable to that among signs. The painting in Figure 9.1 seems to show a structural system of squares, whereas that in Figure 9.2 seems to show a constructive system. The painting in Figure 9.1

is considered representative of artists in the op-art movement, which seeks interesting visual illusions formed from simple shapes. The relation of the squares as a whole produces the illusive effect. Here, the relation of the squares is relatively robust, and random removal of one square would probably still produce the same effect. In contrast, the painting in Figure 9.2 is composed in a constructive manner. The squares seem to be placed according to the fundamental relation of placing them one on top of another, and the whole painting is constituted by use of this fundamental relation. Squares here cannot be randomly removed: certain squares must stay to maintain the composition. Kazimir Malevich was an artist noted as an adherent of (Russian) *constructivism*. It cannot be said whether the term constructivism has the same meaning in art as in this chapter, but the compositional aspects of Malevich's painting are reminiscent of the structure of computer sign systems.

An important aspect of the relation between a structural system and a constructive system is that the former may include the whole of the latter, whereas the latter may include only part of the former. The self-referential factorial function can be included in both systems, but many natural language terms, defined self-referentially, can work in a structural system but not in a constructive system. Such differences derive from the difference in how human beings and computers interpret self-references.

Thus, a programmer – a human being used to applying the robust structural system of natural language – writing a program is forced to think in a constructive manner. The programmer must generate a program that will halt despite using self-reference; the programmer does this by knowing exactly how the sign will acquire its final value. Programmers must fully administer all signs, remaining completely aware of how they are related. Since computer software applications are generated through programming, the users of current computers naturally face a similar challenge. Neglecting one sign could instantly lead to disastrous behavior. Many software applications have safeguards against nonhalting execution and restrictions on sign manipulation. Such measures may cause users to feel awkward or unnatural when working with computers.

To make a more human-friendly computer language, a fully constructive system should be restructured so that it can handle structurally formed signs. The key lies in the method of processing reflexivity, inclusively of self-reference. Studies related to this question in the computer science domain have been made since the birth of computer science, as will be seen in Chapter 11. Devising such a path towards a *structural computer* would be the key to stopping HAL 9000 or Speedy and would lead to a more natural computing environment, including the creation of more natural artificial beings.

9.6   Summary

Through observation of the nature of signs having reflexivity and analysis of how humans and computers process self-reference differently, natural language, as an example of a structural system, has been compared with programming language, a constructive system. The difference between them derives from the different interpretive strategies for self-referential expressions in these two sign systems.   Natural sign systems handle self-reference by leaving ambiguity as is, which generates a structural system where the signification of signs exists in the holistic system and the whole sign system operates reflexively. In contrast, in computer sign systems, since self-reference directly concerns the halting problem, programs must be constructively generated by using procedures that are guaranteed to halt. Alternative handling of reflexivity in computer systems holds the key to developing a more natural computer environment and would also enable greater understanding of human thought.

10

Sign and Time

Time present and time past
Are both perhaps present in time future,
And time future contained in time past.
If all time is eternally present
All time is unredeemable.
What might have been is an abstraction
Remaining a perpetual possibility
Only in a world of speculation.
What might have been and what has been
Point to one end, which is always present.

Excerpt from "Burnt Norton" in FOUR QUARTETS
by T. S. Eliot, copyright 1936
by Harcourt, Inc. and renewed 1964
by T. S. Eliot, reprinted by permission
of Houghton Mifflin Harcourt
Publishing Company. (Eliot, 1968)

10.1 Interaction

So far, the discussion has proceeded by only looking inside sign systems, without considering other sign worlds existing outside the system (see Figure 3.8). Parts I and II examined the computer signs present within a computer program, and the previous chapter considered the structural aspect of a sign system. Every sign system is significant, however, since it communicates with the external world. In the case of humans, communication typically corresponds to communication via natural language, whereas in the case of computers such communication corresponds to interaction. In other words, communication is an important feature of a sign system for both machines and humans.

FIGURE 10.1. Soejima Taneomi (1828–1925), *Kiunhiu,* Saga Prefectural Art Museum. Image courtesy of Saga Prefectural Art Museum.

The last two chapters of this book are dedicated to looking at the nature of a computer sign system within an environment. In these chapters, the pansemiotic view is taken, in which the environment is also considered pansemiotic. That is, a sign system may only interact with or handle the environment via signs. For a computer system to interact with an environment, the interaction must be described in a program. To start with, therefore, this chapter focuses on the description of interaction within the sign system, whereas the next chapter considers a sign system communicating with other sign systems inclusively of itself by using the interactive function. The underlying questions of this chapter are how a sign system relates with the outer world and represents it and how a sign is involved in this process.

Like the other chapters, this chapter can be introduced by considering its theme intuitively through paintings. Any work of art is constructed through interaction with a medium, typically starting from a blank canvas in the case of painting. A painter with content in mind starts painting, stroke by stroke, seeking the desired representation of the content. In classic Western traditional paintings, this ipso facto process is often invisible in the completed artwork. In contrast, in many Eastern paintings and works of calligraphy, and also in modern art, the process is shown explicitly. For example, Figure 10.1 shows an example of calligraphy by Soejima Taneomi, the representative artist who initiated modern Japanese calligraphy. The movement of the stroke in this work can be followed, which allows one to relive the concentration and expectation of the painter during creation of the work. Similarly, some modern paintings also have a similar feature, such as the example shown in Figure 10.2. Action paintings like this remind us that behind painting is always a time flow along which the painter worked, stroke by stroke. While such strokes are made, the artwork is still being born and the artist interacts with the canvas. When the action terminates, the painting is finished and becomes fixed.

FIGURE 10.2. Jackson Pollock (1912–1956): Untitled (ca. 1950), The Museum of Modern Art. © 2009 The Pollock-Krasner Foundation/Artists Rights Society (ARS), New York. Digital Image © The Museum of Modern Art/Licensed by SCALA/Art Resource, NY.

It is hence this interaction along the time flow that constitutes art, and the same applies for human and computer sign systems. For a sign system to evolve into something heterogeneous, it must interact with something heterogeneous. In this sense, interaction is necessary for a sign system to evolve. This applies to computer systems too: without interaction, unless some other random procedure is involved, computation is mere deduction, and the beginning and end of the computational state are essentially homogeneous. A sign system evolves through interaction with a heterogeneous outer world, and this requires the time flow. Therefore, consideration of interaction is the basis of examining what a sign system is and what it is founded on. This chapter looks at the role of signs through interaction and the way time is involved in this process.

To enable interaction in a computer system, it must first be described within a program. Describing interaction in a program means describing events that are unexpected and unpredictable for the system. Currently, such uncontrollable events are described through *sign value changes*. Briefly, a sign is allocated for interaction, with its value initially undefined; the value is later obtained from somewhere outside the system and stored at a memory location represented by the sign. The value triggers further calculation within the system, and the system outputs the result based on the input.

How to deal with such value change in computers has long been a problem, especially for researchers who take formal and theoretical approaches. Rationally, humans want machines to stay mechanically logical and consistent.

Value change, however, means that at one time a computer says this, whereas at another time it says that. Studies have been made on how to implement a computer system that always remains consistent, through a limitation called *referential transparency*: a restriction that any expression must have a unique value independent of time. Interaction then becomes a problem to be described under transparency. There have been studies that have sought an answer to the question of how to describe interaction under transparency, which has led to an ironical consequence. This chapter explains this consequence, and in this explanation we consider the significance of interactions and time for a sign system.

10.2 The State Transition Machine

A modern computer has von Neumann-type hardware, which is based on a state transition machine. A *state* is a sequence of zeros and ones inside the CPU registers, the main memory, and the secondary memory (e.g., the hard disk). The machine performs an operation via the CPU and the state changes to reflect the result of the operation. The state of a computer thus changes over time.

To conform to this hardware scheme, primitive computer programs have been written to take the form of state transitions and are generally modeled as Turing machines. Each such program includes a description of the state changes in memory space. For example, the following program is based on state transition, using identifiers:[1]

```
1: x := 3
2: print x+1
3: x := 5
4: print x+1
5: x := 7.
```

In line 1, the value 3 is assigned to the sign x, which causes the computer to store the value 3 in the memory location attached to x. In line 3, the value stored at x is changed from 3 to 5. The value change is not restricted to occur only once; in line 5, the value of x is once again modified. Naturally, the first and second print operations output different results (i.e., 4 and 6).

Thus far, program execution has been assumed to proceed from top to bottom. If this order is changed, say, by reversing execution to proceed from bottom to top, then the outputs from the program will be 8 and 6, differing from the case when the program is executed from top to bottom. Thus, when

---

[1] Recall that : = indicates assignment, whereas '=' indicates definition (see Chapter 6 and glossary).

value change is freely allowed, the outputs of a program depend on the *order* of execution of program statements. Also, the value of x at a particular point depends on the order of program execution up to that point.

This feature of changing values within programs makes it difficult to verify a program's actions. The correctness of a program cannot be verified without considering the order of the expressions being executed. When a bug is likely to exist in a program, the programmer must read the program to check whether execution occurs in the correct order, verifying the correctness of the value of every sign. A program cannot be verified only by checking the correctness of each expression. Debugging thus almost resembles the virtual execution of a program.

The critical problem seen so far underlying computer programs is related to the arbitrariness of signs: even for a constant value, the signifier is arbitrary. This arbitrariness means that the content can change with the whim of the moment. In natural language, the meaning of a word can also change, which corresponds to the value change of signs in a computer program. Change in natural language, however, is effective only after it spreads globally. This condition of globalness serves to restrain easy value changes and as a consequence natural language values are relatively fixed. Considering the same example appearing in Section 9.3, the term 'spam' was once only the name of a processed meat product, but its content has changed to also signify unwanted, mass-generated e-mail. By now, this change has occurred globally; therefore, a phrase such as 'I received 100 pieces of spam today.' signifies a standard signification. This globalness in terms of social convention prevents sign values from easily changing. As Saussure says, signs are arbitrary but bound (de Saussure, 1911). In contrast, in the case of computer signs, change easily occurs, since a computer language system does not have any restrictions corresponding to the social conventions that stabilize sign values.

10.3   Referential Transparency

There is an artificial restriction prohibiting value changes in computer programs, which is called referential transparency. Programming systems using a language based on a purely functional paradigm,[2] such as Haskell, introduce this constraint.

Referential transparency is a restriction applied to a programming language system to ensure that every expression has a unique value (Bird and Wadler,

---

[2]   The term *pure* signifies a functional paradigm subject to the constraint of referential transparency.

1988). This ensures that the value of a sign can never again be changed once the value is set. For example, suppose that a sign x is introduced into a program; its value is set at some time during program execution and the value remains the same until the end of execution. The values of any expressions using x are calculated consistently by using this fixed value throughout the execution of the program.

The restrictions introduced by referential transparency generate two advantages in a system. First, in a referentially transparent system, the result of execution does not depend on the order of evaluating expressions. Execution of a program in any order leads to the same result if the calculation halts, since every expression has a unique value.[3] Program verification then requires only checking the correctness of each expression, without checking the order of execution. Second, the introduction of referential transparency enhances the reorganization of signs and procedures. The reorganization of procedures is discussed in the following section, but for now we look at the reorganization of signs. Consider the following program, written in a state-transitive manner, with execution from top to bottom:

```
1: x := f 1
2: print x
3: y := g x
4: print x
5: print y.
```

If this was a program *without* the referential transparency restriction, the function g in line 3 could modify the value of x itself. In such a case, lines 2 and 4 would print out different values. In contrast, if this was a transparent program, then such value modification in g would be disallowed, and the same values would be printed out in lines 2 and 4. The introduction of temporary signs such as x and y then becomes meaningless, and these temporary identifiers can be removed (except for the purpose of printing). Such removal of temporary identifiers for assignment was also seen in Section 7.5. Reorganization of signs and removal of temporary identifiers increase calculation efficiency, since memory allocation and memory access for storing values slow down calculation. Removal of self-referential signs, however, requires further sophistication, as was seen in both Chapters 4 and 7. One field of study in pure functional programming is aimed at automatically transforming programs to remove signs that decrease the execution efficiency.

---

[3] This feature was introduced as the Church-Rosser theorem in Chapter 4, Section 4.2.

The restriction of referential transparency thus seems ideal at first sight, because signs are reorganized, program verification becomes easy, and automatic transformation is provided, thus generating an efficient program. Still, this restriction is rarely included in the most widely used programming languages because the description of certain fundamental procedures that are necessary for programs is nontrivial under the condition of referential transparency.

10.4   Side Effects

In a referentially transparent system, nonreferentially transparent procedures should all be rewritten transparently. Therefore, another effect of introducing referential transparency is to decompose computer procedures into those with and without value changes. The latter are transparent procedures, whereas the former are procedures with *side effects*.

A side effect in the computer science domain is broadly defined as a situation in which the value of a variable is unexpectedly changed, despite the programmer's intentions, during evaluation of an expression. Thus, a side effect in this broad sense occurs in carelessly written programs as a bug. At the same time, however, there are procedures that cannot be easily described without handling such unexpected changes, a fact that becomes apparent under referential transparency. A side effect in this narrower sense (Hudak, 1989, 1992) (of pure functional programming) thus signifies a genre of procedures that, by nature, is founded on value changes. Side effects include exception handling, nondeterminacy, concurrency, and, above all, interaction – the focus of this chapter. From this point on, the term side effect is used in this narrower sense.

The natural question raised by the introduction of referential transparency into a system concerns the need to express side effects transparently. Since the final solution is essentially the same for any form of side effect, this chapter focuses on examining the consequences through the interaction procedure.

Interaction consists of all kinds of communication with a program, including mouse motion, keyboard entry, the display of calculation results, and the playback or recording of sound. Interaction is described through a program by using procedures that interact with the operating system (OS), the main software that administers the computer hardware and any applications running. The description of interaction within a program is limited to supposition of how the outside world, including the user, might interact with the system.

The following exemplifies the simplest interactive program typically written in a state-transitive manner. The program reads a character by using the

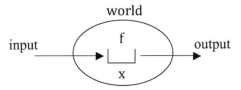

FIGURE 10.3. Simplest interaction in a state transition machine.

function `read_c`, processes it with the function `f`, and outputs the result by using the function `write_c`.

```
1: interact = {
2:   repeat
3:     x := read_c
4:     write_c (f x)
5:   end
6: }
```

(10.1)

When the program above is executed, a memory space inside the main memory is allocated to store the value x, the sign dedicated to handling the side effect. Every time an input is read into the system it is stored in the same memory space corresponding to x, the function `f` is applied, and the result is output. As the read and write operations are repeated, x takes different values. Thus, this is a state-transitive program requiring value changes of x, and it is invalid under the referential transparency restriction.

The situation seen while running this program is illustrated in Figure 10.3. The figure shows the *world*, which represents the surrounding environment in an abstract sense. This includes the status of the OS, since all interaction with the system is conducted via the OS. Inside this world is located the sign x dedicated to interaction. When there is interaction, this affects not only x but also the world: for example, keyboard entry into the system also changes the state of the OS by eliminating the entry after confirming that the system has received the value. This whole, consisting of the world and the program running within, is thus affected by interaction.

A side effect can be described in a referentially transparent manner by using a common trick, namely, making signs *disposable*. Whenever interaction occurs, a new sign is allocated to represent the new value. In the previous example, the sign x was used at the moment of each read operation, but if the sign x differs at these moments, every value will be used once for all cases. Naturally, the execution remains transparent when a different sign is used for every different value. This might seem too artificial and unnecessarily

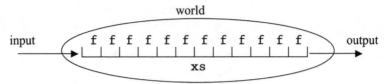

FIGURE 10.4. Referentially transparent interaction using a list (or a dialogue).

grandiose, but for the case when the formal constraint of referential transparency – unique assignment of content to a sign – must be met in a computer sign system, this is the primary solution proposed thus far.

There are two ways to implement disposable signs:

- by generating a new sign for every changing value, and
- by generating a new world for every changing value.

The former method is called a *dialogue* (Hudak *et al.*, 1992; Hudak and Sundaresh, 1988), whereas the latter is called a *monad* (Wadler, 1992).

In the first solution, using a dialogue, the sign x is implemented as a *list*, a sequence of memory spaces represented by the sign xs, corresponding to x in program (10.1). Every time there is interaction the new unused space within the list is used once and only then, and referential transparency is thus met. Program (10.1) can be modified as follows to take the dialogue approach:

```
1:  interact =
2:    let
3:      xs = read_s                               (10.2)
4:    in
5:      write_s (map f xs).
```

This program does nothing more than write_s (map f read_s), but the list xs is temporarily introduced to explicitly indicate the correspondence with program (10.1). For this, the let-expression is used as introduced in Chapters 4 and 7. The operation of this program is illustrated in Figure 10.4. As noted above, the sign xs signifies a list of successively changing values read through interaction by use of the function read_s, and every new input is stored in the subsequent unused location in the list. The trick for dealing with side effects is implemented by changing the type of x from a single value to the list structure xs and, correspondingly, by changing the functional application of f to apply to every element of xs through a higher-order function map.[4]

---

[4] The function map was introduced in Chapter 7.

After applying `f` to each element of the list, the elements are output by the function `write_s`.

In the second solution, using the monad[5] (Wadler, 1992), the idea is to generate the whole world every time a new value is given through interaction, where the world here equals the world indicated in Figure 10.3, or the whole surrounding environment of the system. The resulting program can be written as follows, with `w`, `w'`, and `w''` indicating different worlds.

```
1:  interact w =
2:    let
3:      (x,w') = read_m w
4:      (r,w'') = write_m (f x) w'
5:    in
6:      interact w''
```
(10.3)

The difference from the previous program is that here the read and write results form pairs consisting of the value and the newly modified world. Program (10.3) is executed as follows:

a. Require world `w` for interaction (line 1).
b. Apply the function `read_m` to `w`, read a value into `x`, and generate world `w'` from `w` (line 3).
c. Apply `f` to `x`. Note that the function `f` does not generate a new world, since it is referentially transparent. Output the value of `f x` through the function `write_m`. The world is newly generated as `w''` after the write operation. Here, `r` indicates whether the output was successful (line 4).
d. Repeat the process by going back to line 1 with the new world `w''` (line 6).

The execution of this program through steps **a** to **c** is illustrated in Figure 10.5. Time flows from left to right, showing how the world evolves from `w` to `w''` via `w'`.

The function `interact` repeats because of the recursion in line 6. Successive repetition of the procedure through steps **a** to **c** is illustrated in Figure 10.6. Time again flows from left to right, and world1 becomes world2 after one

---

[5] The name monad comes from the concept of a monad in category theory, a branch of pure mathematics. The mathematical monad bridges two different mathematical structures under a condition defined as a triplet (Barr and Wells, 1995; MacLane, 1998). In computer science, Wadler's monad bridges the OS and the system, and mathematically it has a monadic structure. This monad has nothing to do with the philosophical monad, which is defined as an inseparable, self-evolving being and is seen in works such as Leibnitz (1908). The concept of a monad in this latter signification is discussed briefly in Section 11.2.

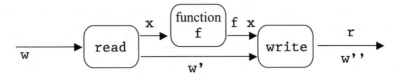

FIGURE 10.5. One interaction using the monad.

execution of the function `interact`, with world1 and world2 corresponding to w and w'', respectively. Subsequent execution of the function `interact` in step **d** modifies world2 into world3 (again corresponding to w and w'', respectively), and so on. In the previous case of the dialogue, the sign with a side effect was transformed into a sequence of disposable signs, whereas here the whole world is disposable. The input is a value signified by x, which is stored and processed in the same way in each world, but x itself is not the same among worlds, since the whole world is newly generated throughout execution.

Even though the signs are reorganized and the unnecessary signs are eliminated, as seen in the previous section, many new signs need to be generated on the fly to describe interaction transparently. Moreover, if Wadler's monad was implemented literally, the resulting system would be unworkably expensive, since it copies the whole system at every interaction. The key to making this approach realistic, according to Jones and Wadler (1993), is to apply interactive operations immediately to the real world in a state-transitive manner. That is, instead of copying the whole world every time an interaction is made, as indicated in the program text, only the places requiring modification are modified using the value changes. This results in a program that theoretically is referentially transparent but in reality uses value changes, and thus, the

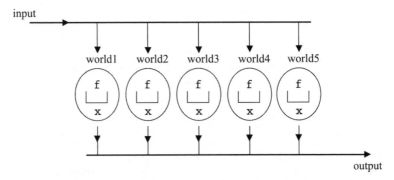

FIGURE 10.6. Referentially transparent interaction using the monad.

program text does not show what the computer really does. Even then, the number of disposable signs will still be large in a referentially transparent system, and execution will be aided by automatic collection of freed memory for further use in allocating signs. In general, referentially transparent systems remain computationally costly and are thus slower than a normal state-transition system. As a result, the application of such referentially transparent programming language systems remains limited mainly to educational use and theoretical studies.

The consequences of changing values, discussed so far, can be summarized as follows:

1. State change is a problem, since calculation results depend on the order of evaluation.
2. Referential transparency is introduced. Then, the execution order no longer matters, signs are reorganized, and computational procedures are decomposed into transparent procedures and nontransparent procedures.
3. Procedures with side effects are described transparently through the use of disposable signs representing changing values.

Does referential transparency solve the problem of changing values introduced in Section 10.2? The problem was that program results depend on the order of execution, which must be administered. By applying tricks using the dialogue and the monad, changing values that were originally indicated by a singular sign must be represented using an ordered structure of signs along the time flow. Therefore, instead of the execution order, the order of the signs representing changing values now must be administered. In other words, the attempt to get away from value changes started from one ordering problem and returned to another ordering problem. Writing an interactive program thus means administering some order for both cases, with and without transparency.

10.5 Temporality of a Sign

The consequences of a somewhat paradoxical attempt at handling side effects in a transparent manner have thus highlighted the significance of value changes and their ordering. Since both changes and ordering are inherently related to time flow, interaction should be reconsidered fundamentally in terms of the temporal nature of signs.

In a dyadic sign model, a sign consists of a signifier and its content. Considering their semantics at the hardware level (Section 2.4), the signifier denotes the memory address, whereas the content denotes the value contained at the address. Analyzing their roles from a spatiotemporal viewpoint, the signifier carries the spatial aspect of the sign, whereas the content captures the temporal side of the sign, in addition to having a spatial side. The signifier of a computer sign identifies a location within a memory space, indicating the place where the content is stored. On the other hand, the content is the value stored in a space of a certain bit length, and its existence is temporal, since it can be modified to another value. Such value modification involves two constraints: that both values must be represented by a single signifier and that the two values must be exclusive and not coexist.

The relationship between the spatial and temporal aspects of signs is that spatiality precedes temporality: without allocation of a sign, its value cannot be changed. Naturally, to use a computer sign at the hardware level, the sign should first be allocated and then values can be stored. For computer signs, to introduce a signifier is to allocate memory space, and a signifier can be allocated without consolidated content. In contrast, plain content without a signifier can never exist on a computer, since content does not exist on a computer without being stored somewhere in memory: within the CPU registers, the main memory, or the secondary memory. Some might suggest that in LG, from Chapter 4, signifiers are attached to content a posteriori to the definition of explicitly articulated content as a lambda-term. Such an introduction of content first, followed by the signifier, only *seems* possible when considering the semantic level within the programming language: in reality, implementation of LG requires providing memory space to every lambda-term so as to allow the expressions to exist on a computer. In other words, lambda expressions cannot exist without signifiers at the hardware level. Therefore, at the hardware level of a computer, signifiers are always primordial in relation to their content. As discussed in Chapters 4 and 9, a sign is speculatively introduced and signifies content to be established in the future. The elements with undefined values appearing in the list xs used in the dialogue example in the previous section exemplify such speculative introduction of signs. The reader might then wonder, what is the signification of such a sign without consolidated content? This is exactly the point of the subsequent discussion in terms of the *role* of a sign within interaction.

Signs are used after allocation by storing a value in bits and then successively changing the value according to the results of further calculation, as depicted in the upper part of Figure 10.7. At the time of allocation, the content consists of an *undefined value*, or random value, which is represented as $\perp$[6] (Bird and Wadler, 1988) in the figure. In this sense, any signifier always has a signified,

---

[6] $\perp$ reads as *bottom*.

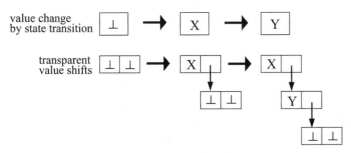

FIGURE 10.7. Value changes of computer signs.

and they are two inseparable sides of a sign. After a while, ⊥ shifts to a concrete value, represented as X. This value can further change to another value, denoted as Y.

Thus illustrated, the two changes, from ⊥ to a value and from this value to another, appear the same, but they have different natures. In the former case, ⊥ expresses that a sign is in the state of waiting for a value to emerge in the future. This shift relates to the halting problem introduced in the previous chapter. Whether the sign will really be altered to a concrete value cannot be judged, since it is theoretically impossible to judge by means of a program whether a calculation actually halts and shifts the sign value to a concrete value.

The second shift, from one value to another, can be decomposed by using the disposable signs introduced previously to meet referential transparency. Successive value changes are performed as indicated in the lower part of Figure 10.7. When a sign is allocated and ⊥ has shifted to a value, the successive change is considered to *restart* through allocation of a new sign (the second section from the left in the lower part of the figure). The newly allocated cell indicates a new sign, whose content is ⊥ waiting to be shifted to a defined value. Since the second value comes *after* the first value, this dependency – the order – is indicated by the value X followed by ⊥. After this new ⊥ changes to a concrete value (denoted as Y), a new sign is allocated (the rightmost section in the lower part of Figure 10.7). Thus, the change from one value to another is decomposed into the following two components:

- the shift of the value of a disposable sign from undefined (⊥) to a defined value, and
- the dependency among signs.

Note how the allocation of disposable signs and the dependency among them are spatial. In other words, transparent representation of a sign change entails maximally extracting the spatial aspects of the temporality of the change.

What remains temporal is the essence of temporality in the kind of calculation described by computer programming: namely, the shift from $\perp$ to a value.

10.6   Interaction and a Sign

As noted in the previous discussion, temporality in calculation is uniformly described only by the shift of a sign from $\perp$ to a value. This in fact is the case for every kind of computation, inclusively of procedures both with and without side effects. There is a crucial difference, however, in the nature of $\perp$ between procedures with and without side effects.

In the case of calculation without side effects, the moment when the content of a signifier is $\perp$ is the period of waiting for the calculation to finish. Although the halting problem prohibits proper judgment as to whether a procedure halts, a typical programmer usually tries to avoid generating non-halting programs and expects the procedure to halt. The $\perp$ then signifies a calculation conceived within the sign system as a value to be generated and to replace the $\perp$ in the near future.

In contrast, in the case of calculation with interaction, $\perp$ does not represent the period of waiting for the calculation to finish, but rather the period of suspension, of waiting until the value comes from somewhere external. The system cannot conceive of what value will emerge but can only wait until the value arrives. The value is provided by the outer world to the sign system. Since the outer world is beyond the control of the sign system, interaction with it requires indicating something *unknown*. It is necessary, therefore, that a sign is speculatively introduced with its value starting from $\perp$, since what will be provided from the outside is unknown. In other words, since the outer world is unknown for the sign system, the means to communicate with it can only be speculative. A sign is the means to articulate an unknown something from the outer world.

The signification of $\perp$ is also different at the level of a sign system. In a sign system without side effects, if everything goes well and the calculation halts, the system experiences no further shifts or sign changes. Such a properly terminated system ceases being temporal. Calculation without side effects always aims toward this atemporal state. In such a system, the beginning and the end of the computational state are essentially homogeneous.

In contrast, to the extent that the system interacts, at every interaction the system acquires something heterogeneous from the outside, which renews the system. The interaction continues to influence parts of the system. Interaction causes the sign system to remain temporal and keep changing. The nature of this change is utterly different from the case without side effects.

Therefore, the role of a sign in interaction is to introduce heterogeneity from outside.

10.7 Sign and Sein

Thus far the temporal nature of a sign has been discussed solely for computer sign systems. The consequence reached is fundamental: the discussion so far seems to suggest the role of a sign as a transcendental medium for communication with the outer world, unknown and heterogeneous. This discussion could be considered as a starting point for examining the general nature of interaction in a sign system. Thus far we have seen two premises within interaction. The first is that a sign must possess a speculative nature. We have already seen that this is the case for computer signs. Second, the sign system must operate within the surrounding, external world. Every computer system runs in the world of its OS and, beyond that, in the surrounding real world. Wadler's monad makes the essentialness of the world explicit in interaction, indicating how interaction concerns not only the system but also the whole in which it is situated.

These two premises indeed hold for human sign systems too. In the last chapter, it was seen how a sign of a natural language is speculatively introduced and how its use reflexively stipulates its content. As for the second premise, it is trivial to note that human sign systems work within their surroundings.

The role of a sign suggesting a similar transcendental view in a general sign system is in fact present in Heidegger (1927). Heidegger writes about signs as follows:

A sign is not a Thing which stands for another Thing in the relationship of indicating; it is rather an item of equipment which explicitly raises a totality of equipment into our circumspection so that together with it the worldly character of the ready-to-hand [7] announces itself. [Section 80]

In other words, a sign is a medium carrying foresight of something that exists in the outer world and is perceived through involvement. The parallelism of this quote with the discussion thus far suggests the nature of signs as a transcendental means to grasp the outer world. A sign is a speculative medium, a means for a sign system to interact with the outside. We must also recall here that such a speculative nature was also the basis for implementing self-reference by requiring the speculative introduction of a signifier.

---

[7] See Chapter 5.5 for the signification of *ready-to-hand*, appearing as *ready-at-hand*, due to the difference in term choice by the two translators.

The magnum opus is unfinished and the book ends with the question: "Is there a way which leads from primordial time to the meaning of being?" (Heidegger, 1927, Section 438). One clue for contemplating this question, in my opinion, is to consider the semiotic nature of a being. Interaction with the outer world through signs of a temporal nature is the starting point for any sign system to be generated and to evolve. The reflexivity of signs and sign systems plays a crucial role in this process, by transforming use (ready-to-hand) into meaning, as seen in the Harder's statement of Chapter 4, and structurally enlarging a sign system, as seen in the previous chapter. Such a procedure can be compared to the process of creating artwork introduced in Figure 10.1 or Figure 10.2, where one stroke stipulates the next stroke, and this repeated articulation finally crystallizes into the final form.

We also saw in Chapter 8 how humanistic values are produced through reflexivity. The subject of Heidegger's masterpiece is Dasein, conditioned as a being that "always understands itself in terms of its existence" (Heidegger, 1927, Section 12), which is the most intelligible reflexive status of a being. Current computers are of course far from humans in this respect, and the most attractive element of Heidegger's work therefore does not yet apply to computer systems. The slightest reflexivity, however, at the level of the system is indeed present in computer systems too. This aspect is considered next, in the last chapter of this book.

10.8 Summary

The nature of interaction in computer sign systems has been examined in relation to the questions of how a sign system relates with the outer world and represents it and of how signs are involved in this process. The analysis was first made in terms of the consequences of an attempt to describe interaction in a referentially transparent manner: specifically by prohibiting sign value changes. These consequences highlight how the nature of interaction cannot avoid ordering along a time flow. Signs were therefore analyzed from a spatiotemporal viewpoint regarding value changes. We verified the speculative nature of signs, whose existence starts with a signifier signifying content that is yet to be confirmed. The signifier is primordial to its content at the hardware implementation level and also in terms of the theoretical consideration that any value change of a sign can be summarized as the shift of an undefined value of $\perp$ to a concrete value. This change from $\perp$ to a defined value is the key aspect of a sign's temporality. The difference between signs having a value of $\perp$ in procedures with and without side effects revealed two roles of a sign within interaction: first, as a medium to represent an unknown outer-world target; and second, to introduce heterogeneity, which triggers the sign system to evolve. A similar nature of temporality was also hypothesized to be present in human systems, as a consequence of this fundamentally temporal nature of signs.

11

Reflexivity and Evolution

Doesn't the analogy between language and games throw light here? We can easily imagine people amusing themselves in a field by playing with a ball so as to start various existing games, but playing many without finishing them and in between throwing the ball aimlessly into the air, chasing one another with the ball and bombarding one another for a joke and so on. And now someone says: The whole time they are playing a ball-game and following definite rules at every throw.

And is there not also the case where we play and – make up the rules as we go along? And there is even one where we alter them – as we go along.

From *Philosophical Investigations*, 3rd ed., by Ludwig Wittgenstein. Translated by G. E. M. Anscombe and E. Anscombe. Oxford: Wiley-Blackwell. (Wittgenstein, 1953, p. 83)

11.1   Reflexivity of Natural Language

This last chapter considers the reflexive nature of a sign system again, but this time from the viewpoint of the whole system. The analysis is made through a notion already introduced in Section 8.4.3: reflexivity, the feature of a function or a system to interpret that which is produced by itself. Since the focus of Part III is the system, reflexivity is considered as the self-referential nature at the level of a system. Here, the notion of reflexivity is a special case of a system's interaction with itself via the external world, and thus the argument assumes the concepts of the discussion in the last chapter.

Interaction of a system with other systems can be compared to a painting that represents another painting. For example, the painting in Figure 11.1 shows a room full of representative Renaissance paintings. A painting that as a whole constitutes a visual system is now indicated as content and adds meaning through such reciprocal presentation of *systems in a system*. D'Ors interprets Teniers's painting as representing the epilogue of the Renaissance

FIGURE 11.1. David Teniers the Younger (1610–1690), *The Gallery of the Archduke Leopold William*, Museo del Prado. Photo credit: Scala/Art Resource, NY.

(d'Ors, 1973). Other such paintings using this technique frequently occur in Vermeer's work, of which an example is shown in Figure 11.2. According to Snow (1979), the baroque painting of the Last Judgment hanging on the rear wall provides a signification of conventional moral and religious judgment that plays an important role within the allegory signified by the painting. These two examples show interpretation of *other* paintings in a painting, which can be compared to processing *other* systems' output within a system. There are also examples of a painting that includes itself, which can be compared to the reflexivity of a system. In Escher's painting of *Print Gallery*, appearing on the front cover of this book, the central part is left blank. De Smit and Lenstra (2003) attempted to fill this blank part and found that the blank part is connected to the painting itself, thus causing infinite recursion of the painting itself toward the center.

Natural language systems are reflexive at various levels. At the level of the human being, a language system evolves by producing an output interpretable for itself. The common understanding that *to state/write is to understand* shows that the production of an expression[1] objectifies a thought as a composition of signs, which reflexively becomes the input influencing the thought, thus fostering understanding. Above all, it is arguably very seldom that a person produces an expression that is non-interpretable to himself or herself. It could be that the individual is only copying some expression without understanding,

---

[1] The term *expression* in this chapter denotes a linguistic expression and, in particular, a word or phrase in the natural language case or an expression in the computer science sense (cf. Glossary).

FIGURE 11.2. Johannes Vermeer (1632–1675), *Woman Holding a Balance*, Widener Collection, National Gallery of Art. Image courtesy of the Board of Trustees, National Gallery of Art, Washington.

but even then such a phenomenon of production usually leads toward a deeper understanding of the expression. Therefore, the act of phrasing is considered evidence of understanding or, at least, of trying to understand. Through this reflexive reconsideration of self-produced output, a human being can change, improve, and evolve.

Reflexivity occurs among multiple natural language systems, namely, among multiple people. Reflexivity facilitates mutual understanding, since it guarantees that an expression has an almost equivalent influence among the people involved in communication. Through communication among people, human beings mutually affect one another, and the system as a whole changes, improves, and evolves. Therefore, reflexivity is effective not only for one system but also for a system consisting of multiple systems. In units consisting of the self, a pair, or a community, self-augmentation occurs, and such activities reciprocally form an organic system that evolves by referring to itself at multiple levels.

A natural language system is naturally reflexive because of its structural nature, as was seen in Chapter 9. The very capability of leaving the content of a sign ambiguous facilitates new expressions that reflexively modify the interpretive system. Consideration of reflexivity in natural language is thus abundant; a representative example is seen in the philosophy of Willard v.

O. Quine (1960, p. 3f). His famous metaphor of Neurath's ship conveys the idea that the language embedding every human theory and belief is like Neurath's ship, which is built and modified while remaining afloat. This notion of reflexivity can also be seen in the thoughts of Ludwig Wittgenstein, as shown in the epigraph at the beginning of this chapter. Self-interpretation is frequently addressed for biological systems too, as seen in autopoiesis (Maturana and Varela, 1980) and biosemiotics (Hoffmeyer, 1996; Hoffmeyer and Favareau, 2009).

In computer languages, however, reflexivity at the system level is not obvious, with one reason for this lying in their constructive nature, as seen in Section 9.4. A constructive system has a much clearer distinction between a set of interpretable expressions and those that are non-interpretable. Even so, in computer languages too, reflexivity forms a criterion for the expressive power of the language system: powerful computer language systems are all reflexive. The objectives of this chapter are to look at various computer language systems with respect to reflexivity.

11.2 Reflexivity of a Sign System

The term reflexivity, as defined in the previous section, is related to *homoiconicity*, which appeared in computer science literature in the 1960s (Mcllroy, 1960). Homoiconicity is a feature of a programming language system that denotes that a computer program has the same form as the data that are input and output by the program. The programming language Lisp typically has this feature, called an S-expression, in which both data and the program code are represented by a simple structure using parentheses. For example, data consisting of a triple of the three numbers 10, 5, and 30 are represented as (10 5 30), whereas program code in Lisp is also represented in an S-expression such as (add 2 (mul 4 5)), which calculates $2 + 4 \times 5$. Although such uniformity of form of data and programs does not seem to be common in high-level programming languages, data and programs both ultimately consist of zeros and ones, so today's computers are fundamentally homoiconic.

Since data form the input and output of systems, a program as data means that it becomes input and output similar to data. The term homoiconicity could therefore signify whether computers can produce self-interpretable programs. Thus, in this chapter, I could have extended the signification of the term homoiconicity to signify reflexivity. The term *iconicity*, however, has a specific usage in the domains of linguistics and semiotics. The systems discussed in this chapter include natural systems, so the term homoiconicity could

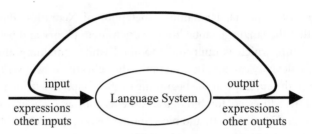

FIGURE 11.3. Reflexive language system.

potentially puzzle readers from those domains. Thus, the term reflexivity is used in this book as defined at the beginning of this chapter and is explained more in general in the rest of this section.

First, the term *sign system* in this book, as defined at the very beginning, signifies a relation among signs and their interpretations. Interpretation in this book means processing an expression according to the predefined interpretive rules of the sign system. A *language system* is a kind of sign system consisting of a relation among linguistic signs and their interpretations. Natural languages and computer languages both constitute language systems. Some sign systems, including language systems, are produced by using a language system. In the case of computer systems, most are written in some computer language.

A *reflexive language system* acquires some expression as input and produces another as output, and parts of the output form expressions interpretable by the system itself (see Figure 11.3, and also Figure 3.8). As mentioned before in Section 8.4.3, reflexivity is the basic step of the procedure to obtain the fixed point of the function or system. Natural languages are reflexive language systems, as was seen at the beginning of this chapter. Using such a reflexive language system, a reflexive system can be produced by embedding the interpretive system of the language. Thus, precisely speaking, reflexivity is an attribute of such systems, as well as an attribute of language systems.

The capability of a sign system to interpret its own output involves *self-augmentation,* that is, the capability of the system to change or modify itself, to extend, to improve, or, possibly, to evolve. Self-augmentation is enabled because a reflexive system can produce output that affects itself. This augmentative feature, which is derived from reflexivity, is not limited to self-augmentation. Let us consider a pair of reflexive systems, X and Y, that mutually interpret the production of the self and the other. X produces an expression interpretable by Y, knowing how Y interprets the expression, based on its self-interpretation. Reflexivity not only guarantees that Y interprets what X outputs but also guarantees that X and Y have the same consequence from the expression. The pair can thus augment together by exchanging expressions. The degree of communication between X and Y is different when X and Y are nonreflexive. If X outputs an expression for Y that is not interpretable by X itself, the status change applied to Y will not be shared by X. Such communication can be compared to an assembly line, where each system does some work and then sends the result to the next system without being able to interpret what exactly the output is. Mutual augmentation also occurs among more than two systems. Similarly to the case of natural language systems, mutual augmentation occurs at different scales ranging from single to multiple systems.

When multiple systems are involved, an important issue must first be considered: whether a language system is *open* or *closed*. In this book, a language system is defined to be open when its interpretation scheme for expressions in the language is public, whereas a language system is closed when its interpretation scheme is kept private. This notion of closedness is distinct from that of having no interaction with the external world. A closed sign system can interact by exchanging linguistic expressions, but these expressions' effects cannot be verified directly, since the interpretation scheme for language is enclosed within the system. The closedness concept, in my opinion, resembles the windowlessness represented in the philosophical concept of a monad.[2]

For open systems, multiple systems may possess exactly the same interpretive system. In this case, the result obtained by using multiple open systems is the same as that obtained by using only one such system. The roles of the systems can be exchanged and the same result will be produced. No additional interpretive effect is thus gained through multiplicity as compared with calculation only by the self (or selves). In other words, mutual augmentation among open systems is qualitatively equivalent to self-augmentation. At the same time, open systems are vulnerable. Openness means that any stranger can ascertain how to destroy the whole system. Publicizing the interpretive scheme directly means publicizing the way to destroy the system.

On the other hand, the two closed systems possess different interpretive systems, formed as a consequence of having been enclosed, and this difference generates additional interpretive influences on the result. The results obtained from closed systems therefore differ even for the same input.

---

2   In philosophy, a monad is an inseparable, self-evolving being, as proposed by multiple philosophers, including Aristotle and Leibnitz. Taking Leibnitz's description (Leibnitz, 1908), his monad is defined as *simple substance*, where simple means *without parts* (Leibnitz 1908, p. 1). Leibnitz's monad has the feature of being *windowless*: "The monads have no windows through which anything may come in or go out" (Leibnitz 1908, p. 7).

Moreover, when two closed systems communicate using language, the influence of an expression remains indirect, since every communicator has its own interpreter enclosed within itself and the counterpart's interpretation scheme is unknown. A speaker can only generate an expression by assuming how the hearer might interpret the expression. Within this assumption, reflexivity plays the crucial role of simulating the other's understanding by using one's own interpretation scheme, as follows:

- The speaker understands its own output.
- The speaker assumes the hearer will understand its own output in a certain way based on its own understanding.
- The speaker speaks, assuming how the hearer will understand its output.
- The speaker understands its generated output by assuming how the hearer will understand this output.

A similar simulation occurs on the hearer's side. Such recursive simulation of the interpretation of an expression could continue to an infinite depth, and the communication between the two sides would be limited to the results of these simulations done on each side. The two could never achieve an equivalent consequence from such communication. If this could be called otherness or alterity, then otherness is conditioned by closedness through the privatization of the interpretation scheme.

Whether or not natural language systems are closed has been controversial, and some philosophers such as Wittgenstein have taken a solipsistic approach. One argument against solipsism is that humans have constructed open systems embedded within natural language as common public systems. For example, explicitly defining the accepted meanings of terms in dictionaries is one appearance of such an effort, so that closed systems work under the same protocol. More trivial examples are logic and mathematics, which are essentially open systems on which computer systems are constructed as introduced in Chapter 8.

The remaining sections examine how computational sign systems fit with regard to reflexivity as seen so far.

11.3 Categories of Reflexivity

Not all computer languages are reflexive: many produce outputs not interpretable by the self but only interpretable by others. For example, markup languages, such as HTML, are not reflexive, since the markup language interpreter cannot interpret its own output. The interpreted output of HTML code typically provides a visual representation intended for human consumption, and the output is not assumed to be fed to a language interpreter. Therefore, there are two kinds of language systems: those that are reflexive and those that are not.

Reflexive language systems produce self-interpretable expressions. Among these systems, a genre similar to markup language is preprocessing language.[3] Preprocessing language preprocesses a certain portion of a program before compilation. It is typically used so that users do not have to reproduce similar code in programs. Examples include C macros for the C language and generic types for C++ or Java. When a program with preprocessing commands is interpreted, it is first put through an interpreter for the preprocessing language that produces the program. For example, when C macros are embedded in a C program, the C macro is first interpreted, which thus produces a C program without macros.

The major function of a preprocessing language is text substitution (Ellis and Stroustrup, 1992). A substitution definition can include another substitution, so the macro expressions in a program might have to be expanded multiple times before the final program is obtained. For example, consider the following example of a small C macro taken from Ellis and Stroustrup (1992).

$$
\begin{aligned}
&\texttt{\#define m(a) a(w)} \\
&\texttt{\#define w 0,1} \\
&\texttt{m(m)}
\end{aligned}
\tag{11.1}
$$

The text to be substituted is m(m), by the substitution rules defined in the first two lines. The first line denotes that m(a) is replaced by a(w). By matching m(m) and m(a), the second m matches with a, so that m(m) is transformed into m(w). Then, using the substitution rule in the second line, the w of m(w) is replaced by 0,1 and the result m(0,1) is produced through the interpretation of this preprocessing language. The point is that the first substitution m(w) does *not* reciprocally continue by matching it with m(a) to produce w(w). That is, rules are not applied recursively within a C macro. This constraint forces the preprocessing to halt, or guarantees that it will, preventing the occurrence of infinite substitution.

---

[3] Usage of the terms preprocessing, macro, and metaprogramming varies widely and depends on the context. This chapter distinguishes between the notion of preprocessing and metaprogramming (the definition of metaprogramming appears in Section 11.4). The term macro is used in the context of a specific programming language, such as a C macro or Lisp macro, since the descriptive power depends on which kind of macro is considered.

Substitution is a simple yet powerful operation and can be equivalent to a Turing machine, as was seen in Chapter 4 in the framework of the lambda calculus as a β-reduction. Preprocessing languages, however, are arbitrarily constrained so that preprocessing halts. Some examples of preprocessing languages, such as a C++ generic type, can handle reciprocal substitutions, but the preprocessing language system forces termination when the number of repetitions of substitution exceeds a certain threshold (Czarnecki and Eisenecker, 2000, pp. 406–413). The point is that the number of times output can be self-interpretable for a given input is limited in preprocessing language by an arbitrary setting. The number of loops in Figure 11.3 is always known for a given input.

In contrast, in a programming language, the number of loops can be infinite. A typical example is the hackers' game *Quine* (Burger, Brill, and Machi, 1980; Thompson 1984), named after the philosopher Quine, who appeared in the first section of this chapter. In this game, a programmer is asked to write a nontrivial computer program, called a Quine, that produces itself. Nontrivial means that a trivial program, such as an empty program producing nothing, is excluded. For example, the following is a nontrivial Quine written in Haskell (Hudak, 2000):

$$\text{main=putStr\$q++show q;q="main=putStr\$q++show q;q=".} \quad (11.2)$$

The first half (before ';') is a program that prints out q twice, and the latter half (after ';') gives the value of q, which is set to the string `"main=putStr$q++show q;q="`. The string `putStr$q++show q` with the *dollar* sign prefixing the first q is equivalent to `putStr (q ++ show q)`. The first q corresponds to the content of q without including it in double quotes:

$$\text{main=putStr\$q++show q;q=.} \quad (11.3)$$

Then, `show q` corresponds to the string assigned to q, this time included in double quotes. These q with and without double quotations are concatenated and printed out. Quines in other programming languages have the same structure of two parts: a definition of the output string and the actual output of that string.

Once a Quine program is input to a language interpretation system, its output is itself. This output can be fed as input, which again generates the same program. Thus, a Quine program forms an infinite repetition of the loop in Figure 11.3. In other words, considering a programming language system as f, its Quine program is its fixed point x = f x. The difference between preprocessing and programming language lies in whether the language system can infinitely produce self-interpretive output for a given input.

Consequently, three categories of computer language can be defined with respect to reflexivity by counting how many times the language system can produce a self-interpretable program:

1. a nonreflexive language system,
2. a finitely reflexive language system, and
3. an infinitely reflexive language system.

In computation, there are two major theories for classifying languages. One is the notion of Turing completeness (Cutland, 1980, p. 175), which classifies languages according to whether the computation described by the language is equivalent to computation on a Turing machine. This classification of languages is equivalent to classification by another theory of computability in which computability is described by the number of repetitions for a given input (Cutland, 1980; Sipser, 2005): computation whose number of repetitions is decidable and computation whose number of repetitions is not decidable. The latter naturally includes computation requiring an infinite number of repetitions. Partial functions[4] belong to the second category too, since the number of repetitions cannot be defined for certain inputs for which the procedure is undefined. In addition, some total functions are known to belong to the second category. Since computation is described by some computer language, this hierarchy directly signifies the hierarchy of languages that describe computation.

The categories of computability and reflexivity somewhat resemble each other in that a distinction is made on whether some number of repetitions is finite or infinite. For a language that is Turing complete, it is formally proved that a nontrivial Quine exists (Kleene, 1938; Rogers, 1987). Many programming languages indeed have a Quine. If a language has a Quine, this means that the language has at least one program that is infinitely reflexive. However, whether the relationship holds in the opposite direction is a controversial question. Even if a language has a Quine, it is not necessarily Turing complete. The set of languages with at least one program that is infinitely reflexive includes the set of Turing-complete languages. Clarification of how much larger the first set is with respect to the second set must be left to future work and will require a more formal definition of the degree of reflexivity of a language.

---

[4] *Partial and total* functions are notions in mathematics and programming. Given two sets and a function considered as a mapping of the elements of an input set to those of the output set (cf. Glossary), the function is called a total function when every element of the input set has a corresponding value in the output set; it is called a partial function when only a subset of the input set has output values.

11.4   Reflexivity of a Computer System

The two fundamental systems of a programming language are the compiler and the interpreter. An interpreter is a system that directly analyzes the expressions of a language and executes them. A compiler is software that translates a program into another language with an interpreter. This target language is typically machine language, and thus a program's source code is first compiled into machine language by the compiler to produce executable code. In this case, the machine itself functions as the interpreter of the machine language, which is defined for the CPU. Usually, execution by an interpreter without compilation is slower than execution of the compiled code, yet the former is handier than the latter in that it does not require compilation. Whether compilers or interpreters are used depends on the need. The creation of a language system therefore fundamentally means producing either an interpreter or a compiler.

Compilers and interpreters are usually constructed by using a preexisting language. Many actual language systems are written in the C language, which provides the full functionality to manipulate computer hardware. Since C is infinitely reflexive, many of the resulting programming language systems are infinitely reflexive.

The interesting question is how the C language system itself was generated. The compiler for the C language was written in C (Kernighan and Ritchie, 1988; Thompson, 1984). Briefly, an interpreter for a subset of C sufficient to build the compiler was first generated in assembly language.[5] This interpreter directly runs on the CPU, since assembly language is designed to control a computer's CPU. The interpreter then interpreted the C compiler program in C to generate a compiling system. Then, providing the C compiler program code to this compiling system generated version zero of the compiler's executable code. By using this version-zero compiler, a version-one compiler program was compiled, thus generating a version-one compiler. Subsequently, version-$n + 1$ compiler code was compiled by the version-n compiler to produce the version-$n + 1$ compiler. Similarly, once the version-zero interpreter for the C language was obtained, a version-$n + 1$ interpreter was obtained from a version-n interpreter. The language system was thus reciprocally enlarged by successively inputting a new program to an old compiler and interpreter and producing a new compiler and interpreter.

---

[5]   Another way to start is by building a compiler. A compiler program that compiles a subset of C is first built in assembly language. By using this compiler, a compiler that compiles the full set of C is written using the subset of C and compiled. This generates the version-zero C compiler for the complete C language.

Augmentation of the C compiler and interpreter was thus performed *almost* by using the reflexive feature of the C language system, except that the new versions of the C compiler and interpreter programs were generated by humans on the basis of the older version. This process has further potential to be automated, which would require two additional functionalities. First, the language system would have to be capable of producing a new version of the self-interpretable program; that is, a version-$n + 1$ program should be automatically produced, given version n. Second, the language system would need a framework for interpreting the modified program on the fly during interpretation of the previous program.

For the first requirement, a self-interpretable program can be produced by a programming language system, as was mentioned before. The key point is the *plan* for updating: how to extend or improve the language. Currently, successive versions of C compiler programs cannot be produced automatically, since each new version has bug fixes and new functions in the language, which are defined by human ideas. It is humans who use the C language, and thus humans have ideas about compiler bugs and new language functions. Such improvement of a compiler is not a matter of mirroring nature, as was seen in Chapter 8. To automatically generate an improved compiler, the scheme for evaluating the compiler should be made explicit.

For some other rare tasks with a clear evaluation function, improved versions of programs can be automatically generated. An example is compiler optimization software (Aho *et al.*, 1986, pp. 887–888). An optimizer transforms a program before compilation so that it requires less memory or has a smaller calculation load. The input is the original program, and the output is an optimized version of the program. Since the optimizer itself is a program, it should be optimized. First, version zero of the optimizer is generated by compiling the version-zero optimizer program. The version-n optimizer program is optimized by putting it into the version-n optimizer, producing the version-$n + 1$ program. Compiling this generates the version-$n + 1$ software. Repeating this procedure may successively optimize the optimizer program. Note that the chain of optimizing the optimizer program might go on infinitely, which makes the process different from the preprocessing mentioned in the previous section.

Similarly, if a new version of the C compiler program could be defined explicitly from an old version, the generation of a C compiler could become automatic. The reality, however, is that there is no well-formulated framework for updating the new version, nor is there an evaluation function, and revision is usually not automated. Thus, the essence of the problem does *not* lie in the lack of a language framework for self-augmentation; rather, the problem lies in the lack of formulation for improvement.

The second requirement has long been implemented via metaprogramming. Metaprogramming[6] is so called because it requires a metalanguage specifying the production of code and its evaluation during evaluation of the original program.[7] The metalanguage used for metaprogramming consists of commands for code generation and commands for run-time evaluation within the overall evaluation of the program. The latter commands are introduced into language systems in the form of a function called eval. The eval function dynamically evaluates a program code fragment given to it by using the language system's interpreter. It may dynamically change the system behavior. The eval function was first introduced in the Lisp language in the 1960s, since Lisp is a homoiconic language (see Section 11.2), and homoiconicity provides the capability for output data to include programs to be evaluated on the fly. Currently, many other languages possess functions corresponding to eval.

The function eval is used together with metalanguages for code generation. Metalanguages include commands to obtain the program code currently being executed. The programming paradigm of *reflection* (Smith, 1982, 1984) provides a set of metalinguistic commands that enable access to the code attached to data objects and redefinition of the calculations therein. Without metaprogramming, all program code should be completed before execution. Code can depend, however, on the calculation result. More importantly, a language system can embed other language systems. For example, a program for binary data generation affects how the user configures data structures, depending on each use. Such configuration is given by a configuration language that is designed in terms of the language describing itself. This user configuration is evaluated dynamically to specify the data structures. This sort of processing of language in language is effectively conducted by dynamically generating programs through metaprogramming.

---

[6] *Evaluation* of a program means interpretation and execution of a program, in order to obtain its final value (or output). The name of the special function eval derives from the term evaluation in this sense. This differs from the use of the term in *evaluation function*, as seen thus far and in Chapter 8; there, it indicates a function for measuring appropriateness under some norm for every input.

[7] Because of the literal denotation of the term metalanguage, namely, as a metalevel language about a language, preprocessing (described in Section 11.3) is often regarded as a kind of metaprogramming. Preprocessing, however, typically signifies static code generation prior to compilation, whereas metaprogramming typically signifies run-time code generation and execution. This chapter distinguishes between preprocessing and metaprogramming according to these typical usages.

It is important to note how metaprogramming makes use of the reflexivity of a language system. Code is dynamically generated to define the next action, according to which the subsequent code is generated. One way to summarize the history of programming language development is to view it as the process of making languages more dynamic by exploiting the reflexive features of a language system.

11.5 Reflexivity of a System of Computer Systems

Reflexivity further plays an important role when multiple systems are involved. It was seen in Section 11.2 that consideration of a system formed of multiple systems must address whether the system is open or closed. Computer language systems are essentially open, unless artificially specified as closed. Each computer can differ in its environment – the CPU, the amount of memory, the installed software, and so forth – but computer language interpretation systems are constructed to absorb such differences, and thus, evaluating an expression of a programming language results in an equivalent consequence on different computers.

In Section 11.2, it was explained how an open system is vulnerable. Computer systems are indeed vulnerable and always suffer from security issues. A computer system is easily compromised by the execution of malicious code. Furthermore, when reflexivity accompanies this openness, it raises the problem of computer viruses. In his paper *Reflections on Trusting Trust*, Thompson (1984) briefly showed how easily a Trojan horse can be constructed from a Quine. Integrating malicious code into a Quine generates a computer virus that reproduces itself indefinitely. Thus, the viruses endemic in the computer world are a result of combining reflexivity and openness.

To tackle such problems, computer systems are often arbitrarily closed. This can be done in at least two ways:

• by closing the system artificially through access restriction, or
• by making the system evolve.

The advantage of the first approach is that the system still functions as though open, thus remaining controllable by the owner and becoming closed only to outsiders. In contrast, the second approach sacrifices controllability.

With respect to the first approach, computer systems are often connected to a network, and within a computer multiple systems coexist. Every system, therefore, should be designed to achieve a balance between what to expose and what to hide. Accessibility is configured at various levels, from the machine level down to each system running on a computer. This configuration also includes the degree of exposure to the outside, from within a machine, a local area network (LAN), a wide area network (WAN), and a public network. At the level of the entire computer, the machine should be protected by security software, and the owner of the machine should take the utmost care to prevent strangers from breaking into it. At the level of individual systems within the computer, the parts to be exposed are configured at both the OS level and the programming level. Since excessive exposure leads directly to vulnerability, computer administrators must configure all of these settings.

Thus enclosed, each system has its own individual processing capability, and multiple computers can form a role-sharing system. Metaprogramming serves well for such connected yet closed systems. For example, when a system finds that it does not have an appropriate calculation program, it can delegate the calculation to another system. Program code is scattered, and intermediate calculation results are handed from one system to another. Such relaying requires searching for program code within a program, so reflection is used to search for functions and software. In other words, delegation is implemented by programs exchanging programs, thus making use of reflexivity. This allows task sharing without the risk of downloading and executing unknown program code from a third party. Multiple systems can thus help each other without exposing their in-depth capabilities.

As for the second approach to close an open system, a system may evolve through interaction, of which the most typical method is adaptation. As briefly introduced in Section 8.4.2, adaptation changes the system settings through interaction or communication with other systems. Such a system is implemented through parameter optimization techniques based on some learning model, but metaprogramming can be utilized if the adaptation concerns the system's more fundamental structure. In this case, a system structurally modifies itself to better match learning data. Adaptation can also be mutually performed by multiple systems: two systems can collaborate to complete a task with their programs adjusted mutually. Such examples are seen in the domain of artificial intelligence, as in studies of pair reflection. Thus, the reflexive feature of systems serves well for mutual augmentation. Adaptation sacrifices controllability, however, and the system becomes unpredictable, since the adaptation depends on what the system has experienced. Thus, when the user tries to control such an adapted system, it might not react as the user intends. Surrounding every adaptive computer system, there is the controversy over whether this form of adaptation truly enhances usability.

Consequently, the reflexivity of computer language systems also provides the potential for multiple systems to mutually augment one another. The typical use of reflection among thus enclosed systems is still limited, and dynamic generation and execution of programs requires further elaboration. Underlying this is the inherent lack of direction for improvement, similar to the case of the C compiler example given in the previous section. Most importantly, such mutual augmentation concerns the vulnerability of systems. Studies are needed to find ways to mutually augment systems under some direction without losing control, while maintaining the security of the systems.

As seen in this chapter, computational sign systems are inherently reflexive, and this is the nature of a sign system in general. It is not known, however, how to harness reflexivity in a specific direction in computational systems, and more importantly, this direction is unknown. Stipulating such a direction starts by situating other sign systems within a sign system, as illustrated in Figure 11.2 and Figure 11.1, and also by situating the sign system within itself, as in the Escher's print gallery on the front cover. In natural sign systems, too, such directions have been found over the course of many years, and stipulation is not a simple issue. The quest for such a direction has been and will continue to be a critical issue in evolving sign systems.

11.6 Summary

The theme of this section was the reflexivity of a sign system. A sign system is reflexive when its own output can be reinterpreted by itself. After summarizing the nature of reflexivity of a sign system in general, various computer languages were examined and three different levels of reflexivity were identified. Further, the nature of the evolution of programming language systems based on reflexivity was seen. Last, reflexivity of state-of-the-art technology for multiple computer systems was discussed, suggesting the potential for making greater use of reflexivity under multiplicity.

Can computers evolve by themselves? In principle, since many computer languages are infinitely reflexive, the potential exists. Two difficulties in achieving this, however, have been explained here. First, there is the difficulty of elucidating the direction of self-evolution. Section 11.4 looked at the example of an optimizer, but formulating a sufficiently clear axis of improvement and evolution is nontrivial. This lack of direction is a common problem when multiple systems are involved. Thus, the difficulty of self-augmentation arises not from the lack of a framework but rather from the lack of a way to formulate a suitable evolutionary direction in which to proceed. Second, technology for securely controlling multiple systems must be devised. Computer language systems are vulnerable because they are essentially open, so *tricks* must be applied to close them, which makes them difficult to control. Finding a good balance between closing and controlling systems under reflexivity will be a nontrivial endeavor.

In addition to these difficulties, there is the halting problem, as noted in Chapter 9, which directly concerns the nature of reflexivity. Overall, today's computers are far from what we have considered to constitute evolution. The discussion in this book, however, has revealed the nature of signs and sign systems as being reflexive. The question of how to exploit such inherent reflexivity in a constructive system will remain one of the main problems of computational systems, and I believe that more evolutionary technology exploiting the reflexivity of programming language systems is inevitable.

12

Conclusion

The aim of this book has been to apply semiotic theory to the field of computer programming and to consider in this light the general properties of signs and sign systems through the concept of reflexivity. Computer programs are described in formal, well-defined languages having interpretive processes that are external to those of human languages. In writing this book, the general properties of signs and the specific characteristics of computer signs were studied in comparison with natural language signs. Certain parts of the semiotic framework were hypothetically reformulated through their application to such a formal system. At the same time, the significances of computer programming theories were reconsidered from a humanistic viewpoint, an approach which brought to light several reasons computer programs are necessarily in their current state.

In Part I, the various models of signs were investigated, and their relationships to each other were considered. Two kinds of sign models were introduced in Chapter 3, the Saussure's dyadic model and the Peirce's triadic model, and the correspondences of their relata were examined by comparing two programming paradigms, the functional and the object-oriented. The analysis then hypothesized a renewed approach to correspondence between the two models and demonstrated their compatibility. This process revealed that a sign, as used in this book, consists of a signifier, with content as its semantics and use as its pragmatics. In Chapter 4, the role of the signifier was examined through application of the lambda calculus, the most fundamental framework for programming languages. Reflexivity is readily present in the lambda calculus in the most primitive form of a self-applicative procedure, but this takes the form of self-reference when sign definition is introduced into it. The content of a self-referential sign is articulated through the use of the signifier, thus unifying the sign relata and showing how pragmatics freezes into semantics through self-referential signs. Moreover, under self-reference, the dyadic and triadic models essentially become equivalent. Chapter 5 examined the way in which the sign model influences the relationships between signs and, further, actually determines the ontology of the sign system. The argument suggests that an ontology based upon either 'being' or 'doing' will emerge depending on which aspect of the triadic sign model is emphasized: content or use. Moreover, in triadic sign modeling, the construction of the ontological framework has the potential to allow either a 'being' or a 'doing' ontology, whereas dyadic modeling is restricted to the 'being' ontology.

Part II was dedicated to a detailed examination of the parts of signs, through which the various kinds of signs and referents were investigated. Chapter 6 first introduced three different representation levels for content appearing in programs and the resulting ambiguities in their signification. The representation levels were formulated by applying Hjelmslev's framework of sign categorization for dyadic modeling and Peirce's framework for triadic modeling. A correspondence between the kinds of signs in the dyadic and triadic frameworks was hypothesized; investigation revealed fundamental sign types existing in both models. The rest of Part II was dedicated to verifying the kinds of content and examined how signs are involved in such representation. Chapter 7 reexamined observations made by a number of philosophers, of which the most representative is Peirce, that any form can be classified into one of the three kinds by considering how many forms it concerns. This statement was verified, in terms of whether it holds in computation, by applying program transformation techniques. It was shown that there are indeed three kinds of content. Examination of each category then showed that the nature of the last kind of form lies in reflexivity. Such reflexivity is realized through description by the use of signs, which provides a means to stipulate thirdness. Chapter 8 further considered the distinction of *an* instance and *the* instance from the viewpoint of haecceity. The chapter showed how the instantiation of *the* instance is a fundamental problem in computing, since *the* instance is usually special because of its uniqueness, yet all instances are easily reproducible on computers. It was argued how *the* instance could be obtained by the two procedures of optimization and interaction, thus restoring the singularity of *the* instance within a class. Underlying these procedures is a scheme of reflexivity, which was hypothesized as a rationale to distinguish *the* instance from *an* instance. Lastly, it was argued that the sheer separation of class and instance requires deconstruction when attempting to understand the nature of significant instances.

In Part III, systems of signs were examined. Chapter 9 presented two typical sign systems: one structural, typically a natural sign system, and the other constructive, typically a computer sign system. The difference between them derives from the different interpretive strategies for reflexive expressions in these two sign systems. Natural sign systems handle self-reference, including any problematic self-referential expressions, by leaving ambiguity as is. This interpretive mechanism generates a structural system where the signification of signs exists in the holistic system and the whole sign system operates reflexively. In contrast, in computer sign systems, programs must be constructively generated by using procedures that are guaranteed to halt, since self-reference directly concerns the halting problem. Making computer sign systems structural was argued to hold the key to developing computer systems that behave more naturally. The last two chapters of Part III considered a sign system's being in a world and interaction with other systems. Chapter 10 attempted to look at the signification of interaction with respect to a sign system, in terms of the questions of how a sign system relates to the external world and represents it and of how signs are involved in this process. The chapter first presented the fundamental problem underlying the description of interaction. It was revealed that interaction cannot be described without considering the ordering of signs along the time flow. The spatiotemporal consideration of signs revealed their speculative nature, in which a sign is introduced by signifying undefined content that obtains defined values through calculation. Through this nature, a sign functions as a transcendental medium to indicate an unknown outer-world target that serves to introduce heterogeneity into the system. Such functions of a sign were hypothesized to also be present in human sign systems, as represented by the quote from a previous writing. Chapter 11 considered the reflexivity of a sign system – a feature of a sign system possessing the capability of interpreting expressions produced by the system itself. Reflexivity holds the key for a sign system to be able to evolve, and this can occur through both self-augmentation and mutual augmentation. After summarizing the reflexivity of a sign system in general, the chapter further presented the classes of reflexivity and the degree of reflexivity that current computer systems can exploit.

Underlying this book is the question of the differences between humans and machines. There have been substantial discussions with respect to *what computers cannot do*, as in Dreyfus (1972). There are obvious arguments based on the fact that human beings have a physical body and also on the fact that the hardware is different, with humans being biological systems. In contrast, this book has attempted to consider this question in terms of the common test bed of sign systems. The computer world ultimately consists solely of signs, and human thought can also be considered a sign system, just as thinkers like Saussure and Peirce have argued. *What computers cannot do* is explored by considering computers and humans as sign systems and by comparing these shared worlds of sign systems. Such a comparison is deemed not to be too much of an oversimplification, given that the precise delineation between natural and computer languages has not been obvious within the domain of the formal theories of languages.

We have seen that there is no difference in the nature of an individual sign between human sign systems and those of machines. A sign is founded on its speculative introduction without any guarantee that it will acquire any final, concrete content. This way of being forms the basis for a sign to function as a transcendental medium for acquiring heterogeneous signification from the outer world. A system formed of such signs becomes naturally susceptible to reflexivity, and the strategy for handling reflexivity determines what kind of sign system it becomes. Throughout this book, indeed, we have seen that a number of difficulties that are not extant in human systems appear whenever reflexivity is processed on machines.

In Part I, we saw how two sign models that are essentially equivalent under reflexivity appear as different paradigms. Part II explored the way in which *the* instance is difficult to obtain on a computer and requires expensive reflexive computation, in a form that is difficult to formalize. In Part III, the differences in handling reflexivity confirmed that the natures of machine and human sign systems differ significantly. Every computational form must be well-formed and explicit, so the ambiguity underlying reflexivity cannot remain without becoming a cause of malfunction. Computer systems have therefore been developed by avoiding ambiguous reflexivity, resulting in constructive systems. The potential for exploiting the reflexivity of sign systems remains limited for machines, and computer systems are far from evolving. Since signs are reflexive, the central issue of computer theories has been reflexivity, and the answer to the question of *what computers cannot do* still lies in reflexivity. In other words, one key limitation of machines still seems to be their limitations in processing reflexivity.

Nevertheless, computer language systems have been potentially reflexive from the time of their invention, like human language systems. By nature, we human beings have known how to make the most of this self-referential character in our language systems, but we have not fully realized how to do so in computer systems. Trying to fill the gap between these two sign systems, however, promises both advantages and disadvantages. If computer signs were articulated like those of natural human language, these signs would become more robust and would suffer less from the problems caused by reflexivity. At the same time, the interpretive scheme would become enclosed within a computer system, which would decrease the system's controllability.

The history of computer language systems can be regarded as a continuing endeavor to discover new ways to apply reflexivity to make such systems more dynamic and evolutionary. This book is thus meant to review this endeavor from the viewpoint of sign systems to understand where we have come from, where we are now, and where we need to go next.

Glossary

This glossary briefly defines the key terms used in this book, both for semiotics and computer science. Many terms have technical usages in each domain, with divergent and multiple significations. Moreover, the topic of the book, in general, concerns terms related to signification, meaning, and sense, which complicates the terminology. To avoid confusion, I have had to use some of these technical terms in particular senses. After certain items, a related, representative part of the book is indicated in parentheses.

Semiotics

connotation: Connotation is defined in a pair with denotation. In the usual sense, the denotation is the stable, material, and logical meaning carried by a sign, independently of its context. For example, the term 'night' usually has a meaning opposed to 'day', referring to the period from sunset to sunrise. In contrast, the connotation is a more subjective, context-dependent signification carried by a sign. A connotation is immaterial, depending on the content of thought, such as the normative, the cultural, the psychological, and the anthropological. For example, the term 'night' could connote sadness or mourning in a certain context.

Hjelmslev, in his glossematics, considered that the dimension of either expression or content could recursively form a sign. When the expression further forms a semiotic layer, the original layer constitutes the connotation for this layer, which constitutes the denotation (Section 6.3). In this book, the terms denotation and connotation are used according to Hjelmslev's sense, not in the typical sense related to materiality and subjectivity.

content: Hjelmslev adopted a dyadic modeling of signs. What corresponds to Saussure's signified, he called the content. In this book also, the relatum that corresponds to Sassure's signified is called the content (Sections 3.5 and 6.3).

denotation: See **connotation**.

expression: An expression, in general, denotes a set of linguistically meaningful elements. Moreover, Hjelmslev adopted dyadic modeling of signs and used the term expression to refer to what corresponds to Saussure's signifier. This term as Hjelmslev's expression, however, only appears at the beginning of Section 6.3.

icon: In the Peircian classification of signs, each aspect of a sign (namely, the representamen, the object, and the interpretant) in relation with the sign is classified by Peirce's universal categories. The icon is Peirce's terminology to denote a sign when its relation with the object is of the firstness category (Section 6.4).

index: In the Peircian classification of signs, each aspect of a sign (namely, the representamen, the object, and the interpretant) in relation with the sign is classified by Peirce's universal categories. The index is Peirce's terminology to denote a sign when its relation with the object is of the secondness category (Section 6.4).

interpretant: In Peirce's triadic modeling of signs, the relata are called the representamen, the object, and the interpretant. The interpretant has the function of connecting the representamen and the object. It also evokes semiosis, or the interpretation of the sign. In this book, the interpretant is considered to possess the functionality that causes the use of a sign (Chapters 3 and 4).

interpretation: Interpretation signifies the processing of a sign or linguistic phrase according to predefined semantics and pragmatics.

object: An object in semiotics, in general, denotes the target to be represented by a sign in an abstract sense, inclusively of both the real-world object and the non-real-world object. At the same time, Peirce used the term object to denote the referent of a sign. The Peircian object denotes the real-world object (dynamical object) placed exterior to the sign and also the concept of that object (immediate object) embedded in the sign. After Chapter 3, whenever Peirce's object is referred to, it signifies Peirce's immediate object. The term object in the computer science domain, as introduced in the next section of the glossary, also has multiple meanings (Chapters 3 and 5).

object language: See **metalanguage**.

metalanguage: Metalanguage is defined in a pair with object language. Signs are often classified through the use of metalevel language. For example, the part of speech is a metalanguage term for the object language consisting of natural language terms. In Hjelmslev's glossematics, it is considered that the dimension of either expression or content can recursively form a further sign. When the content further forms a semiotic layer, the original layer constitutes the metalanguage for this layer, which constitutes the object language layer (Section 6.3).

meaning: In this book the term meaning is used to denote everything attributable to a sign, except for the signifier.

representamen: Peirce applied triadic sign modeling, and the representamen corresponds to the dimension of the signifier of a sign (Chapter 3).

semiosis: Semiosis means the semiotic process formed by multiple signs. Linguistic behavior usually forms semiosis (Chapter 3).

sign: In this book, a sign is a means of signification. Two definitions are given here. One is taken from the *Oxford English Dictionary*: "something perceived that suggests the existence of a fact or quality or condition, either past or present or future." Another definition is given by (Saussure 1911, p. 74): "The linguistic sign is based on an association made by the mind between two very different things, but which are both mental and in the subject: an acoustic image is associated with a concept." I follow these definitions in general, and further, for the case of a computer sign, the definition is given in Chapter 2.

sign vehicle: This term only appears at the beginning of Chapter 3, following the usage in Nöth (1990, pp. 88 and 90). It represents the dimension of a sign, which corresponds to the signifier in this book (Chapter 3).

signified: See **signifier**.

signifier: Saussure adopted a dyadic sign model, as can be seen from the definition quoted in the entry for the term **sign** in this glossary. The dimension of an acoustic image is called the signifier in Saussure's theory, whereas the concept dimension is called the signified. This book also follows Saussure's usage of the term signifier. As for Saussure's signified, I use another term, content (Chapter 3).

sense: The usage of the term sense in the semiotic context is avoided in this book. It only appears at the beginning of Chapter 3, following the usage by Nöth (1990, p. 90), to denote the dimension of what corresponds to Peirce's interpretant in triadic sign modeling. For the more general semiotic meaning of sense, see Nöth (1990, Chapter on Meaning, Sense, and Reference).

symbol: A symbol, in general, has the specific meaning of a thing regarded as suggesting something else or embodying certain characteristics; e.g., the cross is the symbol of Christianity (*Oxford English Dictionary*). In semiotics, the usage of the term symbol depends on the writer. In this book, the term symbol only appears as Peirce's symbol. In the Peircian classification of signs, each aspect of a sign (namely, the representamen, the object, and the interpretant) in relation with the sign is classified by Peirce's universal categories. The symbol is Peirce's terminology to denote a sign when its relation with the object is of the thirdness category (Section 6.4).

system: A system in the semiotic sense in this book means a relation among signs and their interpretations. A language is a sign system. Since computer science also uses this term, when I mean this semiotic sense of the term system, it is always modified by an additional term: semiotic, sign, or language.

universal categories: Peirce's universal categories constitute a framework for classifying forms in an abstract sense (Peirce, 1931). Any logical form is classified by the number of forms in relation, namely, one, two, or three forms. Forms with more than three forms are reduced to combinations of three or fewer forms. There are thus only three categories of forms.

use: The term use denotes the appearance of a sign within semiosis, and the meaning is attributed to the sign through this use. This term is less commonly used in semiotics, and for this reason, I use it in this book to denote the third relatum of a sign, which corresponds to Peirce's interpretant.

value: The term value for a sign in the semiotic sense means all attributes of the sign other than the signifier. In other words, this consists of the signification that a sign acquires. The terms value and meaning in the semiotic sense are considered equivalent in this book. Since there is also the computer scientific term value, which is quite different from this one, I use the term meaning instead and avoid using value in the semiotic sense, except for two cases: when value appears in a quotation, and in the usage of holistic value (in the Saussurian sense) (Chapter 9).

Computer Science

argument: When an operator or function is executed, it might need some additional information. Each piece of additional information is called an argument. For example, application of the addition operator to integers requires two integers to be added; these integers are the arguments for the operator. More generally, in the functional representation of f $x_1 \cdots x_n$, the arguments of the function f are $x_1, \ldots, x_n$ (Chapter 2).

assignment: An assignment is a program statement that replaces the value of a sign with a new one. In this book, an assignment operation is described using : =, in the form of A := B. In assignment, the right side of : = is calculated first and then assigned to the identifier on the left side. For comparison with the case of definition (represented by =), A = B implies that this formula should hold in the mathematical sense, whereas this is not the case for an assignment. When the identifier defined on the left side is included on the right side, then = forms a self-referential definition, whereas : = represents the action of value setting. The two expressions using = and : = have the same effect when the identifier defined on the left is *not* included on the right side, as far as the statement by itself is concerned. (Section 6.1).

In a language where self-referential definition through the use of = is disallowed but must instead be made in another form, assignment is often described by = instead of : =. Java is one such language.

class: A class is a linguistic unit in the object-oriented programming paradigm, which generates and controls multiple instances having the same functionality or features. For example, multiple Shape classes – Rectangle, Ellipse, and Circle – are defined in the Java program in Figure 2.2. A class typically forms a type (see **type**). The term is often used in the object-oriented paradigm but can be used in a more general sense in other programming paradigms to denote a set of instances with common features and functionalities (Chapters 2 and 5).

declaration: A declaration or declarative statement is a statement that declares the introduction of an identifier into a program. A declaration might attribute a type to the identifier. For example, in Figure 2.2, line 2 is a declaration of the member variables width and height, of the type Double. In addition, lines 21–23 declare the introduction of the identifiers r, u, and v, of the types Rectangle, Ellipse, and Circle, respectively (Chapter 2).

definition: A definition is a statement in a program that defines the value of an identifier. In this book, an identifier is defined by using =, in the form of A = B, where A is the identifier and B is an expression whose value is given to the identifier A (Chapters 4 and 7). A = B implies that this formula should hold in the mathematical sense. When the identifier defined on the left side is also included on the right side, = forms a self-referential definition. See also **assignment**.

expression: An expression is the basic element of a programming language for calculation. Signs are defined within definitions and used within expressions. Every expression has a value. Syntactically, an expression includes simple cases such as literals (constant values) and variables, and also complex cases, in the form of combinations of simple expressions manipulated by a function or operator. Since a complex case reciprocally forms an expression, expressions are usually defined reciprocally within the language design. An example of a reciprocal definition of an expression is introduced in the definition of LG in Section 4.2 (see also Chapter 2).

fixed point: Given a set X and a function f that projects to X, and an element $x \in X$ such that $x = fx$ holds, x is called the fixed point of f (Chapters 4 and 7). Corresponding to this mathematical definition, the fixed point of a computational function f is the value x such that x = f x holds.

function: A function in a programming language has the same meaning as a function in mathematics. A function is a mapping of an element x of a set X (the domain) to an element of another set Y (the range). For example, the function `area`, defined in Chapter 2 for rectangles, has a domain X consisting of a pair of decimals (`width` and `height`) and a range Y consisting of a decimal (the `area`). The domain is usually represented in the form of functional arguments. Execution of the mapping for a given element of the domain to obtain the corresponding element of the range is called functional application or, more simply, a function call.

halting problem: The halting problem is a decision problem to judge, given a program's input, whether the program will terminate its execution. Turing proved that an algorithm to solve the halting problem for any possible program-input pairs does not exist. The halting problem is undecidable over Turing machines (Chapter 9).

identifier: An identifier is a basic unit of a programming language, namely, the sign identifying an entity and thus distinguishing it from other entities. The computer signs analyzed in this book are identifiers. A more formal definition of an identifier is given in Chapter 2.

instance: An instance is an element of a set or a class. This usage is more common in the object-oriented paradigm but can be used in other programming paradigms too (Chapters 2, 3, 5, and 8).

interface: The term interface in this book is mostly used in the sense of an abstract data type in the object-oriented paradigm, in which an interface declares a set of functions that only indicate how instances are accessed. More explanation is provided in Chapter 5. The term interface in computer science is ambiguous even within the scope of programming languages. Other than this specific usage, the term can also be used to refer to a software application for man–machine interaction, namely, a user interface (Chapters 5 and 8).

interpretation: Interpretation denotes the mechanical processing of linguistic elements according to the predefined semantic rules of a language system, which typically results in changing the state of the language system (Chapter 11).

metalanguage: Metalanguage is metalevel language about a language. Languages used for metaprogramming are typically considered as metalanguage (Chapter 11).

object: In this book, object in the computational context is used in the sense of the object-oriented paradigm, denoting a basic module in a program or an instance generated by using the module. An object in computer science in general can also signify a portion of data in memory (Chapter 5).

reduction: A reduction is a calculation step in evaluating an expression (Chapters 4 and 7).

self-reference: When an identifier is defined by direct or indirect use of itself, it is defined by self-reference. Recursion has the same meaning (Chapters 4 and 7).

statement: A statement is an element of a programming language for execution and consists of declaration, definition, and assignment (Chapter 2).

system: A system denotes the whole set or a part of computer hardware, or a software application running on the hardware.

type: A type indicates an abstraction of a kind of data or a function. For example, 'shape' is the type of instances of rectangles and triangles, or 'noun' is the type of certain terms such as 'cat', 'flower', and 'vase'. Since identifiers represent data or a function, they can also be typed. If the type is explicitly specified in a programming language, the language is called a typed language. In the object-oriented paradigm, a class usually forms a type. Many functional languages are also typed (Section 2).

value: The value of an identifier is the content that it represents. Depending on the semantic level of concern, a value could denote the content defined within a program or the content represented in bits stored at the memory address that an identifier represents. Semiotically, this term has a different signification (see also the definition in the previous section of the glossary).

variable: A variable is an abstraction of a memory space for storing data. Identifiers that do *not* represent constant values are variables.

References

Abelson, H. Sussman, G., and Sussman, J. (1998). *Structure and Interpretation of Computer Programs*. MIT Press.

Aho, A. V., Sethi, R., and Ullman, J. D. (1986). *Compilers – Principles, Techniques, and Tools*. Addison-Wesley.

Aitchison, J. (1994). *Words in the Mind*. Blackwell Publishing.

America, P. and van der Linden, F. (1990). A parallel object-oriented language with inheritance and subtyping. In *ECOOP/OOPSLA*, pages 161–168.

Andersen, P. (1997). *A Theory of Computer Semiotics*. Cambridge University Press.

Andersen, P., Holmqvist, B., and Jensen, J. (1993). *The Computer as Medium*. Cambridge Universtiy Press.

Andersen, P. B., Holmqvist, B., and Jensen, J. F. (2007). *The Computer as Medium*. Cambridge University Press.

André, E., Binstead, K., Tanaka-Ishii, K., Luke, S., Herzog, G., and Rist, T. (2000). Three RoboCup simulation league commentator systems. *Artificial Intelligence Magazine*, **21**(1), 73–85.

Arnold, K., Gosling, J., and Holmes, D. (2000). *The Java Programming Language*. Pearson Education.

Augustine, Saint (1955). *Confessions*. Westminster Press. Library of Christian Classics, Volume 7. Translated and edited by A. C. Outler.

Backus, J. *et al.* (1963). Revised report on the algorithmic language Algol 60. *Communications of the ACM*, **6**(1), 1–17.

Barendregt, H. P. (1984). *The Lambda Calculus, Its Syntax and Semantics, 2nd ed.* North Holland.

Barr, M. and Wells, C. (1995). *Category Theory for Computing Science, 2nd ed.* Prentice Hall.

Barron, W., Buxton, J., Hartley, D., Nixon, E., and Strachey, C. (1963). The main features of CPL. *The Computer Journal*, **6**(2), 134–143.

Barthes, R. (1970). *Mythologies*. Seuil.

Barthes, R. (1983). *Système de la Mode*. Seuil.

Baudrillard, J. (1976). *The Three Orders of Simulacra*, chapter I, page 50. Sage Publications. English edition published in 1994.

Ben-Chaim, M. (2004). *Experimental Philosophy and the Birth of Empirical Science*. Ashgate Publishing.

Benjamin, W. (1935). *The Work of Art in the Age of Its Technological Reproducibility and Other Writings on Media*, chapter 1, pages 19–55. The Belknap Press of Harvard University Press. Translated by E. Jephcott, R. Livingstone, H. Eiland and others, 2008.

Bird, R. (1998). *Introduction to Functional Programming Using Haskell*. Prentice Hall.

Bird, R. and Wadler, P. (1988). *Introduction to Functional Programming*. Prentice Hall.

Bishop, E. (1967). *Foundations of Constructive Analysis*. Academic Press, New York.

Bishop, E. and Bridges, D. (1985). *Constructive Analysis*. Springer.

Breton, A. (1924). *The Lost Steps*. University of Nebraska Press. English edition published in 1996, translated to English by M. Pollizzotti. Originally published from Gallimard.

Brouwer, L. (1927). Intuitionistic reflections on formalism, *From Frege to Göedel*, 1967, pages 490–492. Harvard University Press.

Brouwer, L. (1923). On the significance of the principle of excluded middle in mathematics, especially in function theory, *From Frege to Göedel*, 1967, pages 334–345. Harvard University Press.

Burger, J., Brill, D., and Machi, F. (1980). Self-reproducing programs. *Byte*, **5**, 72–74.

Cann, R. (1993). *Formal Semantics – An Introduction*. Cambridge Textbooks in Linguistics.

Chomsky, N. (1956). Three models for the description of language. *IRE Transactions on Information Theory*, **2**(2), 113–123.

Church, A. (1936). An unsolvable problem of elementary number theory. *American Journal of Mathematics*, **58**, 345–363.

Church, A. (1941). *The Calculi of Lambda-Conversion*. Princeton University Press.

Clinger, W. D. (1998). Proper tail recursion and space efficiency. In *ACM SIGPLAN Conference on Programming Language Design and Implementation*, pages 174–185.

Culler, J. (1982). *On Deconstruction – Theory and Criticism After Structuralism*. Cornell University Press.

Curry, H. B. and Feys, R. (1968). *Combinatory Logic*, volume I. North-Holland.

Cutland, N. J. (1980). *Computability: An Introduction to Recursive Function Theory*. Cambridge University Press.

Czarnecki, K. and Eisenecker, U. W. (2000). *Generative Programming: Methods, Tools, and Applications*. Addison-Wesley Professional.

Dahl, O. and Nygaard, K. (1966). SIMULA – An Algol-based simulation language. *Communications of the ACM*, **9**(9), 671–678.

Dahl, O., Myrhaug, B., and Nygaard, K. (1970). *Simula 67: Common Base Language*. Norwegian Computing Center. Publication N. S-22, Norsk Rgnesentral. Revised version, 1984.

Davis, M., editor (1965). *The Undecidable, Basic Papers on Undecidable Propositions, Unsolvable Problems and Computable Functions*. Raven Press.

d'Ors, E. (1973). *Tres Horas en el Museo Del Prado*. Bijutsu Shuppansha. Translated from Spanish into Japanese by K. Kamiyoshi.

de Saussure, F. (1911). *3ème Cours de Linguistique Générale*. Pergamon. Notes taken by E. Constantin. Translated into English by R. Harris, 1993.

de Saussure, F. (1916). *Cours de Linguistique Générale*. Payot. Edited by C. Bally and A. Sechehaye, 1986.

de Saussure, F. (1968). *Cours de Linguistique Générale*. Otto Harrassowitz Wiesbaden. Edited by R. Engler.

de Smit, B. and Lenstra, H. (2003). The mathematical structure of Escher's Print Gallery. *Notices of the American Society of Mathematics*, **50**(4), 446–451.

de Souza, C. S. (2006). *The Semiotic Engineering of Human-Computer Interaction*. MIT Press.

Deledalle, G. (1979). *Théorie et Pratique du Signe – Introduction à la Sémiotique de Charles S. Peirce*. Payot.

Dreyfus, H. (1972). *What Computers Can't Do: A Critique of Artificial Intelligence*. MIT Press.

Eco, U. (1979). *The Theory of Semiotics*. Indiana University Press.

Eco, U. (1988). *Le Signe – Histoire et Analyse d'un Concept*. Editions Labor.

Eliot, T. S. (1968). Burnt norton, *Four Quartets*, page 13. Harvest Books.

Ellis, M. A. and Stroustrup, B. (1992). *The Annotated C++ Reference Manual*. Addison Wesley.

Floridi, L. (1999). *Philosophy and Computing*. Routledge.

Floridi, L., editor (2004). *Philisophy of Computing and Information*. Blackwell Publishing.

Foucault, M. (1966). *The Order of Things*. Vintage Books.

Foucault, M. (1969). *Archéologie du Savoir*. Editions Gallimard.

Foucault, M. (2002). *Archaeology of Knowledge*. Routledge Classics.

Frege, G. (1892). *The Frege Reader*. Wiley-Blackwell. Edited by M. Beaney.

Gelven, M. (1989). *A Commentary on Heidegger's Being and Time*. Northern Illinois University Press.

Goldberg, A. and Kay, A. (1976). *Smalltalk-72 Instruction Manual*. Technical Report SSL-76-6, Xerox Palo Alto Research Center.

Gunter, C. (1962). *Semantics of Programming Languages: Structures and Techniques*. MIT Press.

Harder, P. (1996). *Functional Semantics*. Mouton de Gruyter.

Heidegger, M. (1927). *Being and Time*. Blackwell Publishing. First English edition published in 1962.

Hindley, R. and Seldin, J. P. (2008). *Lambda Calculus and Combinators: An Introduction, 2nd ed.* Cambridge University Press.

Hjelmslev, L. (1943). *Omkring Sprogteoriens Grundlaggelse*. Ejnar Munksgaard. The original was translated by Whitfield, F.J., published by Indiana University publications in anthropology and linguistics in 1953. This book is the Japanese translation by E. Hayashi for this English version, published by Kenkyusha.

Hoffmeyer, J. (1996). *Signs of Meaning in the Universe*. Indiana University Press. Translated by B. Haveland.

Hoffmeyer, J. and Favareau, D. (2009). *Biosemiotics: An Examination into the Signs of Life and the Life of Signs*. University of Scranton Press.

Hofstadter, D. H. (1979). *Gödel, Escher, Bach, an Eternal Golden Braid*. Basic Books. 20th Anniversary ed., published in 1999.

Hudak, P. (1989). Conception, evolution, and application of functional programming languages. *ACM Computing Surveys*, **21**(3), 359–411.

Hudak, P. (2000). *The Haskell School of Expression: Learning Functional Programming through Multimedia*. Cambridge University Press.

Hudak, P. *et al.* (1992). Report on the programming language Haskell, a non-strict purely functional languages. *SIGPLAN Notices, Haskell Special Issue*, **27**(5). Section R.

Hudak, P. and Sundaresh, R. (1988). On the expressiveness of purely functional languages. Technical Report YALEU/DCS/RR-665, Department of Computer Science, Yale University.

Jones, S. P. and Lester, D. (1992). *Implementing Functional Languages: A Tutorial.* Prentice Hall.

Jones, S. P. and Wadler, P. (1993). Imperative functional programming in Proceedings of the ACM SIGPLAN-SIGACT Symposium on Principles of Programming Languages, pages 71–84.

Kernighan, B. W. and Ritchie, D. M. (1988). *The C Programming Language, 2nd ed.* Prentice Hall.

Kitano, H., Asada, M., Kuniyoshi, Y., Noda, I., and Osawa, E. (1995). Robocup: The robot world cup initiative. In *First International Conference on Autonomous Agents.*

Kleene, S. C. (1938). On notation for ordinal numbers. *The Journal of Symbolic Logic,* **3**(4), 150–155.

Leibnitz, G. (1908). *The Philosophical Works of Leibnitz.* Tuttle, Morehouse & Taylor.

Levine, J. R. (2001). *Linkers and Loaders.* Morgan Kaufmann.

Liu, K. (2000). *Semiotics in Information Systems Engineering.* Cambridge University Press.

Locke, J. (1690). *An Essay Concerning Human Understanding.* Penguin Books, Ltd., Roger Woolhouse. This edition was first published 1997, then reprinted with a chronology and revised further in the 2004 edition.

Lönneker, B., Meister, J., Gervas, P., Peinado, F., and Mateas, M. (2005). Story generators: Models and approaches for the generation of literary artefacts. In *The 17th Joint International Conference of the Association for Computers and the Humanities and the Association for Literary and Linguistic Computing,* pages 126–133.

Lycan, W. G. (1999). *Philosophy of Language: A Contemporary Introduction.* Routledge.

MacKenzie, S. and Tanaka-Ishii, K., editors (2007). *Text Entry Systems: Accessibility, Mobility, Universality.* Morgan Kaufmann.

MacLane, S. (1998). *Categories for the Working Mathematician, 2nd ed.* Springer.

Marsen, S. (2004). Against heritage: Invented identities in science fiction film. *Semiotica,* **152**. 141–157.

Martin, J. R. (1977). *Baroque.* Westview Press.

Maruyama, M. (1961). *Thoughts on 'To Be' and 'To Do',* pages 153–180. Iwanami. In Japanese.

Maturana, H. and Varela, F. (1980). *Autopoiesis and Cognition.* Reidel Publishing.

Mcllroy, M. D. (1960). Macro instruction extensions of compiler languages. *Communications of the ACM,* **3**, 214–220.

Meyer, B. (2000). *Object-oriented Software Construction, 2nd ed.* Prentice Hall.

Montague, R. (1974). *Formal Philosophy; Selected Papers of Richard Montague.* Yale University Press.

Morris, C. W. (1946). *Signs, Language, and Behavior.* Mouton. Reprinted in 1971.

Nöth, W. (1990). *Handbook of Semiotics.* Indiana University Press.

Ogden, C. and Richards, I. (1989). *The Meaning of Meaning: A Study of the Influence of Language upon Thought and of the Science of Symbolism.* Harcourt.

Panofsky, E. (1939). *Studies in Iconology.* Oxford University Press. Reprinted in 1972 by Westview press.

Parret, H. (1983). *Semiotics and Pragmatics – An Evaluative Comparison of Conceptual Frameworks*. Benjamins.

Partee, B. H. and Hendriks, H. (1997). Montague grammar in *Handbook of Logic and Language*, pages 5–92. MIT Press.

Peirce, C. S. (1931). *Collected Papers*. Harvard University Press.

Pooley, R. (1987). An *Introduction to Programming in Simula*. Blackwell Scientific.

Popper, K. R. (1943). *The Logic of Scientific Discovery*. Routeledge. New edition published in 2002.

Propp, V. (1968). *Morphology of Folktale*. University of Texas Press.

Propp, V. (1984). *Theory and History of Folklore*. University of Minnesota Press.

Quine, W. v. O. (1960). *Word & Object*. The MIT Press. Reprinted in 1975.

Rector, R. and Alexy, G. (1982). *The 8086 Book*. Osborne Publishing.

Réunion des Musées Nationaux (2002). Lubin Baugin: Catalogue of an exhibition held at Musée des Beaux-Arts d'Orléans.

Rogers, H. (1987). *Theory of Recursive Functions and Effective Computability*. MIT Press.

Rorty, R. (1979). *Philosophy and the Mirror of Nature*. Princeton University Press.

Rosser, J. B. (1939). An informal exposition of proofs of Gödel's theorem and Church's theorem. *The Journal of Symbolic Logic*, **4**, 53–60. Reprinted in Davis 1965, pages 223–230.

Sipser, M. (2005). *Introduction to the Theory of Computation, 2nd ed.* Course Technology.

Smith, B. C. (1982). Reflection and semantics in a procedural language. Technical Report MIT-LCS-TR-272.

Smith, B. C. (1984). Reflection and semantics in Lisp. In *Conference Record of the Eleventh Annual ACM Symposium on Principles of Programming Languages*, pages 23–35. ACM Press.

Smullyan, R. M. (1985). *To Mock a Mockingbird and Other Logic Puzzles: Including an Amazing Adventure in Combinatory Logic*. Knopf.

Snow, E. (1979). *A Study of Vermeer*. University of California Press.

Snyder, A. (1986). Encapsulation and inheritance in object-oriented programming languages. In *OOPSLA '86 Proceedings*, pages 38–45.

Stroustrup, B. (1986). *The C++ Programming Lauguage*. Addison-Wesley.

Stroustrup, B. (1994a). *The Design and Evolution of C++*. Addison-Wesley.

Stroustrup, B. (1994b). *Lvalue vs. Rvalue*. Addison-Wesley Professional.

Sturrock, J. and Rabaté, J.-M. (2003). *Structuralism, 2nd ed.* Wiley-Blackwell.

Tanaka-Ishii, K. (2006). Dyadic and triadic sign models. *Semiotica*, **158**, 213–232.

Tanaka-Ishii, K. (2008). Narcissus in language: A semiotic contrast of natural and computer language through self-reference. *Semiotica*, **172**, 299–311.

Tanaka-Ishii, K. (2009). An instance vs. the instance. *Journal of Minds and Machines*, **19**(1), 117–128.

Tanaka-Ishii, K. (2010). Reflexivity and self-augmentation. *Semiotica*, **179**, 1–17.

Tanaka-Ishii, K. and Ishii, Y. (2006). Thirdness as self-reference in computing. *Semiotica*, **160**, 327–343.

Tanaka-Ishii, K. and Ishii, Y. (2007). Icon, index, symbol and denotation, connotation, metasign. *Semiotica*, **166**, 393–408.

Tanaka-Ishii, K. and Ishii, Y. (2008a). Being and doing as ontological constructs in object-oriented programming. *Journal of Applied Semiotics*, **20**. Online journal.

Tanaka-Ishii, K. and Ishii, Y. (2008b). Sign and the lambda-term. *Semiotica*, **169**, 197–220.

Tanaka-Ishii, K., Noda, I., Frank, I., Nakashima, H., Hasida, K., and Matsubara, H. (1998). MIKE: An automatic commentary system for soccer: System design and control. In *International Conference on Multi-Agent Systems*, pages 285–292. IEEE Computer Society.

Tanaka-Ishii, K., Frank, I., and Hasida, K. (2000). Multi-agent explanation strategies in real-time domains. In *the 36th Annual Meeting for Association of Computational Linguistics*, pages 158–165.

Tennent, R. (1991). *Semantics of Programming Languages*. Prentice Hall.

Thomas, D. and Hunt, A. (2000). *Programming Ruby: The Pragmatic Programmer's Guide*. Addison-Wesley.

Thompson, K. (1984). Reflections on trusting trust. *Communications of the ACM*, **27**, 761–763. Turing Award Lecture.

Todorov, T. (1977). *The Poetics of Prose*. Cornell University Press.

Turing, A. (1936–1937). On computable numbers, with an application to the Entscheidungsproblem. In *Proceedings of the London Mathematical Society, Series 2*, volume 42, pages 230–265.

Ungar, D. and Smith, R. (1987). Self: The power of simplicity. ACM SIGPLAn Notices. Vol 22. Issue 12, pages 227–242.

Wadler, P. (1992). Comprehending monads. *Mathematical Structures in Computer Science*, **2**, 461–493.

Wittgenstein, L. (1953). *Philosophical Investigations, 3rd ed*. Wiley-Blackwell. Reprint in 1991. Translated by G. E. M. Anscombe and E. Anscombe.

Xu, S., Lau, F., Cheung, W. K., and Pan, Y. (2005). Automatic generation of artistic Chinese calligraphy. *Journal of Intelligent Systems*, **20**, 32–39.

Yamanouchi, S. (2008). *The Problem of Universals – As the Source of Modernism*. Heibonsha Library. In Japanese.

Yonemori, Y. (1981). *Semiotics of Peirce*. Keiso Shobo. In Japanese.

Zemanek, H. (1966). Semiotics and programming languages. *Communications of the ACM*, **9**(3), 139–143.

Index